Keith Anwar

Memories of Afghanistan

by
M. H. Anwar

Edited, with an Afterward, by Keith Anwar

authorHOUSE

1663 LIBERTY DRIVE, SUITE 200
BLOOMINGTON, INDIANA 47403
(800) 839-8640
www.authorhouse.com

© *2004 by Keith Anwar*
All Rights Reserved.

No part of this book may be reproduced, stored in a retrieval system, or transmitted by any means without the written permission of the author.

First published by AuthorHouse 11/05/04

ISBN: 1-4184-5044-8 (sc)

Library of Congress Control Number: 2004093594

Printed in the United States of America
Bloomington, Indiana

This book is printed on acid-free paper.

Preface

Around Christmas in 1973 I received as a gift from my father several sheets torn from a note pad on which he had penciled a story entitled "Rahman." Onto those pages he had poured out a theretofore concealed reservoir of anguish in tribute to a close friend and colleague who had perished in an Afghan prison. Soon afterwards he wrote "The Stoning of Amir Khan," which recounted with understated horror the execution of a beloved schoolteacher. Over the months and years that followed, Dad wrote down one episode of his life after another without regard to chronology, moving eventually from the tragic and traumatic events that haunted him to the picaresque adventures of his youth and the bonds of friendship and family that had shaped his character. As the stories accumulated he began to think about gathering them into book form, and in 1981 he published *Memories of Afghanistan*.

Many readers will find the following pages to be a useful introduction to a poorly understood country, since the social conditions so vividly portrayed here essentially remain unchanged 60 to 80 years later. But *Memories of Afghanistan* is more importantly a record of the fragile hopes of a handful of Afghans who sought to fashion their country's future with the tools of enlightenment and science. Such voices were conspicuously absent when the *Loya Jirga*–an assemblage of warlords and Islamic fundamentalists under the aegis of American-led occupation forces–met in Kabul last winter to adopt a new constitution.

The lives of Hammad and Phyllis Anwar in the United States, both before and after the time they spent in Kabul during World War II, but particularly in relation to the succeeding waves of revolution and counterrevolution that swept over Afghanistan in last quarter of the 20th Century, are discussed in the Afterward.

This second edition of *Memories of Afghanistan* contains portions of the original manuscript that were not published in the first edition. These include a considerable part of the chapter about Rahman and the entire chapter entitled "Pastimes." The text has been edited to correct errors of typography, spelling, grammar, usage and repetition. An effort has been made to eliminate inconsistencies and inaccuracies in the transliteration of names and phrases used in Afghanistan. I would like to thank Bruce Anwar, Sima Zahid and Dr. Faruk Sabet for their editorial assistance. The front cover was designed by Blandine Anwar, using a photograph taken by Dr. Anwar in Kabul in 1982.

–K.A.

Table of Contents

Preface v

Part One

Chapter 1 The Death of My Mother 3
Chapter 2 The Feast of Nowroz 13
Chapter 3 My Partner Taj Gul 17
Chapter 4 Abdul and Koko Jan 35
Chapter 5 Pastimes 44
Chapter 6 Days of the Locust 48
Chapter 7 How to Catch a Chicken 56
Chapter 8 A Summer in Kohistan 63
Chapter 9 The Stoning of Amir Khan 76
Chapter 10 The Valley of the Roses 82
Chapter 11 Bacha-i-Saqao 102
Chapter 12 The Vultures' Turn 130
Chapter 13 Blood Feuds 138
Chapter 14 Nida 147
Chapter 15 A Wedding in Kandahar 153
Chapter 16 Unexpected Ghosts 171
Chapter 17 America at Last 182

Part Two

Chapter 18 A Native Returns 191
Chapter 19 Children of Darkness 205
Chapter 20 Nationalism 218
Chapter 21 Of Sex, Sorrow and Other Things 225
Chapter 22 Phyl's Foibles 232
Chapter 23 My Brother Jwandai 240
Chapter 24 There Is Order in Chaos 244
Chapter 25 A Dream Collapsed 257
Chapter 26 A Message from Rahman 265
Chapter 27 Escape 272

Afterward 278

Part One

Chapter 1
The Death of My Mother

*Childhood and the mother's lap,
What more could heaven offer?
We were dazed and lost
When we started to walk on our own.*

–Anonymous Persian Poet

As far as I can telescope my mind into the past, I cannot visualize my mother fully, since I was only six years old when she died. For the first few years, bits and pieces of her could be seen in other women–a smile here, straight, long, black hair there, a big nose or a sad pair of brown eyes. But years rolled by, washing the childhood memories. However, there are certain things about my mother that haunt me to this day.

I would be mending a broken kite on the floor rug of our combined living, dining and sleeping room, when a whiff of breeze would draw my attention to the familiar figure, clad in dark brown, slowly passing in front of me in a sort of ballet motion. She would bend down gracefully and pick up my younger brother, Jwandai, then walk to the open window, sit, pull out one of her large, droopy breasts and guide the dark protruding nipple into his anxious mouth. Other times, when pickings at our shop were scanty, I would trot myself to our kitchen, where my mother would squat on the dirt floor of the small, smoky room, tending the fire under an earthen jar which contained our family's supper of lamb stew. I would stretch my hand like a beggar, and she would invariably lift the cover of the pot and, with a large wooden spoon, fish out a piece of meat, cool it by blowing on it, and then pass it to my tiny hand, pinching and patting my cheek with her free hand.

Sprawled on the dusty floor near the kitchen door, which provided the only escape route for the bellowing smoke, I watched every motion Mother made.

Memories of Afghanistan

"Why are you crying, Bobo Jan?"* I asked.

"I am not crying. It is the filthy smoke that makes my eyes water. You are getting your clothes dirty lying like that on your belly on plain dirt."

"If I stand up, the smoke will make my eyes water also."

"You little devil, go and play with your younger sister."

So many of her children died before they even managed to walk on their own feet that she thankfully bestowed more love upon those who managed to pull through the scourge of childhood ailments. I remember only snatches of conversation or the hazy outline of incidents involving Mother. Facts such as the delivery of fourteen children, including two sets of twins, or the death of eight of her children before passing their fifth year, were told to me much later by the first-born daughter, who still lives at the age of eighty-eight. But Mother's reality can be grasped for me only through my own personal experiences.

In contrast to Father, who was very religious and rarely lost a day of prayer, Mother was more casual in her relationship with God.

"It is more foolish to think that the Almighty is waiting patiently for me to tell Him how big and powerful he is so early in the morning than to prepare a meager breakfast for my hungry children. And besides, if He is as merciful and just as your father claims, why does He allow so many children to go hungry and diseased practically all their miserable short lives?"

"You are teaching the children disrespect," Father would object with a frown and much shaking of head.

"Respect cannot be demanded. It must be earned."

"How can you utter such blasphemies so calmly?"

"I am not calm. I am boiling inside. At this very moment, two of my children are sick with malaria and are shivering in the next room under a blanket, while the rest of us suffer from the mid-summer heat."

---

* Mother dear.

4

The Death of My Mother

Mother could neither read nor write. In this male-dominated society women were confined to domestic chores. In spite of her sharp wit and keen observation, she somehow did not pursue developing her mind. She watched Father teach only the boys and did not raise an objection. But her heart was heavy and sad. I was told much later that she hated to get pregnant so often, every second year after each delivery.

"Our lives are worse than those of the stray dogs that roam the streets of this dirty town," Mother used to complain. "They are as hungry and diseased as we women, but at least they can walk where they please and are not, like us, chained to an invisible post all their long and miserable days."

Mother was a funny woman. She was not talkative like Father.

"If you have something to say, say it; otherwise rest you tongue," she often said. Her specialty was humming old country songs all day long, whether while she was cutting vegetables for the stew pot, washing clothes or involved in other household tasks. In mid-afternoon, she would often hold me on her lap and lullaby me to sleep. Each song was different from the one before, but all of them fit two or three tunes, wailing monologues. She would set the harmonic tone with a hum and then improvise the words as she sang along.

"Bobo Jan, sing to me about the fairy in the white dress," I begged.

"What fairy?" she would ask.

"The one who had wings and flew into far-off places."

"Oh, that. Maybe some other time. Today I am going to sing about the little mynah who flew out of the nest and hurt its wings because it was not ready to fly yet."

"Then what happened?"

"Its mother came home and not finding the little one in the nest, she searched and searched until she found it on the ground in the thorn bushes. Now listen..."

I would hang onto Mother and fight sleep until the little bird was safely tucked away in the nest next to its mother.

Memories of Afghanistan

At night, it was usually Father who told me stories. His favorite ones were about the famous travels of my grandfather who had covered by foot thousands of miles from his native land of Arabia through Syria, Iraq, Persia and finally Afghanistan, where he settled. Father also liked to talk about the dynastic wars in the Muslim countries, especially in Afghanistan, where he himself participated in some as a young soldier. Father was not a spontaneous storyteller like Mother, who could spin a yarn as short or as long as my span of attention could hold. The expression on my face was her sign to change the story abruptly or to carry it on to climax after climax of resonant pitch of excitement.

Years later, I realized that Father's stories mainly served an educational purpose, while Mother's were for entertainment and for the delightful flight of fancy which served childhood craving. She did not tell me that inflicting pain on another was bad, but many a night I went to sleep with wet cheeks because "the little puppy's leg was bleeding and it was howling in pain." Most of her stories had a happy ending–but not all.

I must have been about five years old when there was a great commotion one morning in our house and also on the street near Father's shop. Our king, the pleasure-loving, moon-faced dandy, Habibullah, had been shot and killed on one of his seasonal hunting trips.

Habibullah had ruled for almost two decades over an unruly kingdom which had been tamed and emotionally castrated by his father, Abdul Rahman. Habibullah inherited a devastated but peaceful land–peaceful in the sense of having been dazed into submission by the previous two decades of tyranny, the like of which is experienced periodically in the dynastic kingdoms of the Muslim countries of the Middle East.

Habibullah's first and foremost hobby was collecting wives. His theory was that in order to unite his kingdom into a common bond, he had to marry the daughters of the most prominent families in his realm. From the number of offspring who claimed him as their father, one could deduce that, even if partially true,

The Death of My Mother

Habibullah must have been a very busy man. For many years, the main topic of conversation in the homes and bazaars of Kabul was the sexual proclivity of our king. No one doubted his potential for procreating, but there was a decided lack of unanimity over all the unjustified claims of so many well-nourished fat little lads strutting on the few clean streets near the royal palace. No doubt their young mothers were in the delightfully furnished chambers behind the high walls of the castle, but every pregnancy could hardly be attributed to the poor king himself.

Mother used to listen to the neighbors gossip about the king, but her contribution consisted of clucking her tongue and shaking her head, followed by, "the poor man."

"Bobo Jan, how could a king be poor?" I would blurt out.

"Be quiet, you don't understand these things," Mother would answer.

The king's killer was not apprehended. There were rumors of all sorts as to who the killer might be. The most prominent was that the anti-British faction in the army was responsible, using as its instrument the king's son, Amanullah, who at that moment was the regent in Kabul. Subsequent events confirmed the validity of this theory. Amanullah proclaimed himself king and promptly jailed any of the few in the royal family who challenged his right to the throne, including his uncle.

The new king's first important act was to declare war on England. A few days later, the people of Kabul saw an airplane for the first time. I climbed up to the rooftop and saw a large, shiny object blinking in the midday sun and buzzing like a living kite. After a short time, it disappeared behind the eastern mountains. When Father came home, I ran excitedly to him and asked, "Baba Jan,* did you see the shiny airplane?" He brushed me aside with the back of his hand and solemnly told Mother that those metal birds were very dangerous weapons.

"What happened?" Mother asked.

---
* Father Dear.

Memories of Afghanistan

"Well, the airplane dropped three bombs in scattered areas not far from one another. One landed near an army stable and killed three horses and wounded many more. The second landed harmlessly in a small brook, producing a rather large crater. But the third fell on a small house, killing everyone–father, mother and three children."

"But what do they gain by killing children and horses?" Mother asked.

"Woman, you are asking military questions rather than finding ways of protecting our family."

The pros and cons of various options were discussed among the adults without coming to any definite plan of action. So we children anxiously waited day after day for the shiny plane which never came again. We heard that a war was fought somewhere near the Afghan-Indian frontier, and after a while a peace treaty was signed.

To be objective about one's own father is an exceedingly difficult undertaking. Peeling off emotional layers so that one can have a good look at the real personality actually destroys the father image. To say that my father was more honest than most, more sexy than average and more hungry than necessary would all be true but would not explain his entity. Maybe what I should do is let events speak for themselves–some that I shared with him and others that impinged upon me through his influence or mode of living. There were, of course, other events during my early growing period that I would find hard to trace to my father, such as becoming an expert gambler and a petty thief at the age of ten, and an uncompromising foe of monarchy and the priesthood by the time I was fourteen.

My father was a most devout Muslim. He prayed five times a day facing Kaaba. After my eighth birthday, he insisted that I was old enough to pray and fast during the month of Ramadan. These, as I found out, were difficult tasks. Before every prayer session, one had to wash his face, hands to the elbows, feet and genitals. One washing could be carried to the next prayer session provided

The Death of My Mother

one had not gone to the toilet or even passed gas. I remember going through agonies of conscience about whether this rule applied to all farts or only to the ones that emitted a distinct sound. I decided on the latter, and then became an expert noiseless gas passer.

At the age of four, I sat on my father's lap to learn the alphabet. By the time I was seven, I could read almost any Persian printed book. Winters were harsh and cold in Kabul; families would huddle under a common blanket next to the short, square table under which the small brazier burned to supply us with heat. My sister, Diljan, who was two years younger than I, and my brother, Jwandai, two years younger than she, would go to sleep shortly after dinner. My father would nod his head and I would pick up the heavy book and read aloud as many as ten pages of the recent history of Afghanistan. Some nights he would disagree with the printed events and, in an emotionally-charged voice, give his interpretation.

But what I loved most was to be wakened before sunrise by my father and skip along behind him for two miles to the fruit market to buy supplies for our grocery shop. We had to be there early so as to select the best melons, watermelons and grapes. He taught me how to know whether a watermelon was ripe by recognizing the pitch it emitted when struck by a finger blow.

Haggling is a way of life in the Middle East, no matter how dear or how cheap the article. I was constantly fascinated by my father, who was one of the best hagglers in town. He would pile up the melons in a huge mound and casually turn to the owner, asking, "How much?"

"Six rupees."

"Did I hear you correctly...?"

"Yes, you heard me correctly."

"But that is highway robbery. I am prepared to give you three-fifty for the lot."

"Are you trying to ruin me?"

"God forbid," my father would console him. "I have been accused of many crimes, but not of ruining an honest man's life. So I'll add another half and make it a round figure of four rupees."

Memories of Afghanistan

"For the sake of your poor, tired son, I'll cut my price to five rupees, and no more arguments."

"My son is neither poor nor tired." I would stretch my chest as far in front as I possibly could. "And besides," my father would continue, "we are not in the habit of accepting charity. That is my price–take it or leave it. Let us go." And my father would put his large hand on my shoulder.

"At least put these melons in their proper places."

"I don't see you busy doing other things," my father would snap. As we moved briskly a few paces, the merchant would call us back.

"You are a shrewd man, but as you see, we are not very far apart. How about splitting the difference and calling it four-fifty?"

"By God, you are a tough one," Father would say as he put two more melons on the pile. "I am not going to cut your price further." Then he would order me, "Go and find a donkey to carry our load, my son."

Our home was situated in the very heart of the old city of Kabul, a city full of mud houses with common, cracked walls topped by wobbly beams. As kids, we learned to run over these beams expertly and covered miles of dusty rooftops, while pilfering any edible or other article that could be disposed of safely in the dark alleys of the town. Bedbugs and body lice were our constant companions in our walled-in adobe abodes.

One tepid morning in the month of June, I opened my eyes and saw my father's face hovering above my tiny bed. His eyes were red and tears were streaming down his cheeks. Having never before seen my father in such a state, I jumped and grabbed his legs and started bawling. He picked me up and carried me to the next door neighbor. My younger brother and sister were already there on the floor covered with a blanket. Depositing me there, my father hurriedly left the room after whispering with Mrs. Rustom. While she calmed me down, her daughter, who was a few years older than I, brought a tray of tea with bread and cheese. Mrs.

The Death of My Mother

Rustom told her daughter, Rabia, to entertain us after we had had something to eat. It was mid-afternoon when Rabia told me that my mother was dead. I told her she was lying, and began to fight with her. She answered that if I didn't believe it, I could go to the rooftop and watch for myself. Rabia and I climbed to the roof.

In our yard I saw a coffin and next to it a long board. A woman, covered to the neck with a white sheet, was stretched on this board. A short woman was washing the feet of the corpse, using buckets of steaming water passed to her by another woman. The dead woman on the board did not look like my mother at all. Her face was a yellowish-white. I told Rabia she was a liar. Running downstairs on my way to find my real mother, I found the main gate locked. I began to cry and repeatedly hit the door with my head. Days later, when I came out of a delirium, I found myself in the house of my oldest sister, two miles from our town. Sitting around me were my sister, Dada, and her daughters. Then I knew in the depth of my being that my mother had been taken away from us. Oh, how the dreadful image of the corpse with the yellowish-pale face wrapped in a white sheet pursued me for many years!

Days merged into months and seasons in their unchanging pattern paraded through the snug valleys. In our little enclosure of mud walls and crawling insects, the three of us, aged six months, two-and-a-half years, and six years and a half, crept, cried and carried on a daily impoverished existence. Father would wake me in the morning and we two would prepare breakfast, which consisted of tea, bread and occasionally a chunk of soft cheese. Together we would clean the "children" and feed them. Then he would go tend to his shop, leaving us once again to our own devices. At noontime, he would reappear to partake of a lunch of leftovers or bread and tomato with a walnut for each one. The baby was fed the same foods, but only the soft portions.

Before leaving us for the rest of the day, Father would unwind the long striped cloth from his waist and extricate a piece of lamb surrounded by strips of fat. These he put into a pot with one or two

Memories of Afghanistan

vegetables or fruit, and spices. He would build a small fire under the pot, lock the kitchen door, and leave.

We felt our mother's loss so terribly in the beginning that we often would cry ourselves to exhaustion. Sleep was disturbed by all the ghosts and goblins that roamed around us as soon as we closed our eyes.

Gradually, time began to erase the rough outline of painful memories. The winter months, with their sharp winds, were behind us. The mountain of snow which had accumulated was melting very rapidly inside our four walls, producing mires of sticky slush.

Chapter 2
The Feast of Nowroz

Preparation for the celebration of Nowroz* was in progress. My sister and I talked a great deal and agreed on a secret plan. We saved all our pennies and collected as much bread, cheese, dried mulberries and walnuts as we could. On the first of the three-day holiday, our Dad woke us in the morning, kissed us and served us the famous traditional Nowroz breakfast of *haft mewa*,† a stew of dried fruits and nuts, a large cookie for each of us and tea. A few hours after he left us, we were plodding our way to Sakhi, a holy shrine built in memory of Ali, the son-in-law of Mohammed. Almost half the inhabitants of the city of Kabul celebrated the holiday there for three days. I carried my brother on my shoulder and my sister carried the bag of food and our dilapidated shoes which had already blistered our feet. Sakhi was in the adjoining valley about three miles from our home. The town was dotted with tents from which protruded sofas constructed of mud and slabs of stones, on which the shopkeepers spread their wares of cooked *mahi jelabi*,‡ the dish typical of this holiday.

Colorful toys, ribbons and splashes of red, green, yellow and orange streamed through the bright sunny air. The noise of the food venders merged with the multiple pitch of the sounds emanating from various toys, producing an atmosphere of gaiety that elevated one's soul. The odor of mahi jelabi combined with that of human sweat and animal manure so excited our appetites that we spent most of our money for a portion of the food spread on freshly cooked bread, topped and seasoned with ground hot red pepper.

After washing down our delicious hot meal with rose-scented sweet water, we roamed around. At one point we pierced through a crowded circle to watch a striped cobra dance rhythmically to the

* New Year's Day, which falls on the 21st day of March.
† Seven fruits.
‡ Fish and candied dough fried in deep oil.

Memories of Afghanistan

tunes played by an Indian flute player. Then, for a long time, we listened to a lady fortune teller. My sister was fascinated. Finally, I entered the shrine, dragging my little brother, who was frightened of the shimmering candle-lights lined along the dark corridors and of the people who were whispering to God. At just that moment, it occurred to me that it would be quite impossible for poor God to hear and attend to all the problems spoken at the same time. Because my brother continued to whimper, I took him outside. We waited for what seemed a long time for my sister Diljan. Concerned, I carried my brother and searched for her among the various exits and entrances of the building. He was heavy, so I gave him a fistful of fried chickpeas and sat him carefully in a sunny spot near the wall of the shrine. Then I trotted briskly past the rows of shops and back alleys, calling, "Diljan, Diljan."

By this time, most of the crowd had left and the sun was about to dip behind the mountain. I panicked and started to cry. In passing the tent of the fortune teller, it occurred to me that she might be able to help me. I lifted the dark curtain. In the dim light, the fortune teller was explaining the lines of fortune in the open palm of a young man and there, in the corner of the tent, stood my sister, mouth open, still totally fascinated.

But she darted out of the tent with me and we ran toward the shrine to find our brother, Jwandai. He was where I had left him, but crying and complaining of stomach ache. He had eaten all the chickpeas.

I put him on my shoulder and we ran for home. When we arrived, Father was there. As quickly as possible, we told him what we had done. Without a word, he undressed us and put us to bed. When I woke up it was the afternoon of the next day. The other two were still curled up in bed.

This incident was a landmark in our lives. From this day on, we became children of the street. Home was used for three purposes only: to sleep, to eat, and to hide from danger. The narrow, dirty streets with their dark alleys and dilapidated shops, the sluggish pedestrians jostling against donkeys and camels, or

The Feast of Nowroz

congregating to watch a cockfight or a loud argument, were of unending fascination to us. We best liked to join others of our age and soon learned how to steal small things–mostly fruits and other edibles which could be disposed of quickly.

We had an uncle who was well-known throughout the country, particularly in the gambling joints. He never shunned a dishonest bit of work in his whole life. We called him Kaka; everyone else knew him as "The Gambler." When the weather became too cold, or if the police were too hot in pursuit, he would escape to other towns. His specialties were to mark cards and load pairs of dice and rent them to various gamblers for a percentage of the winnings. Whenever he came to Kabul, there was a room in our house reserved for him. On those occasions, he had to promise my father that he would "keep himself clean with the law." That contract meant that he was broke when he was with us.

A little more than a year after my mother's death, in the middle of the summer, we found Kaka asleep, a red bandana covering his face, on the rooftop near his assigned cabin. My sister and I were excited at the prospect of having him in our house, but Jwandai withdrew from him and sat in a corner, and our explanations failed to calm his fears. It took some time before Kaka woke up from his noisy sleep. He kissed Diljan and me, picked up the crying baby and sat him on his lap. He opened his dirty canvas knapsack and fished out an embroidered head shawl for Diljan, then slipped a string of colored beads around Jwandai's neck. Then he leaned against the wall and asked, "What is for supper tonight?"

I jumped up and asked, "Kaka Jan, what did you bring for me?"

"When I left Kabul two years ago, there were two children in this house, so I brought two presents," he answered.

"But I was here when you left."

"So you were. Then the bead necklace must be for you."

The baby clung to his beads, and I was about to burst into tears when he pulled from his bag a small object wrapped in tissue

Memories of Afghanistan

paper and handed it to me. With shaky fingers, I opened it and found it to be a round yellow pencil with a shiny metal clip on it. I grabbed his red head and kissed his green eyes.

Kaka's stay with us turned out to be a mixture of good and bad. He was a *chursi.** Daily the sweet odor and the pungent smoke curled and permeated the zigzag corridors of our house. Once a week on the afternoon of Thursday, a day before the day of rest, Kaka invited all three of us to his room for an "occasion." We were each assigned a task. I built the fire in a small brazier. My sister cleaned the sheep's innards (liver, pancreas, heart, kidneys and testicles) which were freshly bought. These delicacies were broiled on red hot coals. Meanwhile, Kaka would solemnly put a dark rubbery substance in the palm of one hand and press with the other. The hubble-bubble was already prepared with moistened tobacco leaves and set to one side within reach. Finally, the marijuana was ready to be cut into small pellets and embedded in the tobacco. It was the job of my young brother to take the live coal with a small pair of tongs in his shaky hand and, with shiny, bulging eyes, press the coal against the mixture, while Kaka whiffed and puffed the smoke all around us. The mixture of smoke and the aroma of the cooking meat, the smell from Kaka's mouth and the hubble-bubble intoxicated us all for the rest of the afternoon. I remember the hot chunks of meat sprinkled with salt and hot pepper as the most deliciously memorable meal in my life.

The disadvantages of having Kaka in our house were many, but the worst were the restrictions he imposed on our freedom of movement and the deadlines in the evening when we had to be back at home. I suppose he felt he was responsible for our health and safety since he was our uncle. Although Father told him many times that he was the last person in the world to undertake the teaching of good behavior, Kaka enforced his rules harshly and we carried the black-and-blue marks of his strappings for many days and weeks.

* Hashish smoker.

Chapter 3
My Partner Taj Gul

Morality is a luxury the poor cannot afford.
—Kaka, my uncle

I was almost seven years old when a series of catastrophes occurred which changed my whole lifestyle. My father married again–a good-looking lady whose husband had died shortly after my mother's death. My father told us that she would make all the decisions pertaining to the household. She wasted no time making a few rules right away. First, my sister was to stay home and help with the housework. Second, I was to learn a trade, not only to keep me away from street gangs while I was young, but also so that I would be a useful citizen when I grew up. My father promptly took me to a tailor shop that was not far from our own grocery shop and delivered me to a round-faced, stern-looking tailor, who sat cross-legged on a square cushion. While he served Father a cup of tea, he told me how fortunate I was to have come under his tutelage. He had small red eyes which he kept wiping with the sash of the bulbous turban that dangled over his shoulder.

My tasks for the next day were assigned to me. I was to heat two irons by filling them with live charcoal and keep replenishing them with more coal, blowing as the need arose to keep the coals hot. In addition, around the clock, I was to bring tea from the tea shop to two tailors, their relatives, friends and customers. By the end of the first week, while I was plotting an escape from this horrible routine of a tailor, I was told by the master that he was satisfied with my work and that in a year's time I would be shown how to sew on buttons.

Convinced that my stepmother was the cause of my recent miseries, and counting on my father's partiality toward education, I resolved to apply to the primary school, which already a good number of my friends were attending. Next day, instead of going

Memories of Afghanistan

to the tailor shop, I went to the Sidaqat* school for boys. The principal asked why my father was not with me. I explained that Father had no help in his shop and could not leave. Lying had become second nature to us children. We had to protect ourselves against so many adult atrocities–physical punishment being the most immediate form–that we were forced to tell lies. I always felt ashamed, however, when I told lies to Father. His calm, personal integrity was a stronger weapon than any violent action.

So, after school, I went straight to his shop and told Father about my change in plans.

"But I didn't know you wanted to go to school," he said, and added, "you have been so casual about reading and math." I promised to be a good student.

Within a period of three months, I was promoted to second grade. I was very good in reading comprehension and math, but geography was the love of my life. It didn't take me long to learn the name and location of continents, countries, lakes, and the most important rivers and mountains. I loved to sit and look at the globe, with its blue-colored waters and multi-colored countries–some large and some small. I was told that all the countries that were colored pink belonged to a rather "small, pink doll" that sat at the top left corner of Europe, the one surrounded by water, known as Great Britain. We learned more about this unique island in our history book. She was hated and feared by most of the Afghans. She shaped our destiny through her loyal puppets, the Pathan chiefs, who came from the barren hills near the frontier of British India.

I was pleasantly surprised that I began to enjoy school more and more. It provided opportunities of which I had not been aware. Since it took little time or effort for me to be the top student among my thirty-odd classmates, it seemed I could do no wrong at home, at school or in the outside world. At school, I was asked to help tutor some of the well-to-do students. I soon discovered a special bonus for me in these relationships. They brought their delicious

---

* Truthfulness.

My Partner Taj Gul

lunches, wrapped in real paper, in tin boxes. Since food was not an ample commodity at my home, I soon worked out a side racket which not only kept me provided with tasty nourishment but allowed me to hoard some leftovers for my sister and brother, who were also grateful.

The school was in session from September to June. In Kabul, the weather changes at regular intervals. Starting about the beginning of December, snow would fall intermittently and freezing temperatures prevailed for sixty days. The snow had to be cleared from the flat roof tops and was thrown either into the alley in back of the house or, sometimes, into the house enclosure itself. Since most of the houses had common walls with one, two, or three neighbors, the amount of snow inside sometimes reached as high as fifteen feet. By the middle of March, the snow melted, causing pools of stagnant water which, augmented by occasional rain, resulted in muddy water that was knee high in some streets. It was typical that I, like most of the students, managed to live through this horror of cold and slush protected only by a cotton outfit and leaky shoes with no stockings. On my hands and feet there were many layers of burned calluses that came from pressing them against the hot stovepipes in our classrooms to thaw out the numbness in bad weather.

Between our house and the school was a narrow zigzag street that was intersected by other streets. About halfway up on one side was a rather large area where all the flour and rice of Kabul was sold wholesale. The bazaar shops were arranged in such a way that each section featured a special commodity or trade. On the way to school, I passed shops that specialized in selling fruits and vegetables (fresh in summer and dried in winter); then came spice shops, shoemakers, shops of tinsmiths and jewelers. Individually, the butcher, baker, candy and tea shops were dispersed throughout the city.

There were usually two or three of us who traveled to school together, passing through the delightful mixture of odors, noise and pungent smoke. One day, we stopped in front of the chickpea

Memories of Afghanistan

vendor. He had a wooden tray covered with hot paste, spiced with salt and red hot pepper. While spicing our penny's worth of chickpeas, we would dip our fingers into the hot paste and lick them while the vendor was busy with another sale. We would delay our departure until he saw what we were up to, and then we would dash off while, cursing, he called for the police.

In the afternoon, we had more time to waste and often took detours into the side streets. One of our favorite sports was to have a member of our group order a couple of apples for a penny, then walk off with them without paying. Invariably, the shopkeeper would give chase, and when he was almost out of sight, we others would grab whatever fruit was within easy reach and walk in the opposite direction. Meanwhile the original culprit would leave the apples on the sidewalk for the shopkeeper to pick up and then join us a couple of blocks away for his share of the loot.

Some foods were easier to steal than others. It was easy, for example, to get potatoes dipped in spicy batter and fried in oil, or corn dipped in a hot vinegar sauce and fried over charcoal. These vegetables were freshly prepared for quick sale and so were displayed prominently on wooden trays or in flat, woven baskets. Here the trick was for most of us to involve the owner in a loud argument about cost, police brutality, or even as mild a subject as flying kites. Thus employed, his attention was distracted while one of our crowd deftly pierced several pieces of hot vegetable with a long, thin, sharply pointed stick. Other delicacies such as candied nuts or pistachio cookies were kept out of reach and in tightly covered jars, and for these we had to have money, real cash.

Stealing was not difficult, but selling the stolen goods was, at that point, an experience foreign to us. We knew it was possible and debated procedures for a long time before we arrived at even a tentative solution. Finally Taj Gul, our "genius" in matters pertaining to elegant living, proposed that at first we should steal something from our own households to sell. He argued that if we were caught, the worst that would happen would be that we

My Partner Taj Gul

would receive a good thrashing. Lali said that the only thing of value in his home was the copper pot in which his family's daily food was cooked, and he certainly wasn't going to deprive his folks of a hot meal. Listening to the others, I soon realized that none of us had anything of value in our homes. But Taj kept us from being discouraged by saying that what he meant was for us to tell the buyer that the merchandise we had for sale had been privately-owned when it would, in fact, have been stolen. We argued and discussed loud and long before we evolved a workable plan of action.

Now, the people in our small towns and cities in those days had a good deal of time to waste. Generally, they passed away the time by visiting friends in the shops or in their homes. Sometimes they were involved in talk that was always loud, accompanied by sweeping hand gestures; other times they indulged in games of cards or chess–but whatever their activities, the teapots were constantly refilled and cupfuls were continuously consumed.

When these folks went visiting, they observed social custom by removing their shoes before entering the social establishment. Oftentimes one could see shoes of all sizes and shapes piled up at the entrances of favorite shops. This attracted Lali's attention one afternoon as we were returning from a cockfight. In no time he had a fairly new pair of shoes under his jacket. Since he was ten years old and the eldest of the three of us, he was asked to do the selling, which he undertook with some trepidation. Taj and I stayed a block away on the alert for policemen, but Lali came back with the shoes still bulging under his garments.

"What happened?" I asked.

"I told him the shoes belonged to my father."

"You said what, you idiot?" Taj asked incredulously.

Boldly, I then told my friends to wait there, and went to the shop without the shoes and told the owner the true story. He was more than willing to give us two rupees for the shoes. This was more than we had ever possessed in our lives. From then on, the shopkeeper, Mr. Deen, became the source of cash for all our gastronomical necessities.

Memories of Afghanistan

Petty thievery became a way of life with me for the next few years until I entered high school. I always had a partner or two and was considered the "brain," who organized and planned the details. We stole spools of electric wire, cloth, shoes, dishes of all kinds, toys and sometimes even big items like carpets, tools and bicycles.

I remember one day when Taj and I were carrying a heavy wooden box full of electrical supplies we had pilfered from the corner shop. We had just entered a dark alley when I felt someone tapping on my shoulder. Without turning my head, even in the semi-darkness, I knew we had been caught by a policeman. Slowly we put the box down and froze to the ground in a stooping position.

"I saw everything," said the officer.

"What are you going to do with us?" I asked.

"Nothing."

"Nothing!"

"Not a thing. You are poor like me and stealing is certainly better than pimping. All I want you to do is to consider me a friend and a partner. For your own safety, say not a word of this to anyone."

We explained where we normally disposed of the stolen goods. He introduced us to another shop where he claimed we could do much better in price.

So for the next six months, Officer Kareem became our "protector" in our criminal activities. Then, as suddenly as he had met us, he joined his Maker one day on a lonely, sun-drenched street of Kabul. Rumor had it that he had been "bumped off" by a member of another gang of older boys whom he was also "protecting."

The scale for measuring poverty was interesting, to say the least. Our family, for example, was considered poorer than one that could buy at least one pair of shoes a year for each of its members. I never had a pair of shoes of my own until I was eleven years old. During the warm weather–between April and September–I never

My Partner Taj Gul

wore shoes outside the school yard. In the winter time my feet were covered with any odd-shaped object of whatever size. I remember hurrying to school on cold days, and, slowing my momentum as I passed the shoe shops, being awed at the sight of the rows of beautiful footwear. The most expensive shoes, those embroidered with gold and silk threads, were featured on the topmost row. The sixth and lowest rung contained the cheapest ordinary shoes that had no decoration or ornaments. I mentally resolved that some day I would be educated so that I would be able to afford a pair of shoes at least of the quality of those in the third or fourth row.

The margin between life and death was narrow indeed, even among those more fortunate than the members of our family. The wealth of a family was usually measured in terms of the quantity of necessary provisions the family could store for the winter. The most necessary items were flour, wood, charcoal, *ghee** or sheep fat. Those of us who could not afford to buy these provisions in quantity before the cold weather set in were obliged to supplement their needs on a daily basis by buying at the market at much higher prices; the economic rule was, the colder the winter, the higher the prices.

One cold winter when I was in the fourth grade, it snowed for days on end. The city of Kabul was completely isolated from the surrounding farmlands. No provisions of any kind were brought into the city. Schools and offices were also closed. Poor people groaned from hunger and shivered with cold. We were fortunate that we had food and charcoal from my father's grocery shop. During the second week of the storm, the death rate, especially among children, increased to alarming numbers.

One day I overheard an argument between the local mullah and our neighbor, Akber.

"But mullah sahib," Akber was remonstrating, "my son died of hunger and cold."

"I know," replied the mullah, "but how am I going to live in my bare mosque if charity is denied me by the people I serve?"

---

* Clarified butter.

Memories of Afghanistan

The man of God added, "You should have called me before the little one died so that he would have left this world with the words of the Almighty ringing in his ears, as stated in the Koran."

"That would have cost me money. If I had had any, I would have bought food to keep my son alive," Akber argued, with tears rushing down his cheeks.

"Are you disputing the will of God on top of your other sins? How were you going to keep him alive with food if his time to die had come?" the mullah asked.

Akber apologized for his shortcomings. The mullah shook his finger in rage in Akber's face and sternly ordered him to come to the mosque and ask forgiveness from Allah. After he left I touched Akber's hand and told him how sorry I was that his young son had passed away.

"Passed away? Who? Oh, it is you," he said, alarmingly confused. "Why is it that in hard times the children of the rich and royalty do not die?"

Poverty induced an unimaginable vicious cycle of events on a good many of the poor and destitute in Kabul. They were the beggars, who were usually young and of small stature and often malformed as a result of exposure to the elements, constant hunger and disease. Those who were fortunate died early, although some managed to live to be twenty or thirty years old. Their emaciated bodies were wrapped in whatever pieces of cloth they could find, coughing, spitting and shuffling, one hand always extended to snatch a penny or a crumb of food. They inhabited the dark alleys, street corners, river banks and mosques. In cold weather, their favorite gathering places were near bakeries and restaurants where it was warmer and the chances of getting some food were better. Even though I saw them almost every day of my life, I could never tell whether they really were as miserable as they looked or they were faking. Their spindly legs, irritated red eyes, leg stumps and fingerless hands were real enough, but I learned later that many were skilled in affecting lameness, inflamed skin and even blindness.

My Partner Taj Gul

We were children of poor parents, but we had a home and a family and were much more sophisticated in our search for the means of livelihood. We were the unseen scourge of the inner sanctum. We operated from inside houses, our own houses. Since all the houses had common walls, our mobility depended upon how expertly we perfected the art of walking on the long beams that interconnected the walls. Our gang generally was limited to two or sometimes three. Kaka Nabi and I were always together, but we added a third member whenever we had planned a special job.

In the interconnected houses, all the kitchens were located on the top floor. One special day we needed cash and our plan required a third helping hand. We planned to steal dried meat from the kitchens and sell it out in the bazaar. The meat was usually purchased in large hunks, salted, and hung on hooks fastened to poles that hung under the eaves of the top floors. The partner Kaka and I chose was Taj Gul. It was important that he be of slight build, because our operation required him to be dangled upside down while Kaka held him tightly by the ankles. I was on the lookout for the unexpected return of the owner of the house or one of his relatives. Taj Gul's resourcefulness and agility prompted our trust in him.

In a matter of minutes, Kaka pulled him up with two hunks of meat, one in his left hand and one in his mouth. He went down for a second time, and while he was unhooking a chunk of meat, he heard stirring from below and whispered to be pulled up. By this time, Kaka was somewhat tired and his hands began to shake. Taj was agitated and insisted on being hauled up right away. I ran and caught hold of one of his legs and we managed to get him on his feet in no time. With our loot, we picked our way over half a dozen walls to the safety of Kaka's house.

"Oh, what if you guys had let go of my feet, with my head down, watching the cobblestones two stories below?" asked Taj.

"We would never commit such an unfriendly act, my boy," I assured him.

Memories of Afghanistan

"It is a bit risky, though, and I think next time we should take better precautions," Kaka reflected.

Now we had to figure out how to sell the meat. It took a while to dispose of it, but soon we had our money. It didn't last long, and a few days later we were faced with how to accumulate more cash for the upcoming weekend. Taj was reluctant to join us again in the venture, but Kaka explained that he had a foolproof plan this time.

"As further precaution," Kaka said, "we are going to tie a rope securely around your ankles and tie the other end to a beam. This serves two purposes–less exertion of effort on my part trying to hang onto your ankles while I am flat on my belly, and it eliminates the possibility of an unpredictable accident."

Only after much persuasion, Taj agreed to give it a try. We chose a different house for our experiment. We tied one end of the rope securely to one of the exposed ceiling beams over the kitchen. The other end went around Taj's ankles, which had been well padded with odd pieces of clothing. Then we eased him down toward the dried meat. While we were congratulating ourselves on our ingenuity, a sudden noise from the top stairway froze us to the spot. A tall man was advancing toward us, brandishing a heavy stick. We had been so absorbed in the working out of our plan that we had forgotten to guard the approaches. Kaka and I, in an unprecedented show of energy, climbed over the wall away from the man's reach.

"What about Taj, who is dangling from the rope?"

"Don't worry, the man will release him and probably punish him some," Kaka declared. "If it were not for that rope, he could have been down with his head resting inside his intestines just as he was once in his mother's womb." Then another thought struck him. "Oh, my God, I lost my mother's clothes line!"

From an adjoining house, we watched to see what would happen. The tall man threatened to cut the rope, then said maybe he would just let Taj hang there until he dried like meat and thus became food for the household cats. Taj's face was beet red as he

My Partner Taj Gul

groaned and begged for mercy. Then he began to cough and make wild gestures. So the man pulled him up, set him on his feet, and threatened to call the police. We knew this was a useless threat. Any policeman would expect to be treated as a guest of honor when he entered a house. So, for us the show was over.

It was becoming increasingly more difficult to make an honest rupee with one's God-given wit, but I sat down and tried to figure out what the possibilities might be. I set them down on paper and began to mull them over. This is what my list looked like:

1. Carrying heavy merchandise to various houses from the bazaar. Comment: Heavy work, small pay, work not likely to be steady.
2. Buy and sell like my father. Comment: no capital.
3. Begging. Comment: I hadn't the skill and the competition was keen.

There I was, ten years old, in the middle of a hot summer. I was hungry; I had no money, and the prospects were dismal. Suddenly I had another thought. I could buy and sell ice. Only a small amount of capital would be required and the job involved some mobility. I would take orders from a number of householders, then buy a very large chunk of ice and cut it in sizes to fit the orders I had to deliver. I went to Father for his advice and consent. He was delighted as I had expected. Honest work, no matter how hard or boring, was my Dad's idea of how to make a living. That is why he was respected by everyone in spite of the fact that he stayed poor all his life. Some people called him a "sucker" behind his back, because they knew that he could have succeeded in almost anything he tried.

Let me tell you how he came to be where he was–the story that came from his own lips. When he was about eighteen years old, he was a soldier in the army supply corps. He was in charge of all the provisions a camel could carry (they had no trucks in those days). Somewhere outside the capital, two opposing armies clashed. Since the generals didn't know what trench warfare

Memories of Afghanistan

was, the men of both armies became mixed with each other. The officers, as many do today, stayed well behind the lines in safe places with their binoculars around their necks. They started to give orders to the wrong regiments. In this turmoil of unbelievable mix-up, the supply people couldn't find the right person to deliver the provisions to, so they abandoned the camels and horses and fled for their lives. All except my Dad. He led the loaded camel away from the field of battle and then tried for days to find the proper authority so as to return the provisions.

He was advised to give up this search and warned that he would be shot for desertion. It seems that there was a new government ruled by a new king, Abdul Rahman. The word was that he killed first and asked questions later of the relatives of the victim, and, if he didn't like the answers he got, penalized them by fining them to the limit of their resources.

So my father dumped the boxes of food in a friend's house and released the camel outside the city. When he opened the wooden boxes, he found they all contained cookies–"pretty good-tasting" cookies. He rented a shop in the poor section the city and started to sell cookies. Word of these tasty cookies at a very reasonable price spread around town, and his supply diminished at a fast rate. He paid a year's rental for the shop in advance, tied the rest of his cash in a long piece of cloth and wound it around his waist, then took off for Guldara to marry the love of his life, whom he had seen when he was ten years old. He brought his bride back to Kabul and started to produce cookies in his shop. In those days, there were commercial bakeries where people took their food to be cooked. Later on, he added other items to his stock, but basically he was frozen in a tight mold of honest poverty for the rest of his life.

But I have been sidetracked from my own story. My father agreed to give me some money to start my ice business. The warehouses, or ice dens as they were called, were just outside the city proper. Ice was produced in large, deep holes the size of volleyball fields. In cold winter weather, the area would be flooded in increment depths of about ten inches. Each layer was separated

My Partner Taj Gul

by a one-inch thick matting of hay. When the ice den was filled to the brim, more hay was thrown on top and the whole structure was covered with dirt in the shape of a dome. This was left untouched until the following summer, when the ice dens were opened for business.

One hot summer day, I walked the two miles to the ice den. I was barefoot, but I had several layers of padding on my body. To prevent the ice from melting, there was an entrance and an exit, each wide enough to allow only one line to enter and leave with a load. This was the only place of business in the whole country where the buyers stayed in line and, when each one's turn came, paid a definite price for a block of ice about three feet long, two feet wide and ten inches thick. I bought one, but I noticed some older and stronger fellows buying and carrying two and even three blocks at one time. I tied a rope around my block, put my hands through the loops and adjusted the ice on the padding on my back. I found the load not too heavy for me and started moving at a fairly good pace. However, after about fifteen minutes of walking, some of the water from the melting ice began to soak my shirt and drip over my backside into my crotch and down my legs onto my bare feet, so my feet soon became mud-caked as I trod the dusty roads. The spectrum of sensations on the two-mile trip ranged from cool to ticklish and unpleasant.

When I reached my father's shop, I changed into dry clothes. It took me most of the afternoon to cut the block of ice into the proper sizes and deliver them to twenty-five separate houses. I managed to carry in a basket on my head the orders for a whole block of houses.

Two persons gave me tips besides paying for the ice. One was a white-haired old lady, who was rather rich, imposing, and always well-dressed. The other was a teacher from Turkey who was employed by the government and lived modestly in our section of town. He was a short man with very long hands. Often I would find him sprawled on his bed with his door open, and he would look like a frog pinned down for dissection. Except for two

Memories of Afghanistan

or three well-to-do households, most of my customers were of the poor class. In one of the rich houses I saw a little girl about my age who I thought was the pretties thing I had ever seen. She was always polite to me and even smiled at me.

My profit on a block of ice per day was two rupees. I figured it would take me twelve days to buy a fairly good pair of shoes if I didn't spend the money on anything else. However, during the second week, Taj Gul helped me double my ice delivery to two blocks. It took some hard selling to dispose of all that ice. After delivering the orders, I brought the rest to the bazaar and peddled it by yelling, "Ice for sale, ice!" Any unsold ice we gave to some of our neighbors. On the way home with my father one evening, I told him that one day I was going to marry that pretty, rich girl.

"If I know you, the impossible is only a mild challenge in your book," Father said, rumpling up my hair.

At the end of the second week, I found the Turkish teacher lying on his bed as usual. However, he stood up and gave me a large tip. I smiled and thanked him. Quickly, he held my shoulder and kissed me on the cheek. I jerked myself loose and ran for the door, but he tripped me. While picking me up, he stuffed some paper money in my hand and promised not to hurt me. I threw the money on the floor and started to yell. Since his room was practically over the shopping area, he opened the door and asked me to pick up the money and leave. I ignored the money, jumped over the basket of ice and ran as fast as I could. As I ran I kept touching my cheek, which felt as if it were on fire from his ugly lips. I did not sell ice that day nor for two more days; then I resumed the business, but with much less enthusiasm.

The white-haired old lady was still tipping me generously. When she saw me after three days of absence, she was very happy and asked me to come and see her after my ice was all delivered. I asked her what she wanted of me.

"You will see; you will be happy," she said with a wide smile. She noticed my nervousness and told me gently that she was

My Partner Taj Gul

interested in another business and was willing to pay me more money than I could possibly make selling ice.

"If you have a minute, I will explain it to you."

I told her that I had time. She explained that she bought opium once a week from a man who lived at the edge of town, but that the trip was becoming difficult for her. If I would run this errand for her, she would give me ten rupees, plus two rupees for transportation. That was almost as much as I made in a week in the ice business.

I agreed. Two days later, we rented a buggy and she accompanied me to our destination. At the end of town she dismissed the driver. She whispered that we would walk the rest of the way, and cautioned me never to bring the driver to the house. We turned a few corners and then she knocked at a door. A man opened it and let us in. He looked at me rather suspiciously, but left us to fetch a small packet wrapped in soiled newspaper and tied with thread. The old lady took some money out of the sleeve of her long black dress and counted it into the open hands of the man. Then she told him, "This is the young boy I told you about. He is hardworking and honest. I have told him about the precautions he must take when he comes here."

He looked at me furtively, but said nothing. After leaving the house, we again walked a rather long distance before we were able to find a buggy to take us back to the lady's house. We did not talk and I enjoyed the rare opportunity of a buggy ride. After the driver had left, the lady touched my arm and said that she counted the trip as my working day and that she would pay me if I came inside. The money she gave me was two rupees more than I had bargained for. She muttered something about the cost of transportation getting higher every day. Then she fetched some leftover rice and meat stew for me.

"I don't want you to go without lunch because of me, but first I would like you to bring my hubble-bubble from the corner of the room. I asked her if she would like me to fix her a smoke and explained, "My uncle also smokes the stuff and he lets me

Memories of Afghanistan

fix it for him." She seemed somewhat surprised, but said, "As you wish." I rubbed the tobacco expertly in the palm of my hand and stuffed it in the cup. She added the waxy, flat piece of opium she had detached from her week's supply. Ceremoniously, I lit a match and held it gingerly over the mixture. She sucked the smoke in spasmodic puffs through the stem of her tiny contraption. There were certain differences between this lady's smoking and my uncle's. Her hubble-bubble did not contain water, so there was no gurgling sound. Also, the smell that permeated the room was more pungent and not as nauseatingly sweet as the smell of *churs*.*

Soon, I noticed, she leaned against the pillow. Her eyeballs were rolled upward and her hands twitched in her lap. A tiny stream of dirty-yellow saliva trickled from the corner of her mouth. I thought she was getting sick, so I shook her and asked if she needed help.

"I'll be all right in a minute," she groaned in a rasping, dry voice.

I wiped her face clean and then sat down on the floor and ate the cold food that was surrounded by buzzing flies. In a few moments, she began to stir and sit up. Her face reminded me of a ghost I had been reading about–white and fluorescent.

"I smoke only once a day about noontime," she explained. "As you can see, I can use some help around this time."

I eagerly agreed to come every day, hoping to make my weekly job as permanent as possible (selling ice was getting on my nerves). Through the succeeding days and weeks, she told me the absorbing story of her life, sad and preposterous.

Zakia had been a happy girl in Badakhshan. Her father was a small landowner. The land, adjacent to a green, rocky tableland, provided the family with all its necessities. Her family consisted of two girls and three boys. They also had two farm hands, a cook, and a tutor. All the children were taught to read and write, including the younger sister, who was twelve years old.

---

* Hashish.

My Partner Taj Gul

"It was so good to be alive in those days, but we never realized how short the time was when it all ended suddenly."

Her future husband was the chief of the bureau of taxation. He came to the northern provinces to find out how to increase the government's revenue. He was recently widowed, but he was already looking for a young mate. As a gesture of friendship to this important person from the central government, the governor of the province talked to the matchmakers, who provided a number of names, including Zakia's. Shortly, then, with the blessing of her parents, she was wedded to Mr. Yusuf Khan, who was old enough to be her father. Even though she cried for days on end, she was forced to leave everyone she loved. For twenty-two years, Zakia told me, she existed, not lived, in a pretentious house with servants and the luxuries of life, but without love. In spite of the fact that she discovered her husband was a homosexual, she had two children by him, a boy and a girl. The marriage of her daughter and the death of both her son and husband all occurred within a period of ten months.

"I was like a caged animal with the shutters down," she explained. "As you see, even at my age, I am not permitted to go out of this house without covering myself from head to toe."

She continued. After the deaths she became mentally and physically ill. Her recently discovered arthritis exploded into acute and painful inflammation. Only the administration of daily doses of morphine could give her a few hours of rest. "Eventually my craving for the drug became more urgent than the pain in my arms and legs. My maid confided in me that the drug could be obtained for a price."

The summer was almost over and I was making preparations for the opening of school in September. Zakia took an especial interest in my education. However, her physical condition deteriorated and she was in pain most of the time. Even though she put on a brave front, every time she moved she would squint her eyes and purse her lips. More and more often, she spent her time sitting or lying against the pillows gazing into space. I

Memories of Afghanistan

started reading aloud to her–stories from school books–which she enjoyed. One day I bought a brand-new book of stories from the bookstore. I could hardly wait to read it to Zakia and hurried to her house, actually running for the last few blocks.

When I reached the house, I saw several men gathering near her door. No one paid any attention to me as I pushed my way inside. I ran up the steps two at a time to the second floor where her living and bedrooms were. I barged inside and bumped into a fat lady. She shrieked and the other three or four women who were there gave me a surprised look.

"Where is Zakia?" I asked with great agitation.

A young, heavily made-up woman approached me. "So you are the young boy who was helping my mother," she commented. "Unfortunately, around noontime Mother had a fatal heart attack. She was still in bed and her water pipe toppled, burning half the bed. The neighbors smelled and saw the smoke, put out the fire and got in touch..."

"She is dead, she is dead." The phrase echoed in my brain. All my future hopes were dashed. "She is in no condition to be seen," Zakia's daughter told me.

In a daze, I walked out of the house and kept walking. Somehow, I found myself climbing the foothills of Kohe Bala Hissar, covered by yellowish, silty clay soil. My mother's grave was just a little way up the slope to the right. Her grave was somewhat eroded, so I repaired it with stones and sat down to rest.

Chapter 4
Abdul and Koko Jan

When isolated, man will count stars to protect his sanity.
—My father

Sidaqat, our primary school, opened in late September. Thanks to Zakia's generosity, for once I was well provided with clothing to protect me from the cold winds of the coming winter. I had hidden almost sixty rupees that I had saved while I worked for her, and used it sparingly for necessities.

In the same month, my father rented almost one-third of the house to a couple. The husband, Abdul, was lame. Even though he used a cane, he had to put his right hand on his kneecap when he walked, which caused him to lean in that direction, like a ship on a stormy sea. His wife was lean and pretty, with a slightly elongated face, a beautiful smile, and arms like slabs of white marble.

Abdul's difficulty in mobility forced him to find a business that could be handled inside the house. He bought large quantities of sheep fat and rendered it in vats, then scooped the melted fat into stoneware jars. Soon our house looked and smelled like a small factory, with logs piled high against the wall on one side of the fireplace and jars of solidified sheep fat on the other. He completed two cycles a week of shopping for the sheep fat, rendering it and jarring it, then transporting and distributing it to various shops in town. Friday was a day of rest.

While he worked, Abdul sat on a wooden platform close to the fire, scooping melted fat into the jars. All the time, he yelled at his wife, "Why are you so clumsy, you old fool? Prop up the container or we will have melted fat all over the ground." Her job was to keep logs going on the fire and the vats full with fresh fat. She had to bring the melted fat to Abdul, who jarred the fat, and she would then have to carry the full jars away. In addition, all day she fed him tea and food. I was a welcome guest in their midst. "Anwar, my

Memories of Afghanistan

son," Abdul would say, "don't get involved like me with a messy business and a stupid woman when you grow up." He would rumple my hair or poke me with his cane if I was out of his reach.

Every third day, when Abdul was out delivering the rendered sheep fat and collecting his money, Koko, his wife, whose real name was Zainub, would talk to me of many things.

"You are lucky to have been born a man. We women have to wait to receive our rewards on the day of judgment."

"What happens then?" I wanted to know.

"Has no one told you about it? Why, on that day Israfeel will blow his horn and people will be blown out of their graves like popcorn in a dish of hot sand. The sun will come down from the sky and the earth will become as hot as the top of a stove. People will walk around aimlessly, moaning and groaning from the intense heat. Mohammed, the last prophet sent to us by God, will finally prevail upon God to open the proceedings. The people will line up and one by one their good deeds will be weighed against their sins. They will then be told to walk over the bridge stretched over hell. This bridge is thinner than a hair and sharper than a razor blade. If your sins weigh heavier than your good deeds, you will slip and go down into the cauldron of fire, where you will burn until you have paid for your sins. However, if you pass on to the other side, you will be judged good and worthy and the gates of heaven will open to you."

"What happens to the Kafirs?"

"Naturally, they go to hell and stay until eternity."

"What happens to their little children?"

"Oh, they will be put in a place called 'purgatory.' It is located between heaven and hell."

The days Abdul was out, mostly I stayed home. Sometimes my stepmother would join the conversation. She was an expert in ghost stories.

"Did I tell you about my trip to Sakhi?" she would ask without any preliminaries and, without waiting for an answer, would proceed.

Abdul and Koko Jan

"Well, Fatima's mother and I went there for worship one Friday afternoon not long ago. On our way back home, the sky got dark and we could hear the thunder rumbling in the distance; the wind began to blow down the slope of the valley. From far away we heard the sound of drums which became louder as it got nearer. Then suddenly, the valley was crowded with creatures of all sizes. There was a turmoil of motion, some of the creatures were rolling like round balls and some were in tiny carriages drawn by little animals with horns. The tall, thin ones played music and took long strides rhythmically, looking neither left nor right. Then, all at once, they moved away and disappeared in the horizon. I tell you, it was a sight to see."

"I've never seen a show as elaborate as that," interjected Koko, "but about a year ago, I saw an afreat near the skirt of the mountain, at the edge of town where we used to live. I had gone to fetch some water from the well, and there he was clambering up the rocks that crushed as he stepped on them."

"I don't like scary tales," my young sister, Diljan, complained.

"I'm sorry, my little sweet. Go bring your *dayira** and we'll sing songs," said Koko, gently pushing the small girl toward the living room.

Diljan squatted on the floor and started to play while my stepmother and Koko sang melodious sad songs. In a short time, various neighbors began to peek down on us from second story buildings. A couple of young girls came through the door and joined the singers. I suddenly realized that I was the only male there and withdrew sheepishly from the singing circle, hoping that no one had noticed me.

One day, when Abdul was out on business, Koko beckoned me from the window of her bedroom. When I joined her, she whispered furtively, "Anwar Jan, I need your help with something. Diljan and Bobo [my stepmother] have gone shopping and I am all alone in the house."

* A tambourine-like instrument.

Memories of Afghanistan

"What do you want me to do for you?"

"Oh, it is a simple thing for you and a great favor for me."

She put a key in my hand and asked me to go to the locksmith and have a duplicate made.

"That's no problem. I will get it for you right away."

"Yes," and she seemed to be unusually secretive, "but I want you to promise me that you will never mention this to anyone."

This seemed more serious than I had thought.

When she noticed my hesitation, she said, "My flower, I am in a desperate situation. You are entitled to know it all and then tell me whether you want to help me or not. You are young, but you are smart. Also, I have noticed that you believe in justice, and that is why I turned to you. As you have seen, there is no love lost between Abdul and me. He is a bully and a loud mouth. See that huge wooden box in the corner? The key you are holding opens it. Inside, there are bags full of money, but I am not allowed to touch any of it. I am just a slave, he tells me, and he owns me just as he owns the money. But a while ago, I took some of the money. Look."

She showed me a fistful of coins.

"Then why do you need an extra key?" I asked.

"My dear, I have been in love with another man since long before Abdul married me. My lover is poor and needs capital to start a business. If I had a duplicate key, I could withdraw small sums on a regular basis and pass them to Amin Jan. When he is set up independently in business, I shall make life so miserable for Abdul that he will be forced to divorce me. Now, do you think you will help me?"

"Yes, of course."

"Oh, my heart. I wish you were a little older. I envy the girl who will get you one day." She pushed five rupees into my hand. The locksmith charged me one rupee, and I brought the keys and change back to Koko. She said I could keep the change and that more would follow in the future. She put the original key back on the chain that Abdul had forgotten.

Abdul and Koko Jan

About a week later, Koko told me that it was not safe for her to meet Amin Jan in public places and asked me to be the liaison for transferring money and arranging discreet meeting places for them.

Again, I found myself in clover. She would give me a fistful of rupees and say, "Take your share and give the rest to Amin Jan." My "share" sort of increased proportionally as time passed, especially when I learned that Amin Jan was not building a business at all, but spending most of his spare time flying kites on the foothills south of Kabul. There were days when I had to search hours for him so as to arrange for a meeting place with Koko Jan. On several occasions, I traced him to a tea house that was well known as a gathering place for homosexuals. I should explain that sexual relationships between males were commonly accepted. While there appeared to be a slight stigma attached to the male who played the female role in the affair, the male partner was talked and boasted about among his friends. Any male who could afford it had his *bacha*–any boy who provided sex as a doer, receiver, or both.

The wives of such men generally were either ignored or, in the higher society of the royal court, given a great measure of freedom in which to seek sexual outlets among their confined circle, which often included close relatives.

The affair between Amin Jan and Koko, with me acting as go-between, continued almost to the end of the winter, although its tempo seemed to slow down considerably toward the end. Amin's appetite for more money and less contact became more pronounced. Koko told me that he would become abusive if she asked for details of his business plans. On a cold January day, I searched for Amin in the midst of a snowstorm. I was cold and tired. On my third visit to Amin's favorite tea house, I asked the shopkeeper if he knew Amin's whereabouts.

"Haven't you heard? Last week, he and his bacha left for Jalalabad. He said Kabul was getting too cold for him."

"Is he coming back?"

Memories of Afghanistan

"He didn't say, but he did complain about his father and life in general in Kabul."

When I came home, Abdul was already there, and I was introduced to an imposingly tall lady by the name of Bibi Jan. She was hefty, with well-developed breasts, a large mouth, dark brown eyes and flowing auburn hair. She was quite different from Koko but claimed that Koko was her real sister. I had to excuse myself to go and shovel off the four or five inches of snow from the roof of the house. My father was already there working.

After a supper of lamb stew and bread, I pulled a cover around my shoulders, stretched my feet toward the warmth of the brazier under the *sandali*[*] and went sound asleep.

The next morning, the sky was clear and the wind sharp and cold. As I left the house for school, I found Koko Jan waiting for me near the outside door.

"Anwar Jan, what happened?"

"I'll tell you the whole story this afternoon after school."

"What story? Did you meet him?" she asked, greatly agitated.

"No. Please, I am late."

"All right, come and see me as soon as possible after school."

Late that afternoon, Koko heard of Amin Jan's flight and broken promises. The story did not take long. Tears rushed down her cheeks and she muttered as she covered her face with both hands, "Please tell me no more." I walked away slowly to leave her alone in her misery. During the subsequent days and weeks, Koko Jan ate very little and spent most of her time in bed. In one month she was hardly recognizable; her large brown eyes dominated her shrunken white face. She gazed into space. Often she was attended to by Bibi Jan and my stepmother, but Koko ceased to answer questions or tend to any of her bodily requirements. Finally, one day, she was wrapped in blankets by Abdul, who told my father

---

[*] A square table covered with a large blanket where the whole family slept. The sandali was heated by a small brazier.

Abdul and Koko Jan

that she was being transferred to her parents' house. We never saw or heard of Koko Jan again.

The tall and imposing Bibi Jan frequently visited our house "to serve and comfort" her brother-in-law. The beginning of the most eventful month in the history of our humble house began to emerge. Abdul fell in love with Bibi Jan and wanted to marry her at once (a Muslim could have as many as four wives). He gave her the keys to his wealth and she spent money on clothes, food and presents for everyone. She gave parties two or three times a week. She seduced my nephew, Nowroz Ali, who was only sixteen years old. I was actually invited to watch the sexual act for which I was rewarded with money. I saw her naked body sprawled on a large mattress in the middle of the room; her hands were folded behind her neck as she lay on a long, pink pillow with lips slightly parted and eyes dreamily watching Nowroz clumsily following whispered instructions. I was mesmerized by her huge breasts, one draped slackly over her abdomen and the other hanging by her ribs almost touching the mattress. Every time she changed position, her breasts followed sluggishly like puppies hanging onto their mother's nipples.

On an afternoon of a cold day during the last week of January, I walked into our yard blowing on my hands to keep them warm, when I noticed a small gathering near Abdul's living room. My parents were inside and my sister was craning her neck, peeking through a crack in the door. When she heard me climb the three short steps, she turned to me and whispered, "He is crying."

"Who is crying?"

"Abdul, the poor man."

"What for?"

"I don't know. Hush, they are talking again."

I pushed her out of the way and eased my way inside. Abdul was sitting cross-legged on the floor holding his walking stick with both hands, moving his torso back and forth. With his face pointing toward the ceiling and his Adam's apple bobbing on his neck, he muttered, "She has ruined me, Baba Jan."

Memories of Afghanistan

"Bibi Jan will come back," my stepmother said.

"No, she spent most of my wealth, and took what was left with her. Oh God, what shall I do?"

"You will make money again when Koko Jan is well," my father said to console him.

"Oh, no, Koko Jan died a month ago, and I do not deserve to be alive. Who would marry a poor, ugly, lame man like me now?"

Father was shocked to hear of Koko Jan's death for the first time. He ushered us out of the room and into our part of the house.

"He is an insensitive and selfishly stupid man," Father proclaimed with much shaking of his head.

The next morning, my sister Diljan found Abdul dangling from a rope, and began to scream so that we thought a snake might have bitten her. We found her on the staircase yelling, "There, there," pointing to Abdul's living quarters. We all rushed through his living room door, then stood still in horror.

As though it were a gesture of submission to fate, Abdul hung from the ceiling, his head bent to one side, with the tip of his tongue black and protruding slightly. The shorter of his legs was intersected by the curvature of the other. He was in his night clothes and the exposed parts of his body seemed unusually white.

"Go get me the kitchen knife, quickly," Father commanded. While he gathered Abdul's body in his arms, as if hugging him, he said to me, "Climb on that sandali and cut the rope." Then he gently laid Abdul's body on the mattress, closed the eyes of the dead man with his thumbs and covered him with a blanket. After he had closed the door, he said something to his wife and left the house.

Late in the afternoon. Father came home and told us that he had been unable to locate any of Abdul's relatives and had spent his time lining up a gravedigger and an attendant to prepare the body for burial, and had arranged for four clients of his shop to help carry the body to the cemetery. Early next morning, on a

Abdul and Koko Jan

clear, crisp Friday, we were all awakened very early. Father and Karim-e-Shoda were already boiling water in the big metal pot Abdul had used to render his sheep fat. I climbed on the wooden platform near the fire to keep warm and observe the proceedings.

"Bachim,* don't get the platform dirty, because we are going to wash the body on top of it. If you want to be helpful, wash the platform with a rag and some hot water." By the time we had finished breakfast, Abdul's body, wrapped in a white sheet, was brought out and pushed into the center of the platform. Father then passed hot water in an earthen jar, and Karim-e-Shoda washed Abdul's body, Then a *charpayi*† was brought in and prepared as a bed. Abdul's body was placed on it, a tiny pillow tucked under his head, and then the corpse was covered with a white-striped, gray blanket. Turning to Shoda, my father said, "Well, there is nothing more for us to do but wait for the others to show up." As they lounged near the fire, I went to the living room where I found my stepmother and Diljan still sitting near the window.

"Poor man, all alone, with no one even to cry for him," Diljan said sorrowfully.

"At least he ought to have some professional mourners," my stepmother added.

After the burial, our household settled into its normal routine of boredom. Fortunately, as I grew older, more and more areas of activity opened to me both in school and on the streets of Kabul.

---

* My son.
† A bed on four legs woven of ropes with various designs and textures.

Chapter 5
Pastimes

Most of the houses in Kabul were attached in long rows, creating dark, narrow passageways that zigzagged for blocks at a time. In the center of each block of houses, however, there was usually an irregular opening into which everyone dumped excrement and garbage. Farmers regularly picked up this mess in early morning hours for use as manure on the vegetable gardens just outside the city. We children used these openings as playgrounds, gambling dens, gang headquarters or as plain social hideouts. Our favorite one was Maidani, at least two acres of irregular land surrounded by high mud walls. During the eight months of the year when the weather was warm, all the barefoot urchins who lived within a half mile would gather there.

Gambling was a favorite pastime. We would form a circle and each put a coin on the ground, then watch with bated breath to see whose coin a fly would land on. When we could afford it, we gambled with hard-boiled eggs. Each would smack the narrow end of his egg against his opponent's, and the one whose egg cracked first had to pay for the cost of both eggs. An even simpler game involved betting on whose watermelon would be redder when it was opened.

Cock fights were so popular that all other activities would stop when they were in progress. Ram fighting, though, was rare, with contests held only once or twice a year. The fight would be arranged about a week in advance, and on the designated day a holiday atmosphere would permeate our locality, as people arrived from all over the city to watch and wager. My father never participated in any of these "stupid, cruel" games, but I remember watching my first and only ram fight. As the two animals were led in to face each other, money passed back and forth in the crowd. When all the bets were in, an unexpected calm gripped the crowd until the two rams, heads down, lunged toward each other. At impact there was loud cheering.

Pastimes

"Give it to him!"
"Crack his skull!"
"Kill him!"

Again and again the rams clacked their heads together so loudly that the noise echoed off the walls. Finally, one animal lost his balance, snorted and shook his head, standing at a slight angle from his opponent. The other ram stood still, nailing the loser with his sad eyes.

With rarely any money for gambling, I engaged in other forms of competition, like running, jumping, wrestling and gang warfare. I remember one mock fight across a pile of cow manure. The group was divided into two teams, who then collected stones for the foray. In vain we tried to get the smaller kids to leave the battle scene. Then the stoning commenced. About halfway into the game I threw a sharp stone but the black head of a child bobbed up and intercepted it. The victim turned out to be Jwandai, who was sitting dazed, hands covering his face and blood oozing from an inch-wide gash on his head. When Jwandai saw his left arm soaked with blood all the way to the elbow, his eyes widened into two saucers and out of his mouth came the loudest howling I had ever heard. Patting my pockets I found a packet of sugar, which I poured onto a freshly cut cloth and held to the wound. The blood congealed. Although we managed to wash the blood from Jwandai's body and clothing, we were never able to convince Father that he had merely fallen down and hurt himself "slightly."

One game that Afghans of all ages participated in was kite fighting. Kite making had developed into an art form and was practiced in almost every household that contained a teenager, young man or adult male. The basic requirement was the shaping of a well-balanced bamboo frame to resemble a fully stretched bow and arrow, tautly covered with a quadrangle of paper or fine cloth. The kite could be made to rotate, dive or move in any direction with the slightest twist of the fingers on the fine, strong thread. The thread we used had an abrasive coating made from ground glass and glue. In kite fighting, two rivals would fly their kites

Memories of Afghanistan

at a reasonable distance from each other and then try to position their kites so that one could slash the other's thread. Sometimes the loser's kite would soar away for miles, and chasing it became another game.

Women and even young girls were excluded from games–even amongst themselves. Their sole source of entertainment consisted of musical gatherings in the seclusion of their own homes. Some played on the dayira while others clapped their hands. Since funerals and weddings were the only other social outlets for women, it was understandable that they eagerly awaited someone's death or marriage. Diljan and I often followed our stepmother when she attended these functions.

At a funeral, a guest would enter a large living room where groups of three to six women huddled in small circles, talking and gesturing with their hands. As the newcomer entered, the conversation would stop abruptly while the widow or a close relative greeted her with kisses on both cheeks. Then, drawing her into their circle, they would let loose a frightening howling for the dead, not necessarily accompanied by tears. Periodically the wailing would cease for a few minutes while women moved from one group to another so as not to miss any tidbits of gossip. The put-on wailing, the sarcastic and often vicious remarks, the surprised hurt at having been misunderstood were all culturally accepted. In funerals, the females were participants in the act itself, and the casualness and spontaneity that prevailed made them more enjoyable than weddings.

Weddings were more formal. Even though everyone dressed their finest and wore all the jewelry they possessed, there was a definite protocol that depended on the closeness of one's relationship to the bride or groom. Those who were seated farthest from the entrance received the best food and the closest attention.

The matchmaking that preceded weddings was much more interesting. My oldest sister Dada was considered one of the best matchmakers in the trade. She not only found brides and husbands

Pastimes

for our growing group of relatives, but her success spread far and wide, and she was consequently hired for good wages. To watch Dada's performance was a great treat. Once I listened while Dada delivered her findings about two young girls to a close relative of our family.

"Now, about the two girls, Rabia and Fatima. Both are from good, middle-class families."

"Stop right there," the prospective mother-in-law interjected. "I know the father of one is a low-rank military man and the father of the other is just an office worker."

"Nevertheless, they are of about the same social standing as your family," Dada insisted, "and of the two, Fatima can read and write."

"That's not important. Can she cook and is she strong enough to wash and clean?"

Ignoring the questions, Dada continued, "They are both young–about fourteen or fifteen. But... I think Rabia is prettier."

"In what way?" another woman in the circle wanted to know.

"Well, she has eyes like almonds, a nose like a pen and a mouth like a dot."

I burst into a loud guffaw at this vision, but they all glowered at me and I had to retreat sheepishly from the house.

After many such meetings, one of the girls would be agreed on and a visit would be arranged for the mother of the bridegroom. Then the matter would be turned over to the fathers to settle the bride price. The poor principals would not even see each other until their wedding day, by which time they would be tired, nervous and filled with foreboding. After the couple was congratulated, kissed and pushed into a prepared bedroom, the wedding guests would disperse–except for the bridegroom's mother. She would keep vigil behind the closed door, listening to the whisperings and groans from inside. In case the groom failed to pierce the veil of virginity, she would have a small undergarment soiled with sheep's blood ready to send to the father of the bride early the next morning as testament to her son's virility.

Chapter 6
Days of the Locust

Whatever good visits thee, it is of God
Whatever evil visits thee is of thyself.

–The Koran

I remember the year of the mild winter when I was in the fourth grade. Practically no snow had fallen in the city or, as I read in the paper, most of the country. I commented to my father that it was a good thing that we poor people were not suffering excessively from the cold and the cost of keeping warm. I was surprised that he did not share my enthusiasm.

"The snow is needed to provide water for next year's crop. We shall suffer more by paying high prices for food, if we can afford it, or go hungry if we can't."

"But Father, I always thought that it was the spring rains that provided the water."

"No, my son, the main supply comes from the slow-melting snow. Since our country has no dams to save the surface water for irrigation, it is mostly wasted."

There were scattered clouds to be seen over the mountains that spring, but the ground was dry and dust storms were frequent. No rain came. By April and May, the fields of lettuce, onion, and turnip that had sprouted a month earlier, having been drenched with well water, had shriveled and died. Even the wells began to dry up and what water we had began to taste putrid and salty. Fortune tellers, fakirs, sorcerers, and mullahs gained prestige and were consulted often. The government came up with the bright idea that what we needed was a mass prayer. Shops, offices, and schools were closed and everyone was urged to gather in Bala Hissar for a mass prayer. My friend Kaka Nabi and I went there quite early in order not to miss anything important. Water carriers, with their sheepskins full of a muddy fluid still called water,

Days of the Locust

were there banging their tin cups against a chain, calling all souls to quench their thirst for a small sum. Mullahs in fancy festive clothes were lined up on an incline. Some sat on mats especially spread for them before their arrival. A bedraggled army of barefoot school children lined up in front in a state of semi-exhaustion. Beggars, shuffling with outstretched hands, lamented the state of their misfortune and asked for small favors. Peddlers pushing their small carts of cooked beans or boiled potatoes were in great demand. For a penny, one received a modest spoonful of beans or three small slices of potato on the palm of one's hand.

Office workers came in groups and lined up where space was available. The more important people came later in buggies. Then the police went into action to clear a spot for them, even if they had to crack a few bones with their sticks.

It was a gray May afternoon. The sun was not behind the clouds, but was diffused by a dust storm which had been blowing intermittently for a month now. People were getting restless and tired. Nerves were on edge, and there were some fights, both of verbal and fist variety, in progress. Then a sudden shrill whistle was blown from the far left near the road and was answered by two or three others at the edge of the crowd. A hush permeated the multitude and everyone craned his neck to get a glimpse of the important personages who had just arrived. Two men descended from a black automobile and waddled up the slight incline to where the mullahs sat. Both wore bulbous white turbans, and their short, fat frames were covered with embroidered dark blue *chapans*.* Their short walk so exhausted them that they mopped the perspiration vigorously from their round faces with pink silk handkerchiefs. As things settled down, Kaka and I learned that the older man was the Hazrat Sahib himself, the most powerful holy man in the country and a well-known British agent. The younger was his brother, Sher Agha, who had political ambitions of his own.

The ceremonies started with a chapter from the Koran, sung by a young mullah who had a resonant tenor voice. Sher Agha

---

* Tightly knitted large overcoats.

Memories of Afghanistan

made a short political speech alluding to the fact that Afghans always showed their nobility under difficult circumstances.

"Never forget that you are living in a free and proud country. You are linked with your other Islamic brothers in a tradition of sacrifice and hard work and these difficult days ahead of you are but stepping stones to the future glory that is sure to follow."

The crowd stirred noticeably when the Hazrat Sahib approached the imaginary podium. He raised his right hand and sternly addressed God:

"We are your people, oh Lord. You chose us to spread the seed of righteousness among the sinful and the infidel. Don't forsake us now. Send your angel of mercy to provide us with our bread and water..." He begged and cajoled the Almighty to be in a better mood. Then he finished with a prayer in Arabic that nobody understood.

On the way back to the city, Kaka looked up into the sky and said, "I don't see any rain yet."

"Give Him time, my son, give Him time. The Hazrat will not be so nice to Him the next time," a passerby remarked. A gathering on the side of the road attracted our attention. Kaka and I went there to investigate. A *malang** was addressing the crowd around him. He was half-naked to the waist, the heavily-tanned upper part of him glistening with oil. Ornaments of all kinds covered his ears, neck, fingers, wrists, and waist. Some of the jewelry was copper, some silver, all studded with various colored semi-precious stones, blue and red predominating.

"I'll tell you what is wrong with the whole procedure," he was saying. "It was like a political gathering. No sacrifice of any kind was offered or promised. Not even a lamb or a chicken was slaughtered to mollify the spirits or the rage of God. Then, of course, there is the Devil and his diabolical disciples all around us." So saying, he put a pinch of an aromatic plant seed on the charcoal fire that a little boy with inflamed eyes and runny nose carried in an elongated copper pot. The pot was decorated with

---

* Fakir.

Days of the Locust

angels of all shapes and sizes, with swords poised to strike. The little fellow would swing the pot with his right hand in front of the onlookers, while his left stretched to accept any offering from the crowd. All the while, the aromatic seeds crackled in the fire and emitted a large volume of blue smoke.

"Yes, my friends, right now I can see the little monsters riding on your shoulders urging you to follow the path of wickedness," the malang proclaimed. "Can you bring us rain?" a young army officer asked. The malang ignored him, but answered the question in his own way. "We are being punished for our transgressions. When Allah is sure that we have repented, prayed to Him in humbleness, asked His forgiveness and shared our good fortune with those in need, then the gates of heaven will open and water will pour in abundance."

When he realized that he had squeezed all the pennies he could from the crowd, the malang sat on the ground and ignored them. He was left alone with his little partner. Kaka approached him and said, "I didn't have any money to give you, but I have some special snuff that I would like to offer you." He unwrapped a piece of cloth he had dragged from his pocket and gave a large pinch of the snuff to the malang. The malang thanked Kaka and put the snuff under his tongue, and after a minute or two said, "Your snuff is good and strong, my son." We bowed and left.

"Where did you get the snuff?" I asked Kaka.

"Well, because of the drought, tobacco has become expensive this year. So I have been experimenting with fillers and when I get the right combination, you and I are going to make piles of money. I discovered that two parts of horse and cow manure and one of tobacco was too weak, so my last formula contained some slaked lime also. So far the response has been mostly positive."

It occurred to me then that taste-testing before the introduction of a new product in the market was an ancient art.

In the succeeding days and weeks there was still no rain. The rainy season was usually over by the end of June. School was closed and the city was either in the grip of hot sun rays or gray

Memories of Afghanistan

and suffocating dust storms. People walked about as if in a trance, oblivious to the misery and suffering around them. For the first time in my life, I noticed my father, with his hands folded on his lap, watching the empty walls for long periods of time. Beggars begged less and slept more under the shade of a wall or on the side of a ditch. Months earlier, the merchants who had hoarded food in the hope of obtaining higher prices had decided to keep it for their own use.

One evening. Father gathered his family around him and announced gravely that our already meager supply of food had to be rationed most carefully. He closed his shop and brought home all the edible products, itemizing them on a piece of paper, each by weight.

Infections were rampant and took a heavy toll, especially on the children of the poor. Street dogs roamed in gangs attacking corpses of beggars that were huddled in the nooks and crannies of the dark streets. These incidents produced such a strong agitation that the government declared war on dogs. At first, the authorities proclaimed a rupee would be awarded for each carcass of a dog that was delivered to a police station. This plan was soon abandoned for two simple reasons–people did not have the energy to chase and kill the dogs, and besides, the small number of dogs that were killed ended up either in the butcher shops or in restaurants. The revised plan was to send soldiers to each locality to shoot the dogs and pile them on the backs of donkeys to be dumped into a large ditch dug for the purpose.

Meanwhile, of course, the families of the very rich and those of the royal house had gone for long vacations to India and were taking up residence in such cities as Peshawar, Lahore, Delhi and Karachi. A few brave ones visited such distant cities as Paris and London. The Hazrat Sahib and his entire household had gone to their usual retreat in Simla, where a comfortable house was always at their disposal as the special guests of His Majesty's Viceroy to India. A skeleton crew was left behind to rule the kingdom by edicts and regulations. Personal problems and small legal affairs

Days of the Locust

were left to the discretion of mullahs and their interpretation of the scripture in the Koran.

The main topic of conversation in Kabul, even among us children, was food. Money had lost its value as a medium of exchange, even at black market rates. Since no newspapers were available, there were rumors that the famine was confined only to Kabul and its surrounding areas. People did not have much to do. They congregated in small groups and gossiped. One day some neighbors gathered in front of my father's closed shop and argued heatedly among themselves.

"What are we going to do, Haider Khan?" Mirza Youssef addressed my father.

"Submit or fight back; what else is there to do?"

"How can one fight God?" Ali Ahmad, the carpenter, interjected.

"Our country is large, and behind the Hindu Kush mountains is Mazar-i-Sharif, where water and grain are plentiful," my father explained. "This is the second year that not enough snow or rain has fallen in our area. Everyone knew this–everyone except our government, whose job it is to plan emergency food distribution."

"If you know so much, then why don't you go and tell the authorities what to do," asked Kurban, one of four brothers who operated an ice cream business when milk was available. I was leaning against the familiar smooth column of our shop, watching and admiring my father for his stand. He was alone in his defiance of authority, and yet they knew he was right.

"Drought," Father said, "is the result of natural causes, but hunger and suffering is man-made, caused by the callousness and lack of foresight of those who manage the affairs of our country." This was strong medicine for some, who shuffled away silently from the gathering.

In the fall, dust storms blew through the dry mountains and dumped their collected loads inside the valley of Kabul. Due to the lack of water in streams and ponds, mosquitoes were not a

Memories of Afghanistan

common sight that year, but hunger took its toll in human misery, especially among the young. Pasty in color, with extended stomachs and spindle legs, the forgotten victims would curl up on the sidewalks, doorsteps, or in the sandy shade of the dry Kabul River, and whimper their last breaths.

One day on my way out of the house, I saw a few locusts jumping around. A few hours later more had dropped on the streets. By noontime a black cloud of locusts enveloped the city, raining on the rooftops, alleyways and streets. People began to sweep the dead locusts away into ditches. The locust invasion lasted only a few days, but it was symbolic of yet another calamity.

My father was a very religious man. I knew that there were details of belief and various stories in the Koran that he took with a grain of salt, but his fundamental belief in God was unshaken. In early childhood, I received my religious training at home along with reading and writing. Being a Shia (a minority Muslim cult in Afghanistan), religion outside the house had very little effect on me. My early image of God was that of a super-father, stern and yet kind. I used to picture Him sitting on a golden throne managing all the details of the earth, especially of man. When I was sick or in pain, I would look up at the sky and, with tears in my eyes, whisper, "I am sorry," as if I were being punished for something I was not aware of. Even at a tender age, though, I sometimes considered the obvious contradictions in my father's point of view, blaming the governmental authorities for their shortcomings and yet absolving God of all misdeeds. Was He, or was He not, responsible for the terrible cruelties that were being dished out to everyone around us? If "He knows best," then why criticize those who were but the instruments of His criminal follies? These disturbing thoughts persisted in my receptive mind for many years, urging me to seek new answers to old, unresolved questions.

Is there a hope, an escape? In the big map of the world that hung in our classroom, the colorful patches of land, surrounded by the blue of the oceans, provided me with many daydreams. Surely life was not a predictable journey through disease, hunger and death everywhere on this earth.

Chapter 7
How to Catch a Chicken

Search for knowledge, even if it is as far as China.
—An Arabian proverb

Sidaqat was the primary school where I spent an eventful five years, completing six years of study by skipping a grade. The school resembled a dilapidated prison rather than a house of learning. It faced the Kabul River and was adjacent to the bazaar. On either side of the entrance gate, several gypsy families lived on a sort of rotation basis, so that we encountered new faces there two or three times a year. They lived in small, two-story structures, of which the ground floor was a shop and the upper one the living quarters. We had no playgrounds at the school nor nearby, so during the recess period we either walked back and forth in the school courtyard like prison inmates or climbed the rooftops to watch the bustle of the city.

My favorite spot was on a ledge that protruded toward the gypsy houses. I would lean there in the warm sun and listen to the constant barrage of obscene abuses daily practiced among the female gypsies.

The teaching staff in Sidaqat was a conglomerate of diverse individuals whose common characteristic was that they did not understand children. Their methods of teaching were questionable, and oftentimes their knowledge of the subject matter was inadequate. Corporal punishment was practiced by most of the teachers, especially those who were least confident of themselves in their profession. There were, however, compensating factors that made life more interesting in school than it could have been on the streets of Kabul. For instance, there was Abdul Raheem Khan, our history teacher. He was a young, intense man who impressed us with his conviction that history should deal not so much with kings, their wars and dynastic rivalries, as with the mass of people, their

How to Catch a Chicken

modes of living, their aspirations, beliefs and economic pursuits. He pooh-poohed historic names like Napoleon and Genghis Khan, but openly admired men like Socrates and Darwin.

While we did not particularly love our Persian teacher, we did respect him. He was a poet of a sort and taught us a great deal about great men in literature such as Hafiz and Sadi. The theme of most Persian poetry was love and separation, but Mr. Moshin was an uncompromising foe of "this trash" of romantic poetry.

"A poem should either excite the imagination or say something profound," he would declare. He was especially fond of the skepticism found in Sadi's poetry.

Most of the teachers, however, were not only incompetent, but cruel, sadistic, partial and unfair as well. The cruelty of one of our religion teachers could only be avoided if one were an exceptionally "pretty" boy, or the son of an official or a wealthy man.

"I must familiarize you with the taste of hell here in this world before your Maker sends you to live there forever," Mullah Jabbar would expostulate as he brought the end of a long stick across a shoulder. One student, Abdul Rasul, was not bright and just could not memorize the religious instruction, which was all in Arabic. He was regularly thwacked on the bottom of his bare feet while one student sat on his chest and two others held his legs high in the air.

Besides teaching religion in our school, Mullah Jabbar performed religious duties in a local mosque. His library there consisted of three large, dirty-brown holy books. He lived in a corner of the ground floor, where his straw mat was spread over a padding of hay. One morning, when we were in the fifth grade, we heard that our Mullah's bedding had caught fire during the night. By the time he woke up he had third degree burns; he was not expected to live. None of us students was sad or even disturbed by the news. Rasul even smiled and remarked, "Well, he has his chance to taste the hell he used to scream about!" Fortunately for us, Mullah's replacement was a kind, lovable man, though rather rough in appearance.

Memories of Afghanistan

Our penmanship teacher was a big man. His grey beard covered every feature on his face except his large, shiny nose, which, like a red clay mound in the middle of a dense forest, seemed not to belong there. Hot or cold, Haji Momin wore the same garments all year round. We students played all sorts of pranks on our teachers, but Haji Momin was impervious to our tricks. Even when we once burned the corner of his long overcoat, he merely stomped out the fire without disturbing the rhythm of breaking pine nuts between his fingers, and eating them one at a time, all the while collecting the shells in his lap so that he could dispose of them later. We were hurt and ashamed by his lack of response–hurt to have been so casually ignored, and ashamed to have harmed such a nice man. When he saw our sad expressions, he walked near our desks, messed up one boy's hair, pulled down another's cap, and patted still another on the shoulder. Finally, he stood in front of us and said, "My children, this coat is getting too old. I was waiting for an excuse to buy myself a new one."

Two days later, as he entered the classroom, we noticed that he was wearing the same coat, but it looked a bit shorter. He had tucked it under all around so as to cover the burned spot.

The student body was a diverse representation of the many different types of people who lived in Afghanistan. The Pathans either tutored their children at home or sent them abroad for their education. However, as the conditions in our schools improved, we began to see a trickle of these children in attendance with us. In the last year of my primary sixth grade, Noor Ahmad, the son of Mohammed Wali Khan, the governor of Kabul, joined us as a student. He was driven to school in a buggy and on arrival the driver would conduct him ceremoniously to our class, arrange his lunch box in the corner and place his real leather satchel of books on his desk. I was offended by the presence of royalty, but since I was president of the class, it was I who had to deal with him. One day during our lunch break, he stopped me in the corridor and said he would like to talk to me.

"What about?" I asked impatiently.

How to Catch a Chicken

"About treating me unfairly," he said.

"Well, I am not about to pamper you like the guy who delivers you to school every morning," was my belligerent reply.

"I only want you to be as friendly with me as you are with the other students," he explained.

I broke up the conversation and started to run away, but yelled over my shoulder, "I'll try."

To my surprise, we became good friends for the remainder of the sixth grade. He invited me to his house about a mile away on the other side of the river. We entered through a heavy gate, then through a smaller, ornate one, after which I found myself in a huge garden surrounded by brick walls almost thirty feet high. I followed Noor Ahmad to a stairway that led to the third floor and a series of rooms that faced the river on one side and the garden on the other. There were other buildings and structures inside the enclosure and many tall trees and bushes. There was a fenced-in tennis court in the far right corner and a huge fountain in the center from which radiated flower beds and gravel paths. For the first time in my life, I realized that there was another Kabul than the one I had always known with its dusty roads, dilapidated, cracked-wall structures and dirty surroundings. Lives in this compound pulsated at a different tempo and rhythm and I wanted to know more about them.

Meanwhile, gradually I was shedding the childhood friends of the inner city where my family lived and cementing ties which were school-centered. In spite of my tutorial efforts, my financial resources were still meager. I had not entirely given up stealing to make extra money, but less and less that way of life had appeal.

Our science teacher, Abdul Aziz, was an interesting but limited person. He was a member of one of the royal families and had been sent to Europe as a young man for training as a scientist. Somehow he became more interested in other immediately obtainable pleasures, such as girls, rather than science. He traveled from one country to another either chasing a girl or running away from one. Consequently, he had a passing knowledge of German,

Memories of Afghanistan

French and English. His scientific curiosity led him to practical problems, especially if they had economic value. One thing he did was to extract odorous material from the local flowers that grew abundantly in Kabul and nearby areas and from them produce perfumes. He showed us how to make soap and black gunpowder. He joined our school faculty at the age of twenty-four, when his family realized that they were wasting their money on a foreign education for him.

While it was true that he did not know much about science, he was familiar with the lingo of science and used it with such authority that some of the other teachers in our school regarded him a "profound thinker."

I was fascinated by the fact that events could be predicted before they happened if certain conditions were met. Often at night in my little room, I would sit for hours at a time and contemplate a concept he had presented. "Is it possible for a person to make himself invisible?" I would muse. If so, one could kill tyrants without being caught, or steal a man's wealth. The words "wealth" and "steal" jolted me back to reality, and I remembered that I had agreed to play poker and had not a penny in my pocket. This led to a new line of contemplation. Perhaps I should go to Maidani and steal a chicken. In my limited way, I set up a formula for the process in my mind:

Aim:	To steal a chicken
Problems:	Chicken runs away when approached
	Makes loud noises when chased
Solution:	Catch chicken from a safe distance without attracting attention or causing noise

I pondered this and the solution flashed into my mind with such suddenness that it surprised me. I went to the butcher's shop which was only a few steps from my father's shop. From the container of odds and ends, I fished out the intestine of a sheep. On the way to Maidani, I cleaned it, and as soon as I got there, I found a flock of chickens scratching for food in a pile of cow manure that had been

How to Catch a Chicken

spread to dry. I sat in the hot midday sun, leaning against the wall, and watched their scratching maneuvers. I tied a knot at one end of the intestine, then stretched it and buried about six feet of it in the manure heap, with the knotted end exposed above the surface and the other end of the intestine in my hand. Putting my head between my knees, I pretended to relax, all the while watching the precocial birds and awaiting the outcome of my experiment. Before long, a large chicken started to nibble at the knot and began to swallow it. I waited until he had swallowed a couple of inches of the intestine and then I began to blow air through the open end. That poor chicken raised his head as if to object to the indignity, then plopped onto his side with his mouth open and filled with the blown-up intestine. Having managed to catch the bird with no undue noise, I grabbed it by the neck and pulled the intestine out of his gullet. Laughing quietly at the ludicrous aspect of the experiment, I tucked the bird under my coat before releasing the pressure around his throat so he could breathe.

By the time I entered high school, however, I had completely rejected stealing as an avocation.

In Kabul, there were many grade schools, but only three high schools. Habibia, the oldest and most respected of the three had been established by King Habibullah during the early years of his reign. Most of the second line office holders were graduates of this school. The other two schools, Istiqlal and Nijat, had been opened in the early twenties during Amanullah's rule and served mostly relatives of the royal household or of prominent businessmen. The graduates of these schools later became heads of government ministries and of the army.

On a certain day in June, all students who had successfully completed the courses of study through the sixth grade were gathered in the courtyard of the Ministry of Education. At first the students stood in proper lines, awed by the colorful buildings and uniformed guards. Gradually we relaxed and sat down or sprawled on patches of green grass. By the time we were beginning to feel hungry, tired and in desperate need to use the toilet, a booming

Memories of Afghanistan

voice jolted us back to attention. Names of the top scholars from each grade school were read aloud.

I was among the twelve to fifteen students who were ushered into a large room. Each of us was interviewed by a stern man whose beard almost reached his navel. He had a high, nasal voice that rolled through thick lips, and his sunken brown eyes penetrated, it seemed, the innermost privacy of the interviewees. Two assistants on either side helped him classify the students, writing their names in a special book on the desk. Each applicant was given an overall look and asked one question, then told to stand aside. When my turn came, I was embarrassed. My clothes were dirty and torn in places.

"What is your father's occupation?" I was asked.

"My father is a shopkeeper," I answered truthfully.

When all those in our group had been questioned and sorted, a new batch of students who were the second highest in their schools filed in. We were then told to return to our respective schools and in a week would learn where we had been assigned.

During that week, we learned that students were assigned according to simple requirements. To enter Istiqlal, a student had to come from a rich family and his class standing had to be in the upper one-third. Nijat's requirements were similar except that the standards were somewhat less stringent. All the intelligent riffraff of Kabul landed in the third school, Habibia, where academic standing, but not wealth, was necessary for entry. I was not disappointed to be with this group, since just having been given entry meant that I would be supplied with a splendid uniform and lunch free of charge. But I was surprised to learn that my nephew, Nowroz Ali, who had only an average class standing and whose father, too, was a shopkeeper, had qualified for Istiqlal.

"How come?" I asked him.

"Well, I said my father ran a 'business establishment'."

Chapter 8
A Summer in Kohistan

The weather in Kabul was predictable and sharply divided into seasons. In the spring, the snow changed into rain, interspersed with short hailstorms and thunderstorms. In the midst of this miserable weather, an emerald sky might envelop the valley of the town and sunlight would surround the mountains.

In April and May, my favorite months, I loved to climb one of the mountains. Sometimes I would take with me a few books in a cloth pouch that hung from my shoulder. At this time of the year, the crisp, balmy weather was exhilarating; the early growing low plants hugged the soil, here and there sprouting a rainbow of flowers. The washed, clean air and the flight of the newly-arrived migratory birds blinking in the sharp rays of the sun were delightful. During these moments, my mother, whose grave I could almost point out, would be focused sharply in my mind, and the accumulated pain of daily living would be washed away.

Spring merged into summer when the hot sun rays drove us kids to the polluted water of the river. At night, everyone in the city fled to the flat rooftops to catch the soothing cool of the night breeze. I loved to lie on my back and watch the shooting stars flash like sharp whips against a calm, black, blinking infinity. The intense rays of the moon threw the black shadows of the surrounding objects into elongated forms, twisting them along the patched-up curvatures of the mud walls.

One day as I moodily strained for the summer to pass so that I could get involved in the activities of the high school, my stepbrother, Najaf Ali, tapped me on the shoulder and asked, "How would you like to go to Kohistan with me?"

"Kohistan?"

"Yes, I have been appointed a district officer there. You can spend as much of the summer there as you like."

Memories of Afghanistan

"I would like to very much, but I have to clear it with my father."

"I have already spoken to him and he has no objection. We will leave in one week. I have sent someone ahead to make the necessary arrangements for our arrival."

Our trip to Kohistan was uneventful. Najaf and I dozed most of the way in a congested truck to the rhythm of the creaking wooden seats. In late morning we arrived at the small, dusty town of Charikar. The driver stopped the truck so suddenly that half the passengers landed on the floor. He stood up, guffawed and said, "Now I don't have to wake anyone up from a disturbing dream, do I?" In the next breath, he announced loudly, "Chaaa-reekaaar!" then jumped out of the truck and headed for the tea house. Najaf and I brushed the dust from our clothes and headed for the dilapidated bazaar. It was the season for cherries and plums. We bought a handkerchief full of each, which cost only a few pennies. After dipping the fruit bundles in the cold water of a noisy brook nearby, we had a hearty meal of fruits.

When we reboarded the bus for the second leg of our journey, we noticed a few new faces among the passengers, whose number had dwindled to half. After talking with the driver, Najaf learned that the village we wanted was a good sixty miles further north and about three miles off the road. The truck zigzagged around the skirt of the mountains and climbed steadily as we headed north.

"These mountains are only branches of a much larger mountain range, the Hindu Kush, which cuts Afghanistan into two almost equal slices," I commented, trying to impress Najaf with my knowledge of geography, but he did not respond.

Finally, it was our turn to leave the truck, and we began to talk as we walked along a dusty road lined with tall poplars that led to the village that was our destination.

"The area looks poor to me," Najaf said.

"All of Afghanistan looks poor to me," I answered.

"But I was hoping to have been appointed to a more prosperous locality."

A Summer in Kohistan

"What has that got to do with it? You're certainly not coming here for a vacation. You have been sent to serve these people."

"Are you out of your mind? In this country, one does not serve. One rules. It cost me two thousand rupees to buy this job, and I am..."

"To buy the job?" I asked incredulously.

"Of course. Every government job has a price tag and a duration limit on it. Mine costs two thousand for four years. My salary will not cover the cost of food and other necessities."

"But how will you make a living if your salary is so meager?"

"That depends on my ingenuity and the resources of the community. That is why I commented on the poverty of the surrounding area."

"I still don't understand," I said.

"You will when you watch me operate on a micro scale. On a macro scale, the national treasury is at the disposal of the officials. When you see what I do, you will be getting a practical education that will serve you when you are grown and have responsibilities to meet."

"But isn't this dishonest and immoral?"

"Look who is talking of morality and honesty! I have been told that you are a common thief and a gambler–not that I give a damn one way or the other. We are like fish in the ocean, running after the smaller fish and hiding from the larger ones."

I thought to myself, "Yes, I am a common thief." We walked the rest of the way in silence, but ideas and thoughts crowded my mind as we plodded along. Morality. Honesty. Truth. Compassion. What were they? Who thought of them first? What was the meaning of good and evil? How was one to measure? What is the yardstick? I became completely confused in contradictions. Najaf asked a passerby about the government building and we were told we were on the right road.

"How far is it?" I asked.

Memories of Afghanistan

"Well, if I were to discharge my loaded gun in that direction," he said, pointing the muzzle of his musket up the road, "the bullet would fall just about there."

We thanked him and started walking again.

"He at least confirmed the direction," I said.

"And if we believed the claim about his muzzle loader, we would have been there already," Najaf added.

We finally arrived at the district office as the last rays of the sun were leaving the upper branches of the tall poplars along the road. The huge door of the compound opened and in the enclosed alleyway, the figure of Noorgul, who reeked of marijuana, was discerned.

"In anticipation of your arrival today, there's a big pot of chicken *qorma** simmering in the kitchen," he said by way of welcome.

"You smell as if you have already had your dinner," Najaf commented. Noorgul ignored this remark, shook my hand and said, "Salaam, Anwar Jan, I am glad you decided to come."

"Salaam, Noorgul," I replied.

The building was a square enclosure. In its center was a well and on two sides of it various colored petunias were in full bloom. By this time I was both hungry and tired. We were conducted to the upper floor of the two-story building and shown to our respective rooms.

"If you are dissatisfied with these, you can change rooms tomorrow. You have eight bedrooms from which to choose."

I dropped my small bundle of clothes and books on the floor and stretched out on the bed. I must have slept immediately, because when Noorgul woke me for dinner it was quite dark. With the aid of an oil lamp, he directed me to the dining room on the ground floor, next to the kitchen. All three of us sat cross-legged on the floor around a yellowish tablecloth.

"Badur, come, bachim, and say hello to your boss," Noorgul yelled. A short, loosely-dressed man rushed inside and kissed

---

* A stew with or without one or more vegetables.

A Summer in Kohistan

Najaf's outstretched hand, while his little daughter of seven or eight years stood near the door, one finger in her mouth, gaping at us with big, black eyes. From the kitchen, the mother handed the dishes of our meal to the little girl, who, in turn, handed them to her father, who placed them ceremoniously on the floor. The dinner consisted of chicken-potato qorma, freshly-baked *chapati*,* pickled eggplant, tea and melon. With our fingers, we dug into the common dish in the center for hunks of meat, and were somewhat surprised to find that the claws and head of the chicken were also included in the stew.

"Let us not make a fuss now," Najaf told Noorgul, "but tell the cook to keep the head, claws and innards for her own family."

"They will be pleased," Noorgul answered.

I ate as fast as possible and went back to bed.

I was awakened next morning by the sound of a *robab* greeting a glorious day. Noorgul was plucking the musical instrument as it lay on his lap. The little girl sat on a straw mat watching him. These little incidents were reminders that sometimes life can be fleetingly beautiful even in its barest essentials. The scene of the sun-flooded courtyard where a woman in a red-trimmed black dress was drawing water from the well in the midst of a profusion of pastel leaves and flowers held me spellbound until I remembered that I was hungry again.

After breakfast, Noorgul took me along for a tour of the place. The little girl, Omyra, and a gentle, ugly dog, Zytoon, tagged behind us.

Pointing to a brick square attached structure, Noorgul explained, "This is our prison."

"How many prisoners do you have in there?" I asked.

"None. Najaf Khan just arrived. We don't intend to keep prisoners very long anyway."

"How do you know? You're not the district officer."

---

* A round, flat bread baked on a hot slab of stone.

Memories of Afghanistan

"Oh, I have been involved in this racket off and on for the last twenty-five years. Several times I have even served the *hakim*[*] who has anywhere from ten to twenty district officers under him. You see, here we deal only with small fish. The big ones–murder, inheritance problems involving large estates, or political disputes– are dealt with by the governor."

"Can I look inside?" I asked.

"Yes, you can. But mind you, when there are prisoners there, I want you to stay away."

The structure had no windows. Light entered through a small grate in the center of the ceiling. The room was bare except for four yellowish straw mats on the bumpy mud floor.

"Omyra will show you the rest of the house. I have some other work to tend to now," Noorgul said.

At first, Omyra was shy with me, but within a few days, she and I became inseparable pals. She was pretty, and it didn't take long for me to discover she was also extremely intelligent. When she introduced me to her parents, they asked me not to take her far from the house and always to ask permission first. Her father worked around the house and also took care of the vegetable garden, while her mother cooked, tended to the flowers, washed clothes and performed many other household chores. During my three weeks' stay, never once did I see her idle.

During the first week, I roamed the countryside, sometimes alone, other times with Zytoon. I found her to be a lazy bitch. On level ground, she would run around and bark playfully, but when I attempted to climb the mountains that stretched east to west like a flock of stags with sharp, pointed horns, she would watch me dolefully for a minute or two, then walk away toward the house. The mountains always drew me like a magnet. I loved to be away from all living things, all sounds, even bird songs, alone up there gazing at nothing in particular, remembering the most intensely sad and happy moments of my short life.

[*] Governor.

A Summer in Kohistan

One morning during the last week of my stay I heard shouting in the courtyard. When I reached it, I saw two farmers in a fist-fight over the irrigation water. One accused the other of stealing his water by diverting it during the night. The accused, a big man with fat, hairy arms and a thick neck, was nervously combing his long gray beard with his fingers. His neighbors, who considered him a rich man and a bully, gathered outside the door to find out how the new district officer meted out justice. His accuser, a tall, much leaner man, had had the lobe of his left ear torn in the fracas, and blood was congealed on his neck and shirt. Even though he seemed to have gotten the worst of the fight, he still stood defiantly.

Noorgul took the wounded man upstairs to Najaf's office. When they came down, I asked if I could watch the proceedings upstairs.

"No," he said firmly, "no one is allowed there except the clients and the witnesses." But I could hear the yelling–and the bully was getting in more words than the other.

Suddenly, Noorgul walked briskly across the yard to a room that was always kept locked. I ran after him to see what was in that room. He did not prevent me from entering. It took a moment for my eyes to get used to the darkness and then I noticed that various leather whips, a metal chain and other odds and ends were hanging from the wall. Noorgul adjusted a thick belt with a revolver in it around his waist.

"I think we caught a good-sized fish in the net," he said.

I did not grasp his meaning, but asked, "What are the implements of torture for?"

"Oh, those are the tools of my trade."

"You aren't making any sense today. Where are you going with the revolver?"

"Don't you hear the yelling upstairs? I am going to calm him down a bit." Saying that, he pushed me out of the room, locked the door, and ran upstairs. Soon afterwards, he came down behind the big man, whose hands were tied behind his back. Noorgul marched him to the prison and locked him in. Then he asked if

Memories of Afghanistan

anyone in the crowd had witnessed the fight. The tall, lean man pointed to two men, but they refused to come forward, so Noorgul dismissed them. He then warned the tall, lean man that his case was weak without witnesses.

"They are afraid to speak against that bully, but you don't think I inflicted these wounds on my own body, do you?"

"No, I believe you. But wounds have a nasty habit of healing up. Pronto, no evidence. See my point? Go home now, and we will call on you when we need you."

I followed Noorgul to the prison gate, but he told me to stay out. While he was inside, he talked a few minutes with the prisoner and then went upstairs to report to Najaf. Again this procedure was followed with the voices inside the prison becoming even louder. As Noorgul came out the second time, he was furious and mumbled something like "the bastard needs a little persuasion." I was about to lose interest when Noorgul came back with a short, thick leather whip. Omyra and I tried to find a crack in the door to watch. During the beating, we heard the prisoner cursing Noorgul, but not crying.

Late that afternoon, the prisoner's son came to inquire about his father.

"Why hasn't he been released?"

"We will let him go when we are through with him," he was told.

"May I see my father?"

"You may not."

"He is an important man in this village. You will be sorry if he is mistreated."

Touching his holster, Noorgul snapped back, "Are you threatening me?" The son glared, spat on the ground, and walked away.

Just before nightfall, an old man with a white beard and bushy white eyebrows that almost covered his eyes walked with the help of a cane toward the office. A few steps behind him was a young boy carrying a covered basket on his head.

A Summer in Kohistan

Noorgul met him at the door and said, "We do not accept special food for our prisoners. They have to eat what is given to them." Shaking his head, the old man and the little boy left.

"He will get only bread and water, and we will see how long he can last, the stubborn donkey," Noorgul mumbled to himself. Next day after breakfast, Noorgul went to see the prisoner once more, this time carrying a chain twisted around his arm. Loud noises could be heard all the way inside the main house.

After lunch, I asked Najaf about the treatment of the prisoner. He reminded me that he had promised me a practical education and that now was the time to watch him in action. He called Noorgul and told him to bring the accused to his office.

"You just sit there and say nothing," Najaf said to me.

"If you are going to beat him again, I am not interested."

"No, no more beating."

When the prisoner walked into the office, he seemed to have lost most of his haughtiness. However, he still held his head high and glowered at Noorgul, who was told to leave.

"I apologize for any inconvenience you may have suffered. This is my younger brother. Please sit down." Najaf was pointedly courteous.

"Never in my life have I been maltreated like this. My family is highly regarded and respected in this village!"

Najaf replied dispassionately, "High or low, everyone is treated equally by the laws of our free country."

The prisoner was not so easily appeased. "I have been physically abused by your aide, and I shall appeal to the higher authorities for a redress."

"I am glad that you feel that way, because I am sending you to the higher authority, the governor himself. Your victim and the two witnesses have been informed. As soon as transportation is available, you will be sent to him. Meanwhile, you shall be treated as my guest."

"May I go home, or at least see my son?" the prisoner requested.

Memories of Afghanistan

"I am afraid you cannot do either until you are in one of the governor's isolated cells in Charikar. Then it will be up to him how generous he might want to be with you."

As Najaf talked, the prisoner nervously combed his beard with the back of his stubby fingers. He knew the game was up.

"Could we talk alone?" he asked.

"My brother here is like my right arm. He has promised not to speak to anyone about our conversation."

"All right. How much do you want?"

"Eight-hundred rupees in cash or commodities, and it must be arranged by you and your son in this office, where you will stay with me until the transaction is completed."

I left the office and took a long walk towards the mountain, thinking about my exposure to the kind of corruption that had permeated every aspect of Afghan life. The culprit, I finally reasoned, was poverty. Poverty breeds corruption, uncertainty and fear–fear of going hungry, fear of becoming ill, fear of not being able to provide for loved ones. In a poor society, the criminal elements always seemed to rise up from the poor and the destitute. But if almost everyone was corrupt, why were the prisons full of the poor and the helpless? Wasn't it punishment enough just to be poor? I could find no answer.

I decided to go home to Kabul as soon as transportation could be arranged. As I entered the district office, Noorgul greeted me with a big grin.

"I don't know how Najaf Khan did it, but we have two carpets, a sheep, three bags of flour and two hundred in cash," he said, using his fingers to emphasize each item. I did not respond.

Back home in Kabul, I found two messages from the Ministry of Education. One advised me to appear as soon as possible at Habibia High School and the other to attend a meeting of all the students at the ministry. The purpose of the meeting was to acquaint the students with the educational authorities.

Habibia was located on the outskirts of town, a distance of two miles from the center. It was on a high bluff, surrounded

A Summer in Kohistan

by gardens and green grass. What a contrast to the dirty, smelly areas where we lived! Before school opened officially, I went there almost every day for six weeks. Students were measured for uniforms and advised that a new one would be issued each year. I met many students, some from other provinces. We participated in sports, mostly soccer and gymnastics, and met our teachers, some of whom had recently been hired from India.

Such happy days they were! The country was changing. There were new buildings, new factories, roads, running water in pipes that came right to our doorsteps. We thanked God who had finally given us in Amanullah a wise and concerned king. One of his earliest acts had been to send students to foreign countries for training. My brother was already studying in Germany, and I hoped some day I, too, might go to one of those strange and exotic lands.

Our uniforms were issued a few days before the start of school. This was the first complete set of clothing I had ever owned and I treated it with extra care. The first day I came home wearing it, Father leaned back on a cushion with his arms folded on his chest and said, "Let me look at you, bachim. Now no one would know that you come from a poor family!"

"I am not ashamed to belong to this poor family," I said.

"Come here, then, let me kiss you."

I bent down to receive his token of affection. My stepmother, younger sister and brother watched.

The cloth of which the uniform was woven was domestic wool of fair quality. Each night I inspected it for spots, and before going to bed, carefully folded the trousers at the seams, stretched them on the floor and covered them with my sleeping mattress. The weight of my body served to keep the seams looking freshly pressed. I was even especially careful not to let any body or head lice spread onto my new garments. Once school opened I found that class distinctions of wealth disappeared as if by magic. Everyone wore the same clothes and ate at least one meal together.

Memories of Afghanistan

Much of the subject matter we began to learn was new and exciting–chemistry, physics, biology, algebra, English and drawing. The old standbys like geography, history and religion were continued. I was surprised to find geography and religion as exciting as chemistry, but discovered that it was not so much the subject matter as the personality of the teacher that made this true–the way the material was presented and the way the teacher treated his students.

Our geography teacher was a Muslim from India who had married an Afghan and settled in Kabul. He taught not by rote, but by reasoning and demonstration. A country's agricultural products and climate, for instance, could be determined by its distance from the equator, its proximity to the oceans and their currents, its altitude, and the surrounding mountains. His demonstration of the solar and lunar eclipses (with models in a darkened room) was an artistic accomplishment and even the dullest students were able to grasp the concepts so logically and visually presented. His explanation of the way seasons are caused in the tropics by the movement of the earth around the sun in an elliptical path and slightly inclined in the same direction was a masterful performance. As important as his teaching ability, however, was the fact that Mawlana Hassan was a beautiful human being, kind, helpful and considerate.

Our religion teacher, Amir Khan, was very different. He was like a young boy himself, playing games with other young boys. He was pliable though his profession demanded rigidity, doubtful when he should have been certain. He was a man of God, but had a hard time accepting the gods of man. We loved him because he was so confused, the poor man.

The first six months at Habibia was one of the happiest periods of my childhood. I had to work hard to stay at the top of my class because the competition was keen. I participated in sports and became a fairly good soccer player. Our team was one of two chosen to compete at Paghman during the celebration of Afghan independence.

A Summer in Kohistan

Two catastrophes, however–depicted in the next two chapters–marred this pleasant dream. They opened paths full of obstructions, but were fateful as well.

I felt as if a new life had begun.

Chapter 9
The Stoning of Amir Khan

For six months Amir Khan had been teaching us religion twice a week. He was a tall man, gaunt, with sunken cheeks. He smiled often, especially when we argued with him the intricate problems of religion. With a jerky motion of his hand, he would elaborate upon a theme that was perhaps beyond our comprehension. We were all boys of 12 to 15 in Habibia High School in the city of Kabul, almost 45 years ago.

Amir Khan was a kind man. He enjoyed aphorisms and tossed them around with a twinkle in his eyes:

"It takes courage to be humble."

"Why bother to be good when you are honest?"

"A good soldier is not born, but produced by two requirements: a cause to fight for, and a gun to fight with."

In the following decades, I found myself using some of these unconsciously.

Our school was composed of an ornate dome structure dotted with tiny windows that let in the light and in times of emergency were used as gun emplacements. There was a spiral staircase. The building had large French doors at regular intervals. These led into carpeted chambers that contained decorated columns, carved woodwork and crystal glass chandeliers. These were our classrooms. Around the building for about a quarter of a mile ran a red-brick path. Opposite the school a sharp slope, studded with flower beds, led to a stream, a large orchard, and a playing field. This entire edifice had been built fifty years previously for King Abdul Rahman, the tyrant.

We liked Amir Khan, oh, for so many reasons. Among all the teachers, only he and the geography teacher refused to carry or use a stick on the students. Amir Khan let us talk and shout as loud as we were able to. If our noise disturbed the adjoining classes, he would take us all down the slope on the run to the edge of

The Stoning of Amir Khan

the stream or into the orchard, if we promised not to steal the fruits when they were in season. Musa the blind (he wasn't really, but he had a large cataract on his left eye) and I were the most vociferous debaters. I can still remember Musa, with his elbows on the desk, his face resting on the palm of his hand, questioning the very validity of sin. Amir Khan would smile and, with a sweep of his bony hand, try to marshal his thoughts in response to the questions.

"If sin were justified, then the whole structure of reward and punishment would fall apart, and along with it, the idea of heaven and hell. By the same token, if the civil authorities did not punish wrongdoers and law breakers, then chaos could certainly follow."

"Ah, but the king does not compel us to commit a crime and then punish us," Musa would shout. "You yourself told us many times that all our actions are predetermined by God; if so, it is not justified for Him to punish us for His own doing."

Again Amir Khan would smile and recite from the Koran the eye-for-an-eye and tooth-for-a-tooth passage. I raised my hand and declared: "It seems to me that we are mixing civil law with religious edicts, the former being a contract among equals, in order to have a functioning society, and the latter superimposed from up above, with a built-in element of compulsion and no choice."

"Did I hear you say 'among equals'?" Musa asked.

"Yes, I did imply that," I answered.

"Your implication is unjustified. Let me tell you that our civil laws are just as arbitrarily imposed as..."

"Children, children, please, we are getting too far away from our original topic," Amir Khan would declare.

Amir Khan loved to discuss, reason, question and mull over subjects, not only with us, but with other teachers, especially two other religion teachers in the school. In the middle of the school year, he began to invite Musa and me to walk with him after school and on the weekends. As we walked, he would tell us of his pains and pleasures, of his heroes, like Suqarat (Socrates) and Aflatoon (Plato), and of ideas far beyond our comprehension.

Memories of Afghanistan

"An idea is like a rough, precious gem, freshly mined," he said once. "It is full of debris. It has to be cleaned, polished, cut and shaped to bring out the sparkle. Plato wrote a whole book about the concept of justice. Socrates spent a lifetime on it."

Then, for two whole weeks, Amir Khan did not show up in class. Our inquiries at the principal's office were left unanswered. On the third week, a new religion teacher was appointed, a heavily bearded tyrant who smelled, like most mullahs. He enjoyed beating the students so much that he would invent new excuses so that he could spend more time beating than teaching.

On one occasion, he ordered us to stand and put our hands, palms down, on our desks. He walked around observing our hands and wrote notes as he did so. Then he walked to his desk and read the names of about half the students.

"Those whose names I just read, line up against the wall. Now, it says right here in the holy book," slapping it with the back of his hand, "that one must be neat and clean at all times. Those against the wall have not trimmed their fingernails. For this, each one will receive a punishment of three blows with a stick on the back of his hand." The rest of the period was an exercise in cruelty. He had barely finished when the whistle for recess sounded. As the students rushed out of class, one yelled, "Mullah Sahib, you smell."

"Who said that? Stop." Mullah raised his hand.

No one paid any attention to him. By the end of the month we all settled into a normal routine of rote study, spiced with occasional bodily injury. Amir Khan became a dim memory, creeping slowly further and further into the past history of the savage tribes dotting the unproductive slopes of the mountains that hugged us on all sides.

But I saw Amir Khan again, almost ten months after he left us. He was sitting on a wooden box in the corner of a shop in the section of a bazaar where condiments were sold. His feet were stretched stiffly in front of him and he was engaged in a lively conversation with the shopkeeper. As I neared him, I noticed that

The Stoning of Amir Khan

heavy chains hung from his waist and were fastened to large, shiny rings around his feet. A soldier with a gun leaned against the wall. I was almost paralyzed with fear, but kept slowly creeping forward. Amir Khan saw me and, with a wider smile than I had ever seen on his face, stretched both hands to receive me. I kissed his hairy neck and turned my face away to wipe the tears with my shirt sleeve.

"He is one of my students," he told the shopkeeper. Turning to me, he said, "I have been trying to see you and Musa."

"What is the problem?" I asked, looking at the chains.

"Oh, these? I have been accused of heresy and the two religion instructors in your school are their witnesses."

"Who accused you?"

"That powerful English spy, the Hazrat Sahib and his disciples."

"Aren't you afraid to talk like this?"

"Afraid I am, my dear, but when the water level is above one's head, it doesn't matter how high it is."

"Where can we find you?"

"I am allowed half a day each week. You may find me here again next week at this time."

We parted sadly after a short chat over a cup of tea. The following week, Musa and I came back to the shop. It was closed. We waited most of the afternoon, but Amir Khan never came.

About ten days later, on a warm Friday afternoon in another part of town, I saw a crowd gathering and heard a commotion. A loud voice was announcing the sin of heresy of one Amir Khan, a former teacher, for which he would be stoned to death that afternoon. I struggled through the crowd to where Amir Khan was. His head was bent slightly to one side and his hands were tied behind his back with a dirty yellow rope.

I ran to him and tried to talk with him. I was stopped by one of the four soldiers who were guarding him, who prodded me with his gun and tore my sleeve and bruised my arm. The nature of the crime and the punishment was announced repeatedly every

Memories of Afghanistan

half mile until we arrived at a rocky clearing at the outskirts of town. Nearby was the royal palace surrounded by a moat half-full of odorous water covered with algae. At the site of the execution, a regiment of soldiers was lined up in a semi-circle at the far end. To the left, a dozen mullahs, wearing bulbous white turbans and long shabby beards, were standing. To the right, there were two rather comic characters, one on horseback and one on the ground, looking nervously at each other. They distinctly did not like their assigned jobs.

Amir Khan was brought before the mullahs who asked him some questions, then nodded their heads when he made a request. He walked slowly a few steps, faced Kaaba and prayed in a sitting position for about five minutes. Then he was led inside the circle, soldiers on one side, townspeople on the other, and mullahs sandwiched in between. I forced myself to look straight at Amir Khan's face. As he looked up at the cloudless sky and lowered his gaze toward the men of God, the mounted soldier raised his saber as the signal to commence the "show." Stones flew from all sides, some missing and some hitting Amir Khan. I was mesmerized and kept looking at his face. Blood gushed from every side of his head. My knees began to shake. I sat down and vomited my lunch of bread and watermelon. When I looked up again, Amir Khan was no more. Where he had stood, there was now a large mound of stones.

Townspeople began to leave hurriedly for home, running away from their collective monument of guilt. The soldiers marched dolefully toward their barracks near the royal palace. I walked slowly to the mound of stones. A piece of cloth shimmered in the evening breeze. I bent over to vomit again, but only a blob of sour spit dislodged from my throat and stuck in the roof of my mouth. A dizzy feeling forced me to sit down and lean against the pile of rocks. The memory of Amir Khan's last wide smile hovered in my mind, only to be replaced by the image of his bloody, bobbing head.

I walked southward to the edge of the moat. The croaking of a few frogs in the shallow green water added a disturbing note to the solemnity of the descending darkness. I turned around and

The Stoning of Amir Khan

gazed at the stone mound, whose outline could still be discerned among the creeping shadows. It occurred to me that Amir Khan was indeed a dangerous heretic to the upholders of law and order and their priestly underlings who sanctify them. He even disturbed their dreams in the plush prisons of their own making. I clutched my sore arm and plodded home, sad and confused.

Chapter 10
The Valley of the Roses

One finds his way only when one has lost it.
—Mullah Nasruddeen

Once a year, a night called Show-i-Barat* was set aside for fireworks. Weeks in advance, we children prepared for this exciting occasion. Fireworks of all sizes, shapes and colors were bought and sold in shops, on street corners and from baskets carried on their heads by vendors. Since our sources of money were limited and we wanted to test our own ingenuity, we bought only the essential ingredients and went to work.

Two types of fireworks appealed to us more than any other, because both produced an impressive bang. One was an imitation of an army cannon. Antique guns were sold reasonably at many shops. We would buy one, saw off the muzzle to a length of about ten to fifteen inches, fit it with braces and attach strong wooden bases. The guns were then packed with gunpowder, sand and pieces of cloth wrapped around stones. At the end, there was a tiny aperture through which we could ignite the explosive, using a sturdy match tied to the end of a long stick. The gun barrel was always aimed at a wall to create an even deadlier noise than a regular gun.

The other firework we made was a ball of cloth tightly packed in its core with a mixture of rough sand, gunpowder, sulfur dust and potassium chlorate. We would take these colorful balls into a crowded market place and throw them up into the air. Upon impact with the ground, they created a deafening sound and it amused us to watch people scatter in all directions.

My "cannon" was a fancy one with shiny brass belts wrapped around the barrel. It was tested with spikes that penetrated a hard mud wall to almost two inches. When I was preparing it, I squatted

---
* Barat's night.

The Valley of the Roses

on the ground, holding it like a baby as I filled it with chipped stones and gunpowder. But suddenly there was a blinding flash as two pounds of gunpowder enveloped me in a sheet of flame. I pressed the palms of my hands over my eyes and yelled for help. I removed my hands from my face only after my relatives had pulled off my burning garments and laid me on a cushion in the living room. I was relieved that I could still see clearly with both eyes, even though my eyebrows and the hair from the front half of my head had been completely singed.

But a great deal of damage was done to my body, only to be discovered as new pains, like ripples in a pool, succeeded the ones before and invaded new and unexpected areas. Within three days, my left leg, left forearm, face and forehead had swelled enormously. My face was like a well-baked loaf of bread that compressed my eyes and mouth into tiny slits. I was fed liquids for a couple of weeks. Then the blisters appeared, some large and some small. Some areas on my leg appeared to be infected and patches of raw tissue began to slough off. Pain came in cycles, more intense each day. It disturbed my father so much that one day he wrapped me in a blanket and carried me on his back to a dispensary which had recently opened in the capital. This was some two miles from our house and the trip was extremely uncomfortable for both of us.

A young Indian doctor instructed his assistant to take us to the next room at once. To our surprise, we learned that both the treatment and the medicine would be free. Since the superstitious population thought of modern medicine as the work of devils and infidels, the place was almost ignored. That is why, probably, we were received like welcome guests. Dr. Chawdary and Dad had a rather long and private conversation while I lay flat on the cushion-covered charpayi listening to Aslam, the compounder, read the labels on the medicine jars and explain the miraculous healing powers assigned to them.

Our trip to the dispensary became routine every Thursday morning. I was warned after the first trip that my leg would

Memories of Afghanistan

get much worse before it got better. The treatment consisted of covering the affected parts with a thick yellow paste and wrapping them with many layers of white cloth. By the third trip, patches of raw tissue began to slough off when the wrappings were renewed; all the while the pain was so intense that I had to bite my tongue to keep from crying out. It seemed to take a long time until new wrinkled skin began to form over what not long ago looked like a slab of bare bone. The damage resulted in my not being able to stretch my leg straight, so a long process of daily rubbing with oil began. Every morning Dad gave me my oil treatment before he left for the shop. Diljan, my sister, brought me all my food and helped me hop on my right leg whenever I needed to go to the bathroom.

All my waking hours were spent in reading. My favorites were the books Dr. Chawdary sent me, some in English, that had pictures and beautiful maps of strange lands. I sat near the window for hours watching the snow drift lazily hither and yon while my imagination took me to foreign lands, across lofty mountains, great rivers and unlimited expanses of water. In these reveries, I pictured myself as a medical man who helped people in pain, or a revolutionary who helped destroy tyrants who kept us in perpetual bondage... then I would glance down at my emaciated leg that Father rubbed and oiled daily and stretched to make normal, and my eyes would fill up with tears, obliterating the pleasing images.

The worst of the winter was over; snow began to melt under the ever-stronger sun rays that penetrated the crystal-clear sky. My foot had healed enough so that I could walk slowly with the aid of a walking stick. Dr. Chawdary advised that I recuperate for at least two more months–more school to be missed. Sensing my extreme boredom at home, Father suggested that I spend the spring with my uncle's family in Guldara (the Valley of Flowers). About fifteen miles north of Kabul, my mother's two brothers lived in this beautiful village. Only one was prosperous enough to have his own home, vegetable garden and a rather large fruit

The Valley of the Roses

orchard. In the late summer and early fall, Uncle Hashim brought his produce of apples, cherries, grapes, and shelled walnuts to the capital for sale. While he was in Kabul, he always stayed in our house. During the year, the outlying farmlands provided the city with wood for cooking, dried fruits and other staples.

However, before my trip could take place, two other matters had to be taken care of. I had to have an aching eyetooth pulled by the local barber and also to be "rejuvenated" (bled) to improve my health. Losing one's teeth was a common phenomenon. By the time most people reached the age of forty, they had only a couple of broken molar stumps that the expert twist of the barber's pliers had failed to dislodge, and these stumps often disintegrated in time. The practice was, at the first sign of pain, to apply small sticks of cloves. Then, if the tooth still ached, it was pushed and pulled in every way to dislodge it. As soon as the tooth could be manipulated easily, a strong string was tied around it as close to the root as possible, and the other end of the string was fastened to a doorknob. Then, eyes closed and mouth open, the open door was pushed and *voila!* there was the tooth dangling from the knob in one clean, surgical operation.

My luck was that I was unable to loosen my ailing tooth, so it had to be extracted the hard way by our local barber. Purposely, I left a thick knot of thread on the tooth, because our barber, Kareem-e-Kor (Kareem the blind) was known sometimes to pull some healthy teeth before getting to the right one. Also, I hoped the thread marker would help distribute the pressure of the pliers. I was told to sit on a ledge in front of Kareem's shop. Father draped his hand around my shoulders, while Kareem groped his way into my open mouth. A crowd formed to watch the performance as if it were a cockfight. I grasped the barber's hand and admonished him, "Not that one... but the one with the string around it."

"What is the string for?"

"To make sure you pull the right tooth out, you idiot," my father said.

Memories of Afghanistan

"Padaram,* have I ever charged anyone for pulling the wrong tooth?"

"No, you pull three teeth for the price of one. You are a generous man," a young fellow yelled.

Ignoring the public comments, the barber told me to open my mouth. With my father's help, he adjusted the rusty pliers on the knot and, with a few back-and-forth motions and a jerk of his arm, he had the culprit out. Between my howling and the laughter of the crowd, it proved to be a noisy operation.

Blood-letting was performed exclusively by gypsy women. This was only one of the arts they plied; they told fortunes, dewaxed ears, sold exotic extracts to improve one's health or sexual potency, and sold little wax balls that promised to take care of one's enemies. They said if one pressed sharp objects into the balls, buried them in wet or dirty places, or simply burned them, they could do the damage one desired.

On a scheduled day, the gypsy woman entered our house and spread her faded shawl on the ground in a sunny area. We children were lined up near the open window. She smiled, exposing her toothless gums. In anticipation of this ordeal, I was in such a state of trepidation that one look at me would have convinced her and everyone else that there was not a drop of blood in my system. It didn't matter. My stepmother pushed me gently and I walked down the three steps and stood at the edge of the shawl, watching the old woman unwrap her dirty bundle exposing three objects–a razor, a small, thin aluminum pan, and a brass suction device which resembled a very large smoking pipe. The cup had a diameter of about two and one-half inches and the ornate stem was not less than eight inches long. First, there was a short ceremony of rubbing, cleaning and arranging the instruments and then I was told to take off my shirt, sit cross-legged and bend my head as far forward as possible. An area about the size of a silver dollar was chosen between the shoulder blades and the upper part of the spine. The skin was pinched with the forefinger and the thumb of the

---

* My father.

The Valley of the Roses

left hand into little folds while the razor in the right hand cut little parallel lines all over the circle. Then the gypsy covered the area with the suction cup and she sucked the wound, causing a vacuum and a rush of blood. She repeated the process, filling the suction cup and emptying it into the aluminum pot until it was about half full. The whole process was repeated on the other side of the spine to match the first one. All in all, about a pint of blood was collected, then examined, before the payment in coins was consummated. My stepmother rubbed my back with sesame oil and gave me a warm glass of milk into which a raw egg and sugar had been beaten.

Within a few days, I gained some weight and eagerly awaited the trip to Guldara. It was the month of April and my birthday passed unnoticed. Fast-moving, low clouds rushed east to west, lingering long enough to deposit a load of rain or hail, but before too many days had passed, the sun played hide-and-seek behind scattered fluffy balls of cotton candy clouds. Spring was pleasant and it felt good to expose my body to the warm rays of the sun. On Friday, my father told me after our meager breakfast to pack up the necessary clothes and books because that very morning a friend of my uncle's had volunteered to take me to Guldara.

It was strange to leave my familiar surroundings for the second trip of my life. I found Haji Zaman[*] and his donkey good-natured companions. Zaman was a husky, broad-shouldered man with a bulging dome of a forehead, under which his rather long and thick nose lost its prominence. Under his black, bushy eyebrows, his large brown cow-like eyes also played a secondary role. However, his white-edged, thick beard was impressive indeed. He carried a long, pointed stick. At regular intervals, he emitted a nasal, high-pitched noise that sounded like "eech dyaaa," and at the same time touched the butt of the donkey with his stick. Zaman was a man of few words and brushed aside my interminable questions like so much childish hot wind, or at least his expression and gestures said as much.

---

[*] Haji is a title that any Muslim is entitled to use after he performs his pilgrimage to the Arabian city of Mecca, where Mohammed was born.

Memories of Afghanistan

The distance between Kabul and Guldara was fifteen miles. I was told that four hours of steady walking, not counting the rests in between, was about all the time it would take to get there. We had started before noon and expected to get there by late afternoon. Donkey in front, Zaman right behind him, and I a couple of steps farther back, we walked more or less in a straight line. Since Zaman was not answering my questions, I began to daydream. All of a sudden, Zaman and his donkey were transformed into Mullah Nasruddeen and his donkey, the legendary character of all the countries in the western half of Asia, where the bulk of the Muslims live.

The sounds of Haji Sahib's grunting matching those of the donkey brought me back to reality, and I asked how far we were from our destination. Haji Sahib cleared his throat and pointed to the next hill and assured me it was the beginning of Koh Damen.*

"At every fold of the mountain there is a green valley," announced Zaman, "starting with Shaker Dara,† followed by Guldara. They stretch all the way to Kohistan,‡ a distance of fifty miles." I looked at my friend with new eyes and was ashamed because I had classified him as the village idiot.

"Have you traveled through every valley?" I wanted to know.

"All of them and many more. Once I was a teacher in the primary grade in Charikar. That is a rather large town in these parts, where each village consists of only a couple of hundred houses."

"Don't you teach any more?" I inquired.

"No, the government replaced us self-taught fogies with young high-school graduates."

"My father is also a self-taught man, but I am sure he could teach the graduates a great deal," I said.

---

* Skirt of the mountain.
† Valley of Sugar.
‡ Country of Mountains.

The Valley of the Roses

"You are partly right and partly wrong," he answered. "Your father and I can teach human wisdom; we can also teach the principle of how to pick and choose among alternatives. For that one needs the measuring rod of experience to evaluate all one's actions and beliefs. But when you are ready for the second phase, which is organized knowledge, this we cannot provide for you."

When he noticed I was limping, he asked, "Do you have blisters on your feet?"

"No, it really isn't important."

"Take off your shoes and let me look at your feet."

So I told him about the gunpowder burn on my left foot. He looked at the burned area that looked like a mass of white, wrinkled parchment. With his strong arms, then, he lifted me up and put me on the back of the donkey. Even my ass felt good against the soft bundle of clothes. Suddenly I looked up and saw the greenest, most luscious valley I had ever seen. "Look, look, Haji Sahib, look," I declared breathlessly.

"Yes, from here on we will be going downhill and Kafir Jan won't mind your weight at all."

"Kafir Jan," I repeated with delight.

"Yes, in spite of everything, I love these green rolling foothills, the cool water that comes from the snow at the top of the mountains and seeps through the cracks and crevices of the deep blue volcanic rocks." Now he spoke a language I barely understood.

Man, boy, and animal were happy in anticipation of reaching our destination. Zaman began to hum local songs and interspersed them with comments about the beauty of the land and the problems facing the people who lived in the area. At the bottom of the valley, he stopped the donkey and told me that we would rest at the *chaikhana** and have some tea. The tea house was a basic construction made of beams of various sizes covered with a mixture of hay and mud. As we entered, the odor of green tea with cardamon, tea-pot soup, and freshly-cooked bread made my

---

* Tea house.

Memories of Afghanistan

saliva run. The tea-pot soup was usually cooked for the owner and his family. It consisted of hunks of bony sheep meat that were simmered in water to which onion and spices were added. Every chaikhana worth its salt always had a few extra pots of it for sale. The shop was empty except for a couple who were in a loud discussion about water rights for irrigation. The owner of the shop, Mr. Fakir, and his son, dozed lightly in the corner.

"Fakir, bachim, bring some of your famous soup and a pot of hot tea for us. As you see, my young friend here is both hungry and tired," announced Zaman. The owner approached us and said, "Ussalam, Haji Sahib, and the young man." Returning to the square mattress, he tapped the shoulder of his son and ordered him to serve us. Zaman and I ate from a common pot, scooping hunks of bread soaked in soup with our bare hands and pushing them hungrily into our mouths. The morsels of meat that dripped with fat were something to write home about. We chewed the bones clean of meat and threw them to two gaunt dogs outside. We cleaned the bowl with more bread, licked our fingers and then dried them on a greasy cloth that hung from a nail, on which many flies gathered when not in use.

Once again we were on our way to Guldara, which was about three miles away. My full stomach and the tap-tap of the donkey's hooves mingling with the swishing noise of the wind against the poplar leaves induced in me a light-hearted drowsiness that was difficult to overcome. My eyes closed and my head bobbed back and forth.

"Here we are," said Zaman. "Halfway up that slope to our left your uncle's land begins. He does not have much land, only about twelve acres, but it is good land next to a stream and very well managed."

As we approached a stone-walled fence that ran perpendicular to a rapidly moving stream, a young boy saw us and, realizing who we were, started to run toward the house. Shortly he and my uncle, followed by a barking dog, greeted us with much hugging and kissing. Haji Sahib waited until the formalities were over, then

The Valley of the Roses

he pressed both of my hands in his massive grip and promised to see me often. I put my arms around Kafir's neck and hauled my bundle of clothes off his back. He seemed to snort a goodbye as we walked to my uncle's house.

Inside the dilapidated two-story mud structure, closed on all four sides, was a well. My aunt was sitting next to it on a slab of stone. "I prepared some good hot tea and fruits for you. You must be very tired," she said, pressing my cheeks with the palms of her hands and kissing me on the forehead. "I have to tiptoe to reach your face, you have grown so tall," she added. My aunt was about twenty-five; she had small bones, a slightly oval face with a tiny mouth and nose and large brown eyes. As she walked away, her two long, black braids hung down her back like snakes. I drank the hot tea, and my uncle insisted I take a dish of walnuts and raisins to my room. My cousin, Kadir, helped me to my room with my bundle of clothes. He told me he was eight years old, the only child in the family, and that he walked about two miles to school every day. He also helped his father plant and water the vegetables and gathered wood for his mother's cooking. Some day, he said, he would like to go to the big city.

The room I was given was rather large and elongated; it had two windows that gave a magnificent view of the far blue mountains, the green valley, the rapidly foaming water of the stream and a well-kept vegetable garden that ran right up to the wall of the house below. Before Kadir left, he told me to rest and that he would call me for supper in about two hours. The windows faced directly south and the slanting rays of the sun at the edge of the window frame were slowly creeping out of sight. I pulled the charpayi near the window, pulled a blanket over my shoulders and went to sleep almost immediately.

The next few days I kept close to the house. I watched my uncle work in the field or orchard, planting, watering, chopping wood or tending the fruit trees. My aunt moved from one job to another all day, gathering eggs laid the night before by a couple of dozen hens, milking the three cows, preparing breakfast,

Memories of Afghanistan

cleaning the house, making beds, cooking meals or heating leftovers, making bread and yogurt every other day and washing clothing once a week in the stream. During the afternoon, she would take a pot of tea to the field and socialize with her husband before his afternoon nap, when she busied herself with mending and sewing.

I still limped a little, but my stamina improved day by day as I meandered up the slopes of the majestic mountain which dominated the adjacent valleys. The mountain was rocky and almost bare of trees and bushes, for they had long since been cut for firewood. But patches of low-growing shrubberies and countless small flowers of white, blue, red and violet carpeted the ground. Always, on these walks, I carried some food and reading material with me. One day I climbed higher than I had planned. The sun was shining and under the canopy of the blue sky the green valleys shimmered in the gentle breeze. Far to the right, a shepherd was stretched under a boulder while his sheep grazed aimlessly down the bluff. I ate my lunch, leaned on my elbow and started to read and ponder the solution to a geometric problem. The warm afternoon sun, the fresh air and a full stomach combined with my mental struggle lulled me into a long, deep sleep. When I opened my eyes, the sun was not far from the horizon. As I struggled to get up, I heard a shuffling noise nearby. When I ran around to the other side of the boulder, I saw a young girl with long flowing skirt and a red kerchief wrapped around the lower part of her face skip down the slope. She did not heed my calls. However, when she saw me running after her, she stopped.

"Why are you running away from me?" I inquired gruffly.

"I was collecting kindling down there," she said, pointing with her outstretched arm, "when I noticed you. On my second trip, I found you still in the same position. I was concerned that you had been hurt by falling or had some other calamity."

"It is very kind of you and I thank you for your concern."

"It is nothing, only common decency requires it," she added.

"Let me help you with your load," I offered.

The Valley of the Roses

"Oh, no, please don't even follow me. It is dangerous for both of us." Her face was still turned away from me.

"But I must see you and talk to you. I am all alone and a stranger to these parts," I explained.

Abruptly she turned her face toward me and said, "We shall meet again in the mountain." Her mouth and a part of her nose was still covered, but her dark, penetrating eyes froze me where I stood. She picked up her basket of twigs and skipped down the hill.

Days passed in rapid succession. The image of "her" whose name I did not know, haunted me in my dreams, but she eluded me in wakeful reality. Maybe she was an illusion that initially appeared in my dreams, like those beautiful fairies I had read about in *One Thousand and One Nights.*

On a clear, sharp day a little more than a week after our first chance encounter, I glimpsed her again across the narrow stream.

"I will see you tonight at dusk at the same place we met before," she said, walking rapidly away from the foaming rapids. In the mid-afternoon, I told my aunt that I was planning to go down into the valley and that she was not to worry if I was late. She smiled and said, "It is good to see you walk better and farther day after day. But be sure to eat something before you go to bed; your frame is still as emaciated as the first day you came."

To avoid suspicion, I walked almost a mile down the valley, then cut across to my left for quite a distance before I climbed the shallow incline through the fields of alfalfa and grassland. As I pushed my way through the steeper climb, the sun rays still illuminated a good part of the village. I crossed over many boulders and gigantic slabs of rock. From that vantage point, I could see the village below and judged that I had walked much higher than our appointed place. Until the sun disappeared behind the hills to the southwest, I rested, then walked down toward the meeting place. I could see no one, but soon I heard a soft voice behind me saying, "I am here. Come away from sight, here, behind the rock." My heart pounded violently as I walked slowly toward

Memories of Afghanistan

her. She was sitting on a smooth stone, her face uncovered and her hands loosely stretched on her legs. Her skin was somewhat red, as if it had been freshly scrubbed. With eyes downcast, she asked, "Do I disappoint you? I have heard a lot about you during the past fortnight. I wanted to meet you and to become your friend."

"I searched for you everywhere," I explained, "but it seemed you simply disappeared."

Raising her face to me, she smiled.

"Let me tell you a few things about me which will probably answer a lot of the questions you have. Listen, please, and don't interrupt. My name is Sharifa and I am, I think, sixteen years old. My father is a tenant farmer who owns a small parcel of land that barely provides for our very small family. Four children were born in the family; I was the last. My mother died the day I was born. The two eldest were boys who helped Father greatly before they were conscripted into the army. The younger died within a year's service and no one knows where the older one is now. My sister was married at the age of twelve and she died of dysentery a year later. When she died, I was eleven years old, and for the next four years I took care of the house and my father. All this time I had no friends nor companions. My best memories are from my childhood when I played and laughed with my sister and brothers.

"A year ago, people started to say that it was not right for a young girl to live alone with an old man, even if he was her father. They knew what they were talking about, because I was raped and assaulted constantly by him. Fortunately he was an old man of fifty or even more, and his nightly attacks were not so much due to sexual drive as to loneliness. Finally, eight months ago, the neighbors and the local mullah arranged to marry–nay barter–me for a cow and two-hundred rupees to an old rich farmer. His attempts at being a husband have been terrible failures, and this has turned him into a cruel tyrant. The reality of my life is so horrible, I have begun to daydream, but am an ignorant and unhappy young girl. You are shocked. Please forgive me, but I had

The Valley of the Roses

to tell someone. Now, if you want, you can turn around and walk away from me."

"But I want to be friendly with you," I insisted. "Why did you wait so long to see me?"

"Early this morning my husband left for a four-day business trip to Kabul. I knew he was planning this trip and waited anxiously for this day to meet you. You are younger than I, but I am sure you know a lot more. They tell me you read all the time."

"I am not as young as you think, and besides, I can teach you to read books," I boasted.

"Good, it is getting darker. I cannot see your face any more. Would you like to come and sit next to me?" she asked.

I was thankful for the darkness, because my heart started to pound again and I began to perspire. But I inched closer to her. Gently she took my hand to her face, rubbed her cheek on it, kissed it, and then held it firmly against her hard, round breast. Strange and exciting sensations emanated from my finger tips, my lips and my penis. With one hand she opened my fly and with the other dropped her pants. Then she lifted her billowing skirt and pressed my penis on and around her protruding breasts as I stood in front of her. Using her pants for a cushion, she leaned back and pulled me to her. Reacting to the new sensations that were overpowering, I pulled her head toward my stomach and suddenly felt the semen dribbling from my stiff penis down between her breasts.

Immediately afterward I felt almost as exhausted as if I had climbed the mountain to the very top. Skillfully, she guided me to the ground and laid my head on her lap. I felt I ought to say something, but the words would not come. Almost maternally, she hushed me and told me to rest. A strange calmness descended upon me and I must have dozed off, because I dreamed that she and I were ghosts swooping up and around the mountain in the darkness of the night, laughing at the moon and the stars, perching on the highest cliffs, then hand in hand disappearing into the void. I opened my eyes to make sure she was still there. She was and my head was still on her lap. I pushed myself up and sat next to her.

Memories of Afghanistan

I told her about my dream and she laughed and cried at the same time. I wiped the tears from her face and kissed her mouth. Again, those feelings began to stir.

I spread my jacket and Sharifa's pants on soft ground and asked her to lie down beside me. What happened next was pure instinct. I dropped my trousers, lifted her skirt, spread her legs and penetrated her hairy, moist vagina. The rhythmic motion, the delayed action and hand play–even the moans and groans of physical joy–seemed to come naturally. Without warning, Sharifa stiffened, grabbed my buttocks and pulled me hard into her, rigidly lifting her body up momentarily and then collapsing in a helpless, exhausted heap. I was so fascinated with what she was doing that I lost the desire to continue, so I lowered my body on her, laying my head on her shoulder. I was not sure whether I had ejaculated or not, but my penis seemed to have softened and shrunk.

For two more nights, we indulged in each other. I told her about myself and my future dreams. We walked in the semi-darkness up and around the rocks. She showed me her little stream of very cold water, where she had spent many hours crying with frustration at her loneliness and pain. She cried constantly while we were together.

"What is to become of me after tonight?" she wailed. I held her tightly and promised to come again next summer, but she would not be consoled. She clutched my hands and cried, "I want to die, but I don't know how to manage it."

Finally I walked her to her house. I convinced her not to kill herself. We had a sweet and tearful farewell and parted in hushed dignity.

This incident awakened many hitherto suppressed emotions, which in turn created a new awareness and ability to focus my senses more clearly on my surroundings. I became more sharply aware of the sounds of the water lapping against the smooth boulders in the stream as these sounds merged with the chatter of birds, the crackling of burning wood and the soft swish of the breeze. These became a rhapsody of sweet tones, punctuated by the raw smell of

The Valley of the Roses

horse urine, the feel of freshly upturned soil, the wonder of the tiny green shoots of onions. For no apparent reason, I jumped and ran through the young secondary growth of willow trees.

At the crest of this joyous energy, I ran to my uncle in the field and begged him to give me some work to do. When I finished the small jobs, I asked for more and he assigned me to two rather heavy tasks that kept me busy for days. They consisted of repairing the stone wall that divided the farm from that of the neighbor's to the north and chopping wood for cooking purposes. For three full days I worked from sunrise to sunset. By nightfall of each day, I had drained my last reserve of energy and barely managed to eat my supper and trot to my room. There, wrapped in a blanket, I exposed my face to the sharp evening breeze and my mind to the vast darkness enveloping the universe, including the blinking stars. I would cry of loneliness and of pain. So many years had already passed since my mother died and I had visited her grave only about three times. The last time was only a day before I left Kabul. I remembered hugging the shapeless grave, muttering bitterly about the senseless, wasted lives, each a stepping-stone for pain, waste and isolation, only to be followed by other such lives that kept the cycle of life and death unbroken, but also unresolved.

When I came down to breakfast on the fourth day to do more exhausting work, I was pleasantly surprised to see Haji Zaman in a lively conversation with my uncle.

"Salaam. Here you are. Your uncle tells me that you are working too hard."

"First of all, I am happy to see you and second, I have been told that hard work is a good antidote for boredom and loneliness," I answered, grinning widely.

"Well, your walk is almost normal. How about a climb to the top of our lofty mountain? I am more than fifty years old and have been to the top only twice."

My uncle thought it might be too much exertion for me, but I was more than willing to try. We spent the rest of the day preparing food and the necessary equipment to take with us. We

Memories of Afghanistan

made ourselves *chapli** and gathered together warm clothing, blankets and other odds and ends. That night I slept at Zaman's house and long before sunrise the next day, we set out with our bundles strapped to our backs.

The stars were above us and a gentle breeze blew down the valley to brush our cheeks. Haji Sahib had told me the night before that the climb to the summit would take most of the day, the climb down only a few hours.

The ascent was a gradual one toward the western skirt of the mountain. Zaman alerted me to the ridge coming up of another mountain called Paghman, which intercepted this one, Kohe Chardeh.† This would be our half-way mark and there we would find a plateau. We arrived there about noon. What a view! There was a large valley to the north where the snow glistened on the upper slope of Paghman. Foaming water could be seen and heard on its southern slope, which eventually produced the main body of water for the Kabul River. Snow slides periodically added crackling noises which culminated into roaring thunders. I had never seen anything so magnificent.

Hungrily we gulped down our lunch of bread and cheese and for dessert ate a piece of *talkhan*.‡ Then we leaned back against a large blue boulder that faced the sun and the valley below.

"You are doing remarkably well, Anwar Jan."

"Thank you for sharing this great adventure with me," I said.

"From here on the climb will become steeper and less interesting, but when you see the geological phenomena at the summit, you will admit that the trip had been worthwhile."

At certain elevations, I thought I had arrived at the end of my physical endurance, but somehow a sense of numbness crept into my lower extremities until they felt as though they only half belonged to me. They followed the commands of my brain, and became insensitive to pain or exhaustion. Very interesting,

---

* Footgear made from automobile tires.
† Mountain of the Four Villages.
‡ A mixture of walnuts and mulberries ground into a paste.

The Valley of the Roses

I thought. Maybe this is what is called "getting one's second wind."

It was mid-afternoon when we were examining the rim of a huge bowl in the top of the mountain. It was half full of slate-colored water. In the southern half of the rim, the snow skirt almost touched the water's edge. All around us were scattered black, puffy volcanic rocks. On the northern slope, a huge, black ridge snaked itself down the valley. Many smaller ridges crisscrossed one another like playful pythons following their mother down the mountain. The howling cold wind slapped against the exposed skin of our faces and necks and emphasized the desolation which must have stretched into the aeons of the past.

Haji Zaman tied a scarf around my neck and said, "On the way down we shall talk. I purposely didn't talk to you all day so you could preserve your energy for the climb. We shall start descending as soon as you are ready."

"I am ready now. Someday I must spend more time up here. These mountains hold so many delightful surprises," I answered.

"Yes, we have a lovely country, inhabited by remnants of races that have crisscrossed this gateway to the fabulous land of India, rich in gold and spices. The rich culture and heritage of Tajiks, Uzbeks, Turkmans, Greeks, Persians and Mongolians have made this land unique in all of Asia. And yet, we had the misfortune that our cohesive sense of nationhood coincided with the establishment of British imperialism in India. It is not by chance that the arrival of British troops at the land of the Pathans and the rise of these people as rulers of Afghanistan coincided historically."

"But Amanullah is trying to change all that," I protested.

"My son, we have a king now who is an exception in a parade of cruel bastards that stretch for almost two hundred years, starting with Ahmad Shah. Their family feuds and clan warfare kept our country poor and destitute up to the present time. Amanullah cannot succeed. The British will eventually destroy him with the help of the mullahs and his own tribal chiefs."

Memories of Afghanistan

Haji Sahib was planting the seed of political awakening in my young mind. I had never heard anyone but my father talk like this before. Instinctively, my father knew that there were inequities in the country, but how, why and what was to be done, he did not know.

"Why don't they teach us these things in our history books in school?"

Momentarily ignoring the question, Zaman continued: "The Pathans are mostly a nomadic people and have not developed a unified culture to speak of. Because of their lack of education and their low level of existence, they have been exploited by their own chiefs, the mullahs, and the British. Since these Pathans are part of the royal family, you don't expect them to permit facts like these in the schools, do you?"

"I guess not, but I still have hope that our present king will eventually correct the situation."

"I hope you realize your desire, my son. But it is a risky venture to tie up the destiny of a nation with the success or failure of one man. Look at his army–a rag-tag, dissatisfied mob. Training them are Turkish generals who recently not only lost a war but lost most of their country's possessions with it. In the army, the high-ranking native officers are the sons of the Pathan chiefs who reside in the frontiers. They have compromised this nation in the past and will do so in the future."

"But our people love their king. Go to any part of the country and you will find it to be a fact," I said.

"Yes," he said, "but the people are not armed or organized for defense." He stooped, picked up a stone and threw it down the valley. Gazing at me sadly, he said, "I am too old, but I am hoping that the kids of your generation will see the end of this tragedy. But this will not happen until the greater tragedy of colonialism that is suffocating Asia is ended."

Only dimly did I understand what Haji Sahib was talking about. Noting my blank expression, he rubbed his hands together vigorously and said, "Well, we are almost at your favorite area of the mountain," and then, to my surprise, he winked. Instinctively, then, I realized that he knew about my affair with Sharifa, but thought it wise not to pursue the matter.

Chapter 11
Bacha-i-Saqao

Our skirts are clean.
—British Foreign Office minutes,
Ingram to Sir Wilbert,
Jan. 23, 1928

For some time now I was experiencing unexpected emotional drives. Sex induced guilt and exaltation, daydreaming and helplessness. Masturbating in front of a full-length mirror only sharpened the awareness of the contradictions of life. Emotionally, I was as confused as any teenager, and yet my young mind was mercilessly bombarded by religious contradictions, political upheavals, nationalism, "the outside world," and a dizzying pace of change which was hurling us into the unknown future. Answers were hard to come by. Father was not of much help with his few dos and many don'ts.

"No stealing, fucking or lying" only emphasizes the negative in man, like the ten don'ts in the commandments of Moses. "Positive action for human betterment is what is needed as a guidepost for our young," Zaman used to say. I pined to be with my wise friend, to ask him for his opinions concerning the many riddles and disturbing half-truths that crowded my mind.

At that historic juncture, our king was being received with pomp and ceremony by the leaders and royalty of Europe as one of the leading spokesmen for the emerging nations, Ataturk of Turkey being the other one. Amanullah was our last hope to pull us out of the quagmire of backwardness, ignorance and waste that his own dynastic tribes of Pathans, with the help and encouragement of the British, had put us into. In school, we daily discussed these issues, and teachers and students alike recognized that another failure would be fatal to Afghanistan as a viable nation.

There was talk of freedom for women, a new constitution, the beginning of industrial development and, above all, the

Bacha-i-Saqao

construction of schools and educational facilities. We young students were excited to be forerunners and possibly the leaders of those to come in this fantastic enterprise. Still, many of us were apprehensive. There were rumors of dissatisfaction among the various Pathan clans who lived astride the Afghan-Indian frontier. The religious community was openly and totally against all progressive changes and their leaders were secretly in touch with the Pathan chiefs and the British authority in India. In the religion classes in our school, the topic of daily conversation was Amanullah's heresy of introducing such courses of study as science and geography.

"Isn't it laughable when they claim that the earth revolves round the sun?" Mullah Ayub, our teacher of religion used to ask with a smirk. "Let me tie your geography teacher to that pillar facing west toward Arabia and twelve hours later show me that he will be facing toward China."

Even some of the doubters among the student body would laugh at our teacher's logic. Nevertheless, these signs persisted as nasty reminders of the past treachery of the Muslim priests and the poor, ignorant Pathan tribes.

Kabul was festively decorated in anticipation of the triumphant return of its beloved king. Our school was chosen to give a reception at which Amanullah and his entire cabinet were to be guests of honor. For the next few days Habibia turned into a debating society. Who would deliver the welcoming speech? How many students should participate? The protocol, the timing, the refreshments and on and on...

The day arrived. Lines of students and teachers waited, stiff and apprehensive. We saw the king's car stop just outside the gate. Then Amanullah, a brown-eyed mustached man, dressed in a simple dark blue uniform with high boots, walked toward us with a big grin and outstretched arms.

"Let us sit down on the grass, and tell me how to serve our poor country," he said. "We have no time to waste and I need as much help as I can get."

Memories of Afghanistan

We sat around our king. Forgotten were the formal talks and the reception. Tea got cold in the pots and dishes of ice cream melted long before we parted from him. He told us about the rejuvenation of education for both sexes, about industries soon to open in the country, the legal protection of every Afghan from arbitrary rules and regulations of the past and so many other wonderful schemes. "I will put these proposals before the *Loya Jirga** next month and obtain their approval," he said.

I was among the small number of students chosen to meet the king one night at the first and only girls' school in Kabul. We sang nationalist songs and shook hands with little girls while their fathers and brothers waited in the hallway to take them home. We cheered, clapped our hands, laughed for the future of our country and touched our beloved king to make sure he was real.

The bazaars in Kabul were festively decorated and in our own shop, we made an effort to add to the festive air. My brother, who was a student in Germany, had sent us a large number of colored photos of German army officers. I hung some of these in prominent areas where the light of the hanging electric bulbs shown on them. On one wall was General Hindenburg with his curved mustache and pointed helmet listening intently to General Mackensen, bemedalled from neck to midriff, who pointed to the map of Europe spread on a massive table. Across, on the other wall, hung the picture of King Fuad of Egypt in his long overcoat and red fez looking sadly into space. The place of honor, at the very top, was reserved for a beautiful Arabic handwriting given to my father by a good friend. It read, "There is no God but one and Mohammed is His Messenger."

In the midst of all these festivities, we were informed by the school authorities that Amanullah wanted to meet with a select group of students. The top five students from each class of the three high schools were chosen. I was one. Altogether, there were about fifty of us who gathered the next day in the royal palace. The king met us dressed in the Afghan national costume. He made

---

* Grand Assembly.

Bacha-i-Saqao

a short speech explaining that he would be spending the next few weeks in Paghman talking to important leaders from all parts of the country. "We shall come to an agreement on a great plan for modernizing our country," he said. Then he shook hands with each of us and gave each one of us a gold coin as a token to remember this great day.

When I reached home that evening, I offered the coin to my father. He looked at it and rubbed it between his fingers, then gave it back to me. "Keep this, my son. Its symbolic value is far greater than its monetary one." I punched a hole in one corner, threaded a heavy cord through it, and hung it from my neck.

While Amanullah was delivering his marathon talk to the elders of his nation, uncontrolled events were passing the national landscape at a dizzying pace. The Pathan tribes, now this one, now another, were on the move again. The mullahs became bolder and their demands greater. A common thief, Bacha-i-Saqao,* was walking the streets of villages only a few miles north of the capital, collecting arms and food for his followers. The army generals and the ministers of the realm were feuding among themselves as pro- or anti-Turkish factions. Nobody in authority seemed to give a damn.

Amanullah rushed back to Kabul to find his kingdom on the brink of catastrophe. He was confused and bewildered. The military contingent in Charikar not only surrendered to Bacha-i-Saqao but joined him. There was no reserve to send north; most of the army had been sent east against the Pathans. The king was told that there were no soldiers left to send anywhere. He appealed to the populace to save him. In his final act of desperation, he ordered the military depot to stay open for anyone who wanted to fight the phantoms in the east, north and south.

A friend of mine, Jameel, and I stood in line to get a gun so that we could help protect our king. We were each given a gun with as much ammunition as we could carry. Once outside we didn't know where to go or what to do. So we moved toward the front. Fighting was concentrated mainly on a bluff behind Habibia

---
* Son of a water carrier.

Memories of Afghanistan

High School. A quarter of a mile away, down below, was a military academy. Across the road to the east of the academy was the art school. The most strategic area to defend in the capital was our school on the hill that dominated the whole area. It was empty! The rebel forces believed that the hill was defended so they stayed north of it about a mile away, almost next to the British legation. That is how the rumor started that the British legation was helping Bacha-i-Saqao.

The military school was lobbing a few cannonballs across our school into no-man's land. They knew that they could just walk up the slope and prevent any force from pushing to the capital. It was only discovered later that the Turkish general in charge was drunk and confined in his room with his two Afghan boyfriends.

In the midst of all this confusion, Jameel and I were crawling in a ditch toward the bluff where the school building was located. By the time we had almost reached the school gate, and when no one had taken a potshot at us, we figured that the bluff must be occupied by soldiers defending the city. So we stood up and started walking. At this very moment we heard a whistle and some stray shots over our heads. The shots came from the military academy behind us. We hit the ditch fast. I said, "Damned fools, there is no one in the school and our own soldiers are shooting at us. Jameel Jan, let's crawl back and tell those morons to occupy the school building while there is still daylight." No answer. I crawled a few paces forward and pulled my friend's leg. Still no response. I smelled the blood before I saw it oozing out of his right ear. A closer look showed that a bullet had entered his left jaw and exited below his ear lobe on the other side. His brown eyes protruded in mock surprise on the smooth surface of his ghastly white face. Although the weather was not very cold on this day in mid-January, I began to shiver violently. I lay next to the dead body of my friend until darkness enveloped the area. Then, leaving all the implements of warfare behind, I trudged my weary way home.

My sister Diljan said, "Father is looking for you. He is worried."

Bacha-i-Saqao

I said, "I am hungry," suddenly realizing that I had eaten nothing since the night before. After eating a bowl of soup with chunks of bread in it, I went to bed and didn't open my eyes until noon the next day. There was a commotion in the next room. Throwing the covers to one side, I ran through the doorway.

"Have you heard? Amanullah ran away!"

"Bacha-i-Saqao's soldiers are all over Kabul."

"The royal castle is surrounded."

"Where were you all day yesterday?" Father asked me.

The enormity of the tragic events of the recent past so oppressed me that I sat down and began to gaze into space. My father told everyone to leave and then walked over and put his hand on my shoulder.

"I know how you feel," he said.

In my mind's eye, I saw my friend Jameel's ghostly face and the blood on his neck congealed like a scarf shimmering in the semi-dark room. Inadvertently, I touched my own neck and realized that the cord holding the gold coin was missing.

"I must have lost my gold coin," I muttered to no one in particular.

"You lost more than a gold coin, my son. Your generation has lost the last hope for your country."

"But why?"

"I don't know. It is no different today than when I was your age. Life has always looked like a chess game to me in this country. Most of us are pawns and are supposed to move in a straight line. Deviation to the right or left is allowed only for purposes of killing, mostly other pawns. This goes on until the king himself is surrounded on one side or the other. Then the killing stops and preparation is made for a new game. Today the royal castle is surrounded and in a day or two we shall have a new king."

Father's explanation was very graphic but unsatisfactory to me, but I had no inclination to pursue the subject.

Outside, gunshots could be heard from all directions. I joined some friends to find out what was going on all over the town.

Memories of Afghanistan

Shops were closed. The poor section where we lived was mainly quiet, so we crossed the Kabul River and approached the newer parts of the city where the economically well-to-do lived. Here conditions were chaotic. Looting was common, especially in the houses of the very rich families, who had already escaped to a safer place. Middle-class houses, where the owners mainly stayed put, were mostly spared. I noticed a man who stopped to rest and unload a heavy wooden box, a large mirror, an umbrella and a bundle of clothing. The wooden box contained books, all in the English language. I asked the man if he knew he was carrying books that had been written by the infidels and all of them in a foreign tongue.

"Are they worth anything?" he asked.

"Only the ones that have interesting pictures."

He picked up one book at random and leafed through it. There were no pictures in that one nor in several others he examined.

"My luck is not very good today. Do you want them?"

I didn't want to sound too anxious, so I said, "Well, I will be glad to help you with some of your load."

"I live in Shor Bazaar," he informed me.

"We are practically neighbors," I said.

"I tell you what. You take the box of books to your house, empty it and the books are yours, but I have a good use for that box."

After the stranger left me, I sorted the books and here is the list as far as I can remember:

Jean-Christophe, by Romain Rolland
A book of short stories
Childhood, by Leo Tolstoy
David Copperfield, by Charles Dickens
A book on astronomy by an Irish author
One Hundred Poems of Kabir, by Rabindranath Tagore
Jungle Book and a couple of other short novels by Kipling

Bacha-i-Saqao

These books and a few friends saved my sanity during the next few sad and hectic months. I had had almost two years of tutoring in English by Indian teachers. With this background and a small dictionary, I would be able to take advantage of my "library." But that came later.

After three days of brooding at home, I ventured out to discover the status of social life in the streets of Kabul. Some shops that still had a stock of merchandise began to open. I pushed my way through the thin crowds to see why there was a gathering of people near the river junction. The body of a dead soldier was being slowly pulled by a horse. His legs were tied with rope to the saddle, his head bounced against the stones of the street, and his hands flip-flopped after each obstruction along the way. His uniform was tattered and his crop of black hair was matted with congealed blood. No recognizable feature was discernible in his half-twisted face.

From the conversation around me, I gathered that he was an ordinary soldier who had attempted to loot a shop, even after the proclamation against vandalism and looting had been posted in all the main streets of the capital. Abdul Rahim, who was the new king's close friend, had caught him and used the soldier as an example to other potential lawbreakers.

It was past mid-January. The weather was cold and dismally gray. My cotton garments were not padded to prevent the cold from seeping in. A putrid odor hung over the city. I turned around and started jogging homeward, partly to keep warm, but partly to escape the ugliness.

Since no daily papers were published in Kabul, those who were interested gathered rumors during the day, and at night in the seclusion of their homes with relatives and friends, analyzed, discussed and theorized. Some of these rumors could be verified, but to learn the veracity of others one had to wait for subsequent events to unfold. All schools were closed. Most of the foreigners had left the country. Scholarships for Afghan students who were studying in foreign countries were terminated. Most of these students were forced to cut short their courses of study and come

Memories of Afghanistan

back to Afghanistan. In the middle of March, we were informed that my brother Wahab had left Germany and would be home in a few days.

During the subsequent week there was a great deal of excitement in our household. Wahab had been sent to Germany by Amanullah around 1920. He was a bright student and was selected as one of a small group to study abroad. This was the first contingent that established a pattern that was followed in future years. His field of study was glass manufacture engineering.

Many small factories had been bought in Europe since 1924, and by 1928 some of them, such as weaving, match-making, printing, hydroelectric, machine tools, shoe-making, etc., were already installed and working. A second phase industrial plan called for more ambitious development. Many large factories for the manufacture of cement, glass, cotton products, large-scale spinning and weaving and many others were ordered. Some machineries were not shipped out, but those that were lay rusting in one of the depots between Kabul and Bombay. When Amanullah lost his kingdom, no one cared to claim them.

In the midst of these terribly sad events, I was excited in anticipation of seeing my brother Wahab, whom I remembered only through the large number of photos he had sent us from Germany during the past nine years. My father, young brother and I finally met him on a clear April afternoon. I was surprised to find that he was somewhat shorter than I, even though he was twelve years my senior. With the passage of time, this difference in our heights became even more pronounced.

Bacha-i-Saqao's rule over Kabul lasted less than a year, during which time the country was in a state of turmoil, financially bankrupt, politically isolated and physically exhausted. With the help of the same treacherous Pathan tribes that had caused his downfall, Amanullah tried in vain for four months to recapture his kingdom. One of his generals, Nadir Khan, who had been the Afghan ambassador in Paris, came to tribal territory to raise a force against the Bacha.

Bacha-i-Saqao

In the gloomy atmosphere of Kabul, Wahab and I joined with four or five other students who had been forced to leave Germany because of lack of funds and gathered in each other's houses for gossip and a game of penny poker.

"Ah, Ghulam, my son, what is the situation on the western front?" Wahab asked.

"Here it is the eastern front, you idiot. And the situation is static. The Pathans are dickering for a bigger piece of the pie."

"Why don't we appeal to Hitler to send us a small contingent of his storm troopers to clear up this mess?"

One in the group would be humming, and pretty soon they would all be singing the Horst Wessel Song:

Raise high the flags...
Storm troopers march with steady, quiet tread

"How can one believe that in a matter of weeks I would be thrown out of the beautiful city of München into this shit pot?" Ghulam asked.

"Fellows, let us proceed with our game of poker and drown our sorrow in hot Afghan tea," Brishna chimed in. Brishna was a member of the ousted royal family. We treated him kindly because his beautiful young sister had been forced to marry Bacha-i-Saqao. Eventually the poker game was interrupted by a lunch of thin soup and flat bread with a few boiled potatoes on the side.

One evening, Diljan took Wahab's meager dinner to him. He looked at it and turned to my stepmother and said, "You slut, why don't you cook something decent for a change?"

My father bristled. "This is the first and last time you will utter those terrible words to my wife. I will kick your ass off if I hear them again. As for the food you are getting from us, you either eat as we do, or find and cook your own food."

"How dare you say such things to me!" Wahab sputtered. "Have you forgotten that I was educated by the Germans?"

"They failed to instill any moral judgment in you."

Memories of Afghanistan

Wahab picked up the clay water jug and hurled it at my father. It hit the window frame just short of its target and shattered into innumerable small fragments. In a way, this incident was a turning point in my life. The relationship between my brother and me, which I had hoped to develop into something durable and useful, deteriorated considerably. I stopped associating with his circle of German-educated friends. Watching them day after day going through the same motions, singing the same *lieders*, dreaming of cold beer, docile *fraüleins* and the strut of marching feet, made me bored and unhappy. They sneered at the culture of our unhappy land, our music, our dress, ways of living and our food. I often asked myself, why didn't they bring back with them a little of Beethoven and Mozart, a touch of Goethe and Heine? In all fairness, I could not blame Germany because of my disappointment in these few Afghan students, but I felt helpless, helpless to see our country torn apart and the future of our youth destroyed, while our so-called educated elite in and out of the government callously watched the process with disinterest.

During a mild sunny day in early spring, some of our relatives from Guldara descended upon us. I welcomed this diversion from my boredom and joined the animated circle of noisy adults.

"Anwar Jan, I was just telling your father that you should join and help the present government. After all, it is the first time in more than two hundred years that we Tajiks are free from the oppressive rule of the Pathans," my uncle Munsoor said.

"The present regime has closed the whole school system. I was a student and I have not even finished high school yet. How can I help any organization?"

"I am sure the schools will open again when things calm down. Meanwhile there is a shortage of persons who can read and write. One of your classmates is already working for Bacha-i-Saqao in the Ministry of Interior."

"Who is that?" I blurted out, taken completely by surprise.

"Kabir Ludeen."

"But he is a Pathan."

Bacha-i-Saqao

"Pathans cannot be trusted," my father said. "And long ago the British found out that a Pathan's loyalty can be bought at a price."

"Yes, I agree with our white-bearded elder about the Pathans, but Anwar is half-Arab and half-Tajik."

"My son knows better. He has to finish his learning before embarking on a working career," my father said.

The month of June was hot and dusty in Kabul. Rumors were rampant in the tea shops of the noisy bazaars. Everyone knew by then that Amanullah was defeated and had gone with his family to India, and that Nadir Khan and his brothers were fighting the government troops somewhere on the eastern front. How far from the capital, no one was sure.

"This friend of mine came from Jalalabad, and he swears that the sound of gunfire could be heard there."

"Did your friend see any actual fighting?"

"No."

"Maybe it was soldiers practicing outside the city."

"Could be."

"Let me tell you this. Twenty, thirty years from now we will have white beards and be walking with the help of a cane. We will raise our heads from our stooped and sunken shoulders and with bleary eyes ask the same question: How close are they to Kabul today?"

The heat of the summer and the unpredictability of events drove me more and more into the solitary confinement of my little room on the second floor of our house. I was bored, confused and extremely unhappy. What was there to hope for? The future seemed bleak and all my hopes had been smashed to little pieces. My mind began to evaluate every possibility open to me. What were they? Suicide, running away from the country. But how? Looking around my almost empty room, I saw the pile of English books in the corner. Selecting the bulkiest of the lot, *Jean-Christophe,* I began to leaf through the table of contents and read the Notes and the Preface concerning the author, Romain Rolland, and the

Memories of Afghanistan

commentaries on the book itself. My mind was made up. I would forget myself in the lives of others.

For the next five weeks, Christophe became my guide through his hunger pains of childhood, the tender love of his ignorant peasant mother, his childhood nightmares, the cruelties of his drunken father, and the kindness of his grandfather and a poor uncle. I laughed with him as he roamed the Rhineland forests and hills and cried for him when he was unjustly punished by his father. I compared his uncle Gottfried with my uncle Abbas and his father with mine. He was fortunate with the former and I with the latter. As a young boy, Christophe's emotional upheaval culminated in a series of love affairs. Some were partly successful and some were total failures, but each one contributed its measure toward his philosophy that growth has its pains as well as its rewards.

The one theme that kept flowing through his life as an eternal river flows, sometimes quiet and graceful and other times roaring like thunder, was music. I so wanted to understand the musical side of his life, but unfortunately I could not. Eastern music in its serious form was known to me. The various manifestations of sound, soft and playful, tender and caressing, ethereal and sublime, sad and jovial, were commonly heard in even the most remote villages. The playful duet of a tabla and harmonium, the sad and heart-rending wail of a flute in a dark quiet night were experienced throughout my life. No written music as such existed in Afghanistan or India. It was learned either through long years of apprenticeship or improvised.

Although I was confined to a small room on a burning hot summer day, poor and hungry, in one of the most backward countries in the world, I followed Christophe to France and Germany and dreamed of visiting those distant lands someday. I must thank Mother for this, for her allegorical stories still echoed in my mind, obliterating the dividing line between the realms of reality and make-believe.

Rumors of impending changes that never materialized frustrated me and I began to consider a change in my living

Bacha-i-Saqao

pattern. Of the few obvious possibilities, none appealed to me. I finally resolved to see my friend Haji Zaman and ask his advice. It would mean covering the fifteen-mile distance between Kabul and Guldara and would be very risky and dangerous. To be safe, I planned to avoid normal roads and to travel only at night. This way, I figured it would probably take about three days to get there instead of one if I traveled by day. My sister volunteered to gather some food for me and to tell Father my whereabouts after I had left.

It was far from pleasant dodging prowling soldiers and avoiding the sun on the rocky skirts of the hills north of Kabul. I was thankful that Diljan had hung a round army thermos full of water on my shoulder, for it would have been almost impossible to find drinking water in those hills. My food was not ample for the trip, but the choice of ingredients was excellent–bread, cheese, shelled walnuts, dried mulberries, and a few apples.

From a distance, these dry, rocky and dusty hills looked gray and devoid of life, but on closer inspection one found them teeming with life. I spent hours watching ants, lizards and scorpions.

As the shadows lengthened on the slopes of the mountains, I traveled in a hide-and-seek manner. There was no problem with the direction of my destination, but the darkness held the valleys in a tight grip and the light that emerged from the sliver of the new moon could not detract from the universal darkness. The numerous rocks and boulders that protruded from the ground impeded my movements and took a heavy toll in cuts and bruises. After a couple of hours, I found myself tired and in need of rest, and it occurred to me that it was my normal time to go to sleep. I woke up from a bad dream as the sun's rays were halfway down the mountain. As I folded my blanket, I realized that my food bundle was missing. An animal had dragged it down the slope, torn it to shreds and eaten up or carried away all the food. I sat on the ground, held my head in my hands and tried to think my way out of the morass of my latest predicament. I had left Kabul almost twenty hours earlier and I was no more than a few miles into my journey.

Memories of Afghanistan

Gathering up my blanket and thermos, I made for the road about a half mile away and trudged along it four miles until I saw a small mud-walled tea shop on my left. Inside I met a young man who had black hair and bushy eyebrows that almost covered his brown eyes. Most of his bare chest was covered by his long beard. He greeted me with a polite smile.

"I am on my way to the northern valleys and ran out of money," I said. "I will be glad to give you this blanket for a good meal."

"Sorry to disappoint you, but I am not the owner," he answered.

While I waited for the owner to appear, the young man told me that chaos prevailed only in the capital and that, since no one was running the affairs of the state, the northern provinces were the most peaceful. As we talked, the owner appeared from somewhere in the back of the shop and gave us a hearty meal of fried eggs, cheese and bread. The young man paid for both of us and said, "You may need your blanket during the rest of your trip."

By keeping up a vigorous pace and doing with a minimum of rest, I was shaking hands with Haji Zaman before nightfall.

"If you will wash the dirt off your face, I will prepare something to eat. A cool stream runs right behind the house," he said.

The tomato-lamb stew on brown rice, washed down with a yoghurt and cucumber drink, punctuated with delightful anecdotes of local interest, helped ease the physical and mental pain of the recent past.

"Your uncles and their families are well and happy. Sharifa's husband died about a year ago."

"Sharifa?" I asked, open-eyed.

"Yes, she told me that she knew you and respected you a lot," Haji Sahib said in a calm and controlled voice. "She became a rich woman according to our standards. A couple of months ago, she was married to a very nice boy of her own age. She requested me, as a personal favor, to thank you for your friendship and to let you know that she is very happy now."

Bacha-i-Saqao

"I am glad," I whispered with my head down.

"Now, I will take you to your bedroom. You have had a hard day."

When Zaman handed me the candle and left me, I walked to the large window near the foot of the bed, opened it and listened to the soft murmur of the leaves silhouetted against the starry sky. To my right, lost in the darkness, was the mountain where I had had my first sexual experience. I could almost visualize our painful last parting. I thanked the stars and the mountain that Sharifa was well and happy.

I slept until mid-morning. From the open window I noticed a beautiful garden on both sides of the little stream where I had washed last night. Farther back was an apple orchard, and there was a grape arbor down the slope to the left. When I went downstairs, a young boy ran in to tell me that Haji Sahib was having tea under the walnut tree with a friend and would like me to join him. They were sitting on a colorful Afghan carpet on top of an imposing mud and straw structure about five feet high. I climbed the stairway on the right and was introduced to Mr. Mir Assadullah. His lean body was covered casually in an Afghan costume and his firm grip and penetrating black eyes were impressive.

"I hope you rested well last night," Zaman said.

"It was delightful."

"Assad Jan's family lives in Mazar. He was in Istalif and I sent someone last night to fetch him after you went to bed. His family is what you might call an absentee landlord."

"Haji Sahib is an uncompromising purist. It is either white or black. No shade in between is acceptable to him. We are even supposed to pay for the sins of our fathers and grandfathers."

"No, not pay, but expiate," said Zaman, who continued: "There is an element of regret and suffering involved in expiation. But payment has an element of finality about it which is repugnant to me. One may indulge in wrongdoing as long as one pays for it in cash or through confession. Now I am going to leave you two alone to get acquainted while I tend to a personal problem."

Memories of Afghanistan

After Zaman left us, Mr. Assadullah asked me whether I wanted to talk or play chess. I told him we could do both.

"I know about you," he said, "but has Haji Zaman told you anything about me and my family?"

"No," I said, "except that you are a kind of absentee landlord." He laughed aloud and said, "Zaman has a sharp tongue, but he is one of the most erudite individuals in our country. That is why we are both here. Zaman, being a Tajik, is under great pressure to join the present government in Kabul, but so far he has been able to stay away.

"My family and Charkhi's* are very close. My uncle was assistant to Ghulam Jilani, the governor of Mazar-i-Sharif. As recently as the end of April, I myself was in a great volunteer army under the leadership of his brother, Ghulam Nabi Charkhi. We had crossed the most difficult terrain in Kafiristan and were poised to attack Kabul when the news of Amanullah's defeat at Ghazni and his final flight into British India reached us. The poor volunteers melted into thin air and all the members of the Charkhi family and most of mine crossed the Oxus River into Russia. I came to Kabul to see if I could put the other pieces of the puzzle together."

"Assad Jan," I said, "you have given me more news in the last few minutes than I have had since the beginning of this tragedy. Now it looks as if we have to make our peace with the son of a water carrier and a thief as our ruler."

"No, I don't think so," said Assad. "This is a temporary affair at best. The British will see to it that one of their most favored families, the Musahiban, who had been exiled to India by Amanullah's grandfather, Abdul Rahman, will emerge as our hand-picked rulers."

"But I thought Nadir Khan and his brothers were fighting under Amanullah's banner."

"Amanullah is a sincere but a confused man. Being a Pushtun himself, he never gave up the hope that sooner or later one of these tribes would recapture his throne for him. He was the only

---

* A prominent family, rivals of the Musahibans. See Chapter 13.–*Ed.*

118

Pushtun king that had won the loyalty and love of the other two-thirds of the non-Pushtun population. But somehow he was never able to trust the rest of us."

"Why did he leave the country? Couldn't he have gone to another part of Afghanistan?" I asked.

"Not that he couldn't, but he wouldn't. He was afraid that he would lose legitimacy for his descendants. Ghulam Nabi Charkhi offered to send him a Russian plane to carry him to Mazar-i-Sharif, where he was putting together a formidable army. Amanullah refused and was confident that with the loyal support of some tribes he could march toward Kabul. He actually captured the key city of Ghazni and encouraged Ghulam Nabi to increase the tempo of his attack from the north. However, in a matter of days the house of cards collapsed and Amanullah was in flight for his life–to, of all places, British India. So I came here to find the details of the latest episode."

"Did you?" I asked.

"Yes, at least partly. In early May, the British authorities in India and Kabul were in great panic that Amanullah might succeed, after all, in regaining his kingdom. A series of interesting moves were simultaneously put into operation. One, Nadir Khan and his brothers eased up the pressure on Bacha-i-Saqao to such an extent that he was able to shift some of his forces from the eastern front to the Ghazni area against Amanullah. Two, Sher Agha, the influential mullah who was supposed to have been 'interned' in India, was dispatched to Suleiman Khel tribal territory, where he and his brother, the Hazrat Sahib, had great influence. Around the middle of April, with the arrival of new arms and military supplies from India, this tribe treacherously attacked Amanullah's reargquard at Ghazni. Amanullah's underarmed and underfed army was cut into small contingents and put to flight. He himself barely made it to the border of India."

"Well, here comes Haji Zaman, and we have not played a game of chess yet," I said.

"I hope you two had an interesting chat," Zaman said.

Memories of Afghanistan

"It has been a most interesting eye-opener for me. However, I am confused as to how Assad Jan happened to stumble upon so much important news," I said.

"Bachim, mullahs and Pushtun tribal chiefs are willing to sell their services to anyone. Crucial news is a high-priced commodity. The head of our secret service in Kabul at the present time is a good friend of mine from Charikar. Need I say more?" Zaman concluded.

Zamanuddin had been a brooding, quiet and extremely intelligent youth in his late teens. His face was massively chiseled into protruding bones and thick lips. His inward personality limited his circle of friends to a minimum. However, those few were true friends. When he was in his late teens, he was restless and so, during the following four years, he traveled throughout most of the important landmarks of his native land. He crossed the great Hindu Kush mountain range and settled in Mazar-i-Sharif long enough to learn to read and write Persian and Arabic. His guiding spirit was Khoja Burhan, the great Uzbek teacher. In 1918, after climbing the Roof of the World, the Pamir Plateau, he came back to his village in Koh Damen and stayed a short while before embarking on a foreign trip. With the consent and financial help of his father, he went to Egypt. Not much was heard of him for the next eight years until he came back after being informed of his father's death. Being an only child, he inherited great wealth. Since he had visited Mecca, the word Haji was added to his name. Eventually Haji Zamanuddin was shortened to Haji Zaman.

During the next four days that Assadullah and I spent with Zaman, he told us many details and anecdotes of his eight years abroad. Except for short trips that he took to neighboring countries, he divided his time equally between Egypt and Syria. He reminisced as if to himself.

"I was sad, disorganized and thirsty for knowledge. The Islamic world was in even worse shape than I–divided, ignorant, poor, sick and in bondage from the Indus River to the Atlantic,

Bacha-i-Saqao

ruled by local despots for the benefit of European overlords, who in turn supported them with arms and money.

"My first encounter with education was at the famous Al-Azhar Mosque in the heart of Cairo, where mullahs and their sons from all countries of North Africa and the Near East could be found. Education consisted of rote memorization of the Koran and other holy books. The noise in the corridors of this once magnificent mosque was deafening. European tourists used to come and watch us and take our pictures in our habitat of filth and degradation. The priesthood was a lucrative profession, being the important element in providing the rationale for monarchy on the one hand and contentment for the exploited masses on the other.

"I gave up my formal education and entered a private school that had been organized for the sons of well-to-do Egyptians. The teaching of the English language was the primary concern of this school, although a smattering of distorted history and some math were also included.

"In my spare time, which was ample, I delved into the past history of Arab culture, which is rich in science, history, philosophy and adventure. With the consent of local amirs, khans, kings and the devoted cooperation of the priesthood, this culture stayed dormant, nay, in large measure, was destroyed. At the end of my stay in Egypt, I realized that as long as these two evils, the priesthood and the system of petty kingdoms, operated, the East, including the non-Muslim population of Asia, would be exploited by the Western Europeans. Ah, I was lost in reverie, and like most teachers, I was carried away by the monotonous pitch of my own voice."

"Haji Sahib, your talk today has opened a new horizon and a future hope for me," I declared when he had finished. Assadullah maintained that Zaman was correct in his analysis and concern about contemporary life in the Muslim countries, but what was to replace it and how?

"Amanullah did his best to change the system of inequity and oppression. What other route is there?" Haji Zaman looked

Memories of Afghanistan

at Assadullah intently and said, "No one person can do the job for us. We all must take part in the common goal. Look at our country today. A common thief is our supreme ruler. One king is on his way into exile and Nadir Khan is selling his country to the British in order to establish yet another dynasty. The night is dark and long. Our resources are meager and untested. Our adversaries, both foreign and domestic, possess most of the trump cards. But let me tell you this. History is on our side. Imperialism is dying, causing dislocations in the very fiber of the world's political, economic and social structures. We must try to fill the gap in our limited way, giving meaning to the space of time left to us."

"You are talking of revolution," asserted Assadullah.

"Yes," said Zaman. "But now we must get some rest because Assad Jan is leaving us early tomorrow."

Next day Zaman and I were clicking our teacups and saucers in silence on the mud porch. It was a beautiful day; the sun's rays streamed through the trees and the quietness was punctuated by the murmur of the stream and the melodies of birds.

"You are very quiet today," Zaman said.

"Yes, it has been a wonderful four days. Now I have to go back to that hot mudhole Kabul, where all the stupidities of life and the living converge."

"Have you thought of spending the rest of the summer here with me?"

"It is out of the question."

"But why?"

"I don't even have my books with me."

"Come with me. I will show you something." Zaman walked with long strides through a door into a rather dark inner chamber. I stood near the door while he lit a candle and passed it to me. He lifted the lid of an old dusty trunk full of books. "Here is something to keep you busy for a long time." He handed me three books which the light of the day revealed to be: *The Rights of Man, The Age of Reason, Common Sense.* The author of all three was Thomas Paine.

Bacha-i-Saqao

"Who is this man, Thomas Paine?" I asked.

"He was an Englishman who joined the patriotic forces in the American colonies that were fighting against political and economic injustices and exploitation. He popularized their grievances in simple, revolutionary language. But we shall discuss him in greater detail after you have read his books."

What a delightful two months that was! Schools were closed, but my intellectual knowledge, awareness of the outside world, political judgment and understanding of the clashing of forces which molded the destiny of man and nations increased by leaps and bounds. Thomas Paine, the son of a poor staymaker, pulled the lofty tyrants down to earth and demonstrated to the hungry and barefoot volunteer soldiers what laughable fools these kings were. I cried and laughed at the common pain and joy of men and women everywhere in the world. Zaman opened to me door after door into the beauties and challenges of life, the arts and sciences and the common struggle for decency and dignity.

"Above all, you must protect your life so that you may be able, through many years of hard work, to accumulate knowledge for the task ahead of you. It is the spread of education that will finally destroy the system of domestic and foreign oppression."

"Haji Sahib, where can one obtain formal education when even the schools are closed?"

"It won't be long now. Bacha-i-Saqao is almost at the end is rope. Nadir Khan, with the help of the Pathans on both sides of the frontier and freshly armed by the British, is moving relentlessly on Kabul. He will be our next king and will have no option but to reopen the schools, if for no other reason than to provide himself with officials and technicians for his bureaucracy."

My days were not organized, but they were usually spent in reading, walking and some physical labor. I learned to gather the early fall harvest of grapes, apples, peaches and pears in the orchard and tomatoes, corn and beans out in the field. I learned how to spade, cut hay, collect eggs and feed the animals. The fierce-looking black dog, Ghor-ghory, became my constant

Memories of Afghanistan

companion. He had a questionable family tree and rumbled a low, rolling sound before barking, hence his name. Ghor-ghory loved to roam the mountains with me, where he was allowed to chase small animals with impunity. He never caught one, and I suspect that, like his master Zaman, he had a tender heart inside his massive frame.

Nights were spent in contemplation, reading, and almost always some conversation which would start at dinner time and sometimes continued until bed time. I asked questions incessantly, questions that pertained to topics of interest to me. Zaman provided answers patiently, even sometimes when the questions were of a personal nature.

"Why did you never marry, Haji Sahib?"

"Well, when I was young, I was too restless to be tied down. When I grew older, it became impossible for me to live with a human being with whom I could not share my thoughts as well as my pleasures. Muslim women are treated far worse than those in the most primitive tribes in the history of mankind. They are stunted physically and dead mentally. They live by their wits and innate resources, which are considerable.

"As far as my sexual problem is concerned, I do have an outlet with a woman. But let me give you the background before you hear one of many garbled versions of it. When my father died, I came home and found that one of the four tenant farmers working on our farms in Kohistan, where the bulk of our property is, had died a couple of years earlier. My father supported the wife and her little daughter who, by the way, is about your age. This woman and I have provided sexual needs for each other ever since. The daughter, who is a beautiful, bright little girl, has a little half-sister–my contribution. One of my pet projects in life is to see that these two girls are educated. As soon as things quiet down, I will send Rahila, the older girl, to a school in Lebanon, where in Beirut there are a few good ones."

On other occasions, we discussed Thomas Paine's books, especially *The Age of Reason*.

Bacha-i-Saqao

"Why was he so vilified, especially in America, after writing this book? He proudly believed in one God."

"You have to look at Paine through the perspective of history," Zaman said. "He was ahead of his time, but if he wrote that book today, I don't think he could find a publisher. His main theme, if you remember, was the superfluity of church rituals, with their cozy scheme of heaven and hell and childish fables of miracles. However, it is very important to remember that all three books of his are revolutionary and full of dynamite in today's colonial Asia, but are taken for granted in the West today."

"I am glad you said that because I have copied many passages from these books which I expect to memorize. Haji Sahib, I will be leaving you in a couple of days and have already said goodbye to my uncles and their families. It was the happiest day of my life when I met you accidently only a short time ago."

"That was no accident. Your mother was born here and you were known and well thought of in this rather small village. My surreptitious trip to Kabul was planned and I am very happy that the outcome has been most satisfying. One more thing, tomorrow before you wake up, I will be on my way to Kohistan. Rasul will take care of you for the rest of your stay."

We said goodbye and picked up the two candles that Rasul lit by touching their wicks against the yellow flame of an oil lamp that danced in the soft breeze.

Back to Kabul, back to dusty alleys and empty bazaars, where the shops and shopkeepers looked vacant and bare. Sounds of drums from the mountains to the east penetrated the thin air of the morning, foretelling the doom of those huddled in the royal castle surrounded by nervous soldiers. The end of September, 1929, was bringing closer the end of one kingdom, headed by the son of a poor water carrier, and the beginning of another. Both kings were foisted on us by the vagaries of dynastic politics and imperial forces far beyond our reach and capacity to control.

Many people, including my father and older brother, believed that Amanullah would come back as king in a matter of days.

Memories of Afghanistan

"He will never be allowed to enter Afghanistan," I said.

"How do you know?" my brother Wahab asked.

"Bachim, Nadir Khan has taken the oath of allegiance to Amanullah and will be considered the greatest hero this country has ever produced. Besides, he will with one bold stroke wipe out the allegations and rumors that he is a hand-picked British agent," my father explained.

"My guess is that one way or another Nadir will proclaim himself king and, like Amir Abdul Rahman, rule by terror," I said.

The incessant sound of drums became ever louder on the foothills of Kabul during the first week of October. Soldiers began to shed their uniforms and desert. Bacha-i-Saqao knew his days were numbered and asked for safe conduct while preparing to flee the castle. Nadir Khan made two vital mistakes at this time. He promised that safe conduct but did not intend to keep his promise, and he also issued a fake order to Shah Wali, his brother, to bombard the castle if Bacha did not surrender peacefully. Here was Nadir exhibiting his tribal character, that for a manly cause the lives of women and children had to be sacrificed. The comic aspect of this staged opera was that the people of Kabul knew that Bacha was out of the castle by October 10, after he received his safe conduct. Within hours, the castle was surrounded. The Bacha was pursued and captured six days later. To compound the folly, Shah Wali wrote a memoir of these tragicomic episodes in which he claimed that after the decisive battle of Kabul on October 5 and 6, he was poised to bombard the castle, since besides the order from Nadir Khan, he had received a smuggled letter from his relatives inside the castle not to spare their lives to achieve victory. What a brave family, these Musahibans!

The "decisive victory," as far as the people of Kabul could tell, consisted of sporadic gunshots from behind big boulders halfway down the rocky hills to the south and east. The drum sounds were getting louder and increasing in number. I was among the few adventurous souls who roamed the outskirts of the capital

Bacha-i-Saqao

and successfully dodged the stray bullets that came from the hills. We saw no soldiers defending the capital. The Bacha had lost the decisive battle almost a month earlier when his army ran out of ammunition and had no source from which to replace it, while, for the Pathans, the door to India and British supplies was wide open.

People in Kabul waited impatiently for the "conquering heroes" to descend and end their full year of nightmare. What was keeping them? As it turned out, Nadir Khan and his entourage were still far behind the advancing columns. They had not expected an easy victory and Shah Wali had to wait for Nadir Khan to catch up, because his prestige was needed before the unruly Pathans were let loose on the capital. But the tribal soldiers could not be held any longer. They descended on Kabul and started looting for three full days before Nadir Khan entered the castle. The Pathan chiefs were already there preparing the groundwork for his "unanimous election against his own will."

On October 16, shortly after his entry into the well-guarded castle, Nadir Khan joined a motley crew of tribal chiefs, relatives, some dignitaries of Kabul and a few odds and ends of camp followers, Indians, and intellectual elite who had gathered by invitation. Among them was a rather short young man, Riaz, who had sunken cheeks and bushy, blue-black hair. He wore a faded blue suit and his eyes watered because of malnutrition suffered in jail when he refused to serve under Bacha-i-Saqao. During the reign of Amanullah, Riaz had been editor of *Anees*, a small newspaper. Three days prior to the meeting, the prison guards opened the prison gates and towers and the prisoners walked out into the confused multitude of looting Pathans. Riaz was searched for and was found in his father's house recuperating from his prison ordeal. He was taken to Hashim Khan, who shook his hand and offered him the job of nominating the king in the Loya Jirga.

"But Amanullah does not need nomination or introduction," Riaz said, still wishfully under the illusion, like most of the people in Afghanistan, that their beloved king would somehow walk again among them as in the old days.

Memories of Afghanistan

"I am talking about our new king, Nadir Shah," said Hashim.

Riaz protested, "I am in no shape to make speeches, as you can see."

"As you wish, but we need your presence at the ceremony."

Riaz was at the gathering when Nadir Khan entered the chamber in his new military uniform and proceeded to talk. The gist of his speech was that he had done his duty as an Afghan and eliminated the mark of dishonor from the land of the Pathans and that now he would be satisfied to live peacefully as a common citizen. Cries of "No, no..." were heard from all corners of the room. One old Pathan chief with a flowing white beard lumbered up, raised his walking stick and uttered slowly and distinctly, "We want you and the country needs you. You cannot veto the will of the Loya Jirga." Everyone jumped to his feet and they all started to clap. When the group calmed down, Abdul Ahmad stood up and proclaimed, "From today on, you will be called Nadir Shah [King]. Your past and future deeds will be written in letters of gold. Under your leadership, Afghanistan will plunge into the twentieth century with gusto and determination. You led us out of the darkness into the dawn of a new day. I nominate you as the first king of a new and glorious dynasty." The nomination was passed unanimously. Nadir Shah accepted with humility.

The people of Kabul were perplexed, dazed and in despair. While the new royalty was writing history in "letters of gold," sporadic looting, rape, abduction and arrests were the order of the day, almost a week after our conquering heroes had rescued us from the "reign of terror." Children were exposed to horrible scenes of cruelty and bloodletting, the like of which was hard to contemplate. On a dusty hill south of the capital, two guns boomed constantly. Crowds of people, including the very young, were encouraged to be spectators at the executions. Truckloads of political prisoners–Tajiks who had helped Bacha, Amanullah supporters and plain common criminals–were led to a clearing at the foot of the knoll. With hands tied behind their backs and their eyes covered with dark cloth, they walked up the hill guided by a

Bacha-i-Saqao

rope that zigzagged through their arms and was pulled at the lead by a tired and bored soldier. At the top of the hill, each prisoner was tied to the muzzle of a gun that protruded about three feet off the ground; a flash, a booming noise, a roaring echo from the valley beyond, and a fine rain of crimson blood ended the final chapter in the life of the man unlucky enough to have been born where he was.

Down below was Chamen, the grassy patch of land, about four acres in area, where we used to play soccer in normal times. At the edge of the green grass, not far from the small ditch which separated the greenery from the dusty road, six corpses dangled from ropes tied to the beam of a newly-built scaffold. The victims, Bacha-i-Saqao and his close associates, had evidently been killed elsewhere, because their bodies were mutilated and had marks of burning and bruises all over them.

On my way home, I read the proclamation that four days of holiday would come to an end on the following Friday. On Saturday, government employees were urged to report to their normal places of work. At home, my father reprimanded me for exposing myself to such barbaric deeds.

"Isn't life sad enough that you went out of your way to pile up memories that will haunt you the rest of your life?" he scolded.

"Papa Jan, we, the children of the Age of Reason, are immune from further horror, because we experienced it in its utter nakedness when we first struggled to suck a mouthful of milk from the dried-up parchment of our mothers' breasts, held tightly in our tiny, anxious hands."

Chapter 12
The Vultures' Turn

We are dealing with stupid and ignorant people in this country.
–Hashim Khan,
the Prime Minister of Afghanistan

Well, a new king finally grasped the reins of the kingdom firmly in his hands. Nadir Shah was a stubborn and a primitive man, primitive in the sense that he ruled by animal instinct, striking hard at the first sign of trouble. He loved pomp and ceremony, but only from a safe distance. His mental capacity could not reach beyond a limited tribal philosophy. He seldom kept his word, but paid fully to three sources that put him on the throne–the British foreign office, the tribal chiefs and the mullahs–in that order of importance.

The British not only transported Nadir and most of his brothers through India, but also gave them logistical support in the Northwest Frontier, among the tribes.

The tribal leaders were well known for their sharp bargains. Their demand for arms, food and money could only be provided by British India through Nadir and his brothers.

The mullahs, especially their top leaders who were at this particular time "interned" in India, mysteriously escaped to the tribal territory to help Nadir, but for a price, which involved their complete freedom in handling the religious life of Afghanistan.

It was known and discussed among the small but influential class of intellectuals in Kabul that the fate of small nations was decided by those who were adept in the art of manipulating puppets. Historical events as such did not make sense when the plans that initiated the dynamics of change stayed locked as "secret documents" in England.

Normalcy was once again proclaimed by the ruling family and dutifully confirmed by the only daily paper in Kabul. Foreign

The Vultures' Turn

countries sent their ambassadors back to their empty legations. The Arg* received a new coat of white paint. The two soldiers who marched rigidly in front of its massive door looked like cranked dolls attired in colorful new uniforms. Shops with scanty merchandise opened, but the usual bustle and gaiety were missing after two lootings in one year. People looked thinner and shivered in the cool of the fall breeze. The past year had taken a heavy toll on the beggars. Their numbers were smaller and their demands barely audible. Everyone seemed to be afraid of the cold of the coming winter. The young breed of the Musahiban clan, tomorrow's rulers, crisscrossed the dirt roads of the capital on their motorcycles, leaving behind clouds of dust.

Schools opened as expected. The only school for girls, however, stayed closed for another seven or eight years. Free lunch and free uniforms were abolished in the high schools. This was especially hard on our school, where the bulk of the students came from very poor families. Corporal punishment was encouraged to such an extent that even teachers who did not believe in it had to carry sticks as a job-security measure.

A religious revival with all its medieval trimmings was in full swing. Mosques were full of devout and fake worshipers. The *chaderi*† became compulsory for women and even young girls. *Muhtassibs*‡ roamed the city streets, stopping and asking anyone a religious question. If the pedestrian's answer was wrong, he would be flogged in public. Gangs of kids found this exceedingly entertaining. They began to follow the muhtassibs asking questions, which they ignored. Once some students tripped one of these keepers of the moral code and burned his beard with a flaming paper. Another one was indignantly flogged with his own whip. The government tried to remedy the situation by assigning a soldier to each muhtassib. When the level of violence increased even further, the mullahs called off their unworkable scheme of religious enforcement.

---

* Royal castle.
† A veil covering the body from head to toe.
‡ Religious examiners.

Memories of Afghanistan

Our school was transferred to an unpretentious building located between the foreign office and the prime ministry. Classrooms were all in one row, ending at a small, two-level structure where the teachers and the principal had their offices. The quarter-acre, rectangular land in front of the classes was fenced in and divided into a volleyball court and a gymnastic field.

Some of the teaching staff in our school were the same and some were replacements for those who had died, left the country, or joined other pursuits. There were some significant changes in the Ministry of Education. The perennial talker, Faiz Mohammed, was missing from the roster of the newly-appointed ministers. His former deputy, Ali Ahmad, became our new minister of education.[*]

Significant new additions to our school were two Persian poets[†], Qari Sahib and Bitab. Through the next two and a half years, poetry became one of my major pursuits. Contemporary poetry, both in Iran and Afghanistan, was mainly confined to inane topics such as love and separation or was sentimental and lyrical. Most of the love poems pertained to boys rather than girls. Qari Sahib, for instance, used to read some of his love poems extending back for two decades to us. It was known that he had been in love all this time with Ali Ahmad.

"He used to be beautiful to look at," Qari Sahib would say.

"Was he a good companion in bed?" Rahman would ask teasingly. Qari Sahib would shake his head and add, "My love was and shall remain platonic."

Traditionally in Muslim countries, protest and irony were used against kings and tyrants or religious hypocrisy. But the new breed of rulers, with foreign help and advice, could not tolerate any disturbance of the status quo. Some of the brightest poets were dead or dying in these countries.

Students read Hafiz, Sadi, Bedil, Firdowsi and Omar Khayyam and wrote poems in the seclusion of their own homes. The country

---

[*] The new minister of education was Ali Mohammed, who was replaced by Ahmad Ali Suleiman in 1933.–*Ed.*

[†] I.e., Afghan poets of the Persian language.–*Ed.*

The Vultures' Turn

was sliding backwards economically, socially and educationally while we read our poems of protest and disillusionment to one another. Here is the translation of a fragment of a poem that I wrote and still remember to this day:

> If sky could reflect the tragedy of our people
> When they raise their heads in agony–
> The distended bellies of hungry children,
> The red bruised lines of the whip on tender skin,
> The uncounted bodies rolling in pain,
> The lined faces and the sunken eyes:
> Will be the mute exhibition of their lives,
> Mocking your cruel legacy.

The four Musahiban brothers feasting over the body of a dying land were very different from one another. The king himself was cruel in a narrow sense. He eliminated suspected rivals to the throne in one short operation. He might have enjoyed the exercise of power over his helpless enemies, but he never played cat-and-mouse with them for long. He believed that John Bull would rule over a good portion of the globe for quite a while yet, and that as long as the tentacles of British power were within sight, his dynasty was safe.

The king's half-brother, Hashim Khan, was a different animal altogether. He resented the king and considered him a military man of limited ability and imagination. Since Hashim had never married, his two nephews, Daud Khan and Naim Khan, the sons of his real brother, were very dear to him. After the death of their father, Hashim Khan made himself responsible for their future careers. He did not care for his other nephew, Zahir Khan, the prince. This undercurrent of family feud, which in later decades surfaced into real animosity, eventually culminated in the destruction of monarchy in Afghanistan.

Hashim Khan, the prime minister, was a realist, even if limited in mental capacity. He did not believe in automatic British protection and had a feeling that Asia's colonial days were numbered. During

Memories of Afghanistan

the next decade, he established the widest network of spies and counter-espionage in the country. His agents could be found in all governmental departments, schools and military establishments and among Pathan tribes, nomads and beggars. No stratum of society was ignored or downgraded. People began to suspect friends or even members of their own families. Reports, rumors, gossip and tall tales were pondered over, classified and catalogued. Political reports were pursued relentlessly and suspects were arrested and tortured until they confessed their crimes and named accomplices. Hashim Khan personally supervised the construction of political prisons and the choice of torture implements.

Afghanistan's financial situation during the decade of the thirties was in a chaotic condition. The dislocation caused by constant warfare and the Pathan incursions and lootings left the country exhausted and poor. With young peasants fighting in one army or another, land cultivation was only partially carried out. Staple food was in short supply for a number of years.

In the midst of all this, the biggest land-grabbing episode in the history of the country was taking place. Yesterday's victimizers became today's victims. Large parcels of land changed hands. For a while it looked as if Hashim Khan was becoming the only beneficiary. However, after his agents sorted out the best lands for him, the rest was distributed among underlings, camp followers and individuals who had proven themselves loyal and sacrificing to the monarchy.

Hashim's next move was to monopolize the handling of karakul and carpets. These two items, plus dried fruits, were the mainstay of hard currency in the country. Sheep herders in the northern plains were informed that their karakul skins would have to be sold only to authorized government agents at a predetermined price. The cost was so low (ten to fifteen cents a skin, depending on quality) that karakul production practically stopped. The prime minister then compelled the producers to sell a minimum number of skins to the government or pay an extremely high fine. Karakul

The Vultures' Turn

production exceeded all expectations. Some of the skins were sold in Europe, but the largest number came to the New York market.

Carpet production requires a skill which is acquired after a great number of years of apprenticeship. The government, realizing the futility of force, opened handicraft training centers, hired instructors and encouraged the art of carpet weaving. Female children of poor farmers were then forced in large numbers to weave twelve to fourteen hours a day producing beautiful Afghan carpets.

A large percentage of the sale price of these two items was deposited in foreign banks in the name of individual members of the royal family. In subsequent years, the size of these personal deposits was so huge that the main function of the Afghan consul in New York was their proper investment.

In Kabul, food products were sold as bulk commodities to retailers or rich households, who bought their staple foods in the peak of the season. These food products, such as flour, rice and various legumes, were lined up in Mandawi (a food market) and the animals were then taken to the nearby caravansary, where they were kept in the yard while their owners occupied small rooms upstairs. Since our prime minister was by far the biggest landlord in the country, his products were always on display. Under the watchful eyes of a couple of soldiers, people always spent a few rupees buying his low-quality products. If Hashim's merchandise was not sold within a reasonable length of time, the soldiers were authorized to keep other merchants out of the market until his goods were all sold.

People gathered in small groups, sadly watching this comic performance at their expense. Their comments were pungent and bitter.

One of Hashim Khan's pet projects was to raise turkeys. He consulted Department of Agriculture experts. They translated an American booklet on the subject for him. In a matter of two years, on a farm not far from Kabul, thousands of fat birds were clucking their way to fame. Articles appeared in the daily paper extolling

Memories of Afghanistan

the genius of our prime minister in introducing *feelmorgh** to his hungry people. It was not mentioned that his hungry people considered themselves fortunate if they saw a piece of meat on their tables once a month.

During the hot days of August, these large birds wobbled in groups of thirty to fifty through the narrow streets of Kabul. They were guarded by two peasants with long sticks, who took turns yelling, "Elephant chicks for sale!" By the end of the day, more birds were stolen than sold. The children who stole them knew that they could never find anyone who would buy stolen goods that belonged to the prime minister. So they feasted on turkey kebab in the dark alleys of the town. What was left was cleaned out by the patient dogs that were attracted by the smell. In the first week of September, it was discovered that an incurable viral disease was killing the birds at such a rate that in a few days all five thousand of them were either dead or dying.

"Serves him right, the bastard. My mouth watered every time I looked at those birds parading in front of my empty shop," Momin said to my father.

"I wouldn't gloat so much if I were you. If I know Hashim Khan, he will make us pay for his folly one way or another," my father said.

"Padar Jan,† why does God always punish the poor and the helpless? What have we done to deserve a dose of calamity for lunch and a parcel of catastrophe for dinner, day after day as long as I can remember?"

"Now you are delving into philosophy, my son. Who knows what Allah's ultimate design is?"

King Nadir's other two brothers played very minor parts in the affairs of our land. Shah Wali Khan was dubbed by the royal court "The Conqueror of Kabul"–as a joke, I presume. However, he took his title seriously. With the help of a couple of ghost writers, he wrote his memoirs in pamphlet form. Our legendary

---

* Elephant chick.
† Dear Father.

The Vultures' Turn

hero's ambition was to find a translator, preferably an expert in the English language, so that this historic document might reach a wider public. The late historian Mohammed Ali, who at one time was my history teacher at Habibia, told me that Shah Wali Khan pestered him for years to translate his memoirs into English.

Professor Ali said, "Can you imagine allowing my name to be used as a translator of his hodgepodge of wishful fancy?"

Shah Wali was a gawky character of medium height. The cut of his mustache and stooped shoulders reminded one of Groucho Marx, always in a hurry but going nowhere. On holidays and important occasions, he was bedecked with all the medals and plumes his frail body could carry. The Musahiban brothers were all poor public orators, especially Shah Wali, who never spoke to a gathering of more than two. This haunted him to such an extent that years later he personally trained his sons to speak in public. Whenever he had guests in his house, one of his sons would be hoisted onto a table to jabber about anything concerning his daily living, emphasizing points by clenched fist or raising of voice. The poor fellows grew up to be talkative idiots. No one dared to tell the father that substance was far more important than form–if they had nothing to say, it was wiser to shut up like their father.

Shah Mahmood Khan, the minister of war, was a substantially built man. His thick and twisting formidable mustache belied his soft, rounded chin and large brown, cowlike eyes. Like the king himself, he liked pomp and ceremony. He also liked the company of his subordinate officers' wives, good food and the quiet seclusion of the flower gardens outside the capital.

Chapter 13
Blood Feuds

Because the past two hundred years of the history of this unfortunate nation was largely shaped by dynastic blood feuds, it is fitting that the most recent and the bloodiest be mentioned here as yet another indignity suffered by my people. However, a little historical sketch preceding the story would make it more understandable.

This land, Afghanistan, has had no historical identity as a nation, either geographically, ethnically or culturally. It has been a gateway for thousands of years, to or from India, Persia or Central Asia. Each invasion dumped its troops in minor garrisons to protect the lines of advance; these were then forgotten and were in turn submerged into the local population. They were Greeks, Persians, Mongols, Tartars, Indians, Arabs and many more.

One tribe whose identity is still obscure occupied the sparsely populated desert in the southeast and the rocky hills in the east. The unproductive land and the meager resources had a profound effect on this tribe, known as Pathan or Pushtun. In the course of time, its members became nomads, marauders, mercenaries and spies. Rivalry for material gains and the possession of women splintered the tribe into smaller units or subtribes, which often led to family bloodbaths. The rise of the British Empire in India coincided with the dominant role of the Pathans in Afghan history.

The family of one of the subtribes, the Musahibans, was exiled to India by Amanullah's grandfather, Abdul Rahman. The British took them under their tutelage and educated them in the best schools in India. During the reign of Abdul Rahman's son, Habibullah, who considered Afghanistan a mere extension of India, the young Musahiban brothers were sent back to Afghanistan and were given important positions in the government. The oldest and the shrewdest of the five brothers, Nadir Khan, entered the military field and delved deep into tribal matters.

Blood Feuds

When Amanullah became king (1919), he declared Afghanistan an independent country and attacked the British troops. The third-rate Indian army, which consisted mostly of Pathans and other Indians, was hastily put together by the alarmed officers in the Northwest Frontier. It was not a match against a motivated, well-armed Afghan force led by General Nadir Khan. But he managed only a stalemate. England, exhausted by the First World War and faced with mutiny in India itself, agreed in a 1919 peace treaty, in Rawalpindi, to give Afghanistan complete freedom.

Nadir Khan emerged from this war a national hero, but privately he came under suspicion. Two subsequent events indicated beyond much doubt where his loyalty resided. One, in the early nineteen-twenties, he opposed a plan to modernize the army in terms of firepower and loyalty, discarding the outmoded recruiting system based on tribal choice. Two, as minister of war in 1924, Nadir Khan refused to put down an English-instigated revolt by a minor tribe, the Mengal. He was relieved of his command and sent into semi-exile as a minister to France. His subsequent return to Afghanistan and capture of the Afghan throne for himself has been covered elsewhere in this book. As a king, he acted not with mercy and justice but with malice and cruelty. He could not tolerate disagreement and his opponents were physically eliminated under bizarre circumstances. Our story deals with one of those.

Shortly after Nadir Khan became King of Afghanistan, a very important rival of his, Ghulam Nabi Charkhi, who was languishing as an important exile in Russia, received a letter in his flat in Moscow. It was in Nadir's own handwriting, urging Ghulam Nabi to come to Kabul. Over a year, a series of letters were exchanged between the two most important Afghans. Most of his friends and relatives, including his brothers, Ghulam Jilani and Ghulam Siddiq, advised Ghulam Nabi not to go to Afghanistan. However, the bulk of his family resided in Kabul and other parts of Afghanistan. If he refused the king's request, their lives and livelihood would be in danger. In March of 1931, Ghulam Nabi landed in Kabul in a small Russian mail carrier plane. There was a

Memories of Afghanistan

huge gathering of the members of the Charkhi tribe celebrating the doubly happy occasion–his arrival and the advent of the New Year on March 21. The first disturbing sign was the presence of two spies on the street prominently parading back and forth, keeping tabs on the new arrivals. They had been sent by Hashim Khan, the prime minister. Were they sent to intimidate? The curious passers-by and the shopkeepers wondered. Five days later, Ghulam Nabi entered the confines of the Arg for his audience. No one saw him again, dead or alive.

In June of 1931, a Captain Rahim was spending his three weeks' vacation in Jalalabad, a town about sixty miles east of Kabul. He had had a promotion in rank and was happy that he could now afford to marry his uncle's pretty daughter. On the second day of his stay, he was aducted from the street and released unharmed three hours later. He had been a petty officer only three months before, guarding the king's chamber inside the royal castle. When he was pushed inside a semi-dark room in a house not far from his uncle's, he instinctively realized the predicament he was in.

"I had nothing to do with it," Rahim blurted out at the two men who sat cross-legged in the corner, a good part of their faces covered by wrapped turbans, just like his two abductors.

"With what?" a muffled question floated to him from the corner.

"What am I here for?"

"You seem to know already." The second voice, at a considerably lower pitch, but extremely menacing, hit him.

"I am willing to tell you all I know."

"Then it is settled. Is Ghulam Nabi Khan alive?"

"No."

"Then tell us what happened. And please don't spare us any gory details."

"His fate was predetermined. Three days before the sad event, the special assistant to the prime minister talked to me and the two soldiers from the king's bodyguard contingent. He said that when the king gave a signal to me by raising his hand, I was supposed to call the two soldiers, who would be standing outside with a rope, to enter and tie the victim's hands behind his back. With the second command, they were to re-enter the room with their guns unloaded and commence hitting the victim with the butts of their guns till dead.

"I cannot forget that day as long as I live. As Ghulam Nabi Khan entered the chamber, King Nadir Khan walked halfway across the room from behind his massive desk and took Nabi Khan's outstretched right hand with both hands and greeted him most profusely by saying that he was most happy they were meeting again. I was unprepared for the play-acting."

"What happened then?"

"Well, they sat at the table like two good friends who had not seen each other for a long time and started talking about the past."

"Tell us exactly what they said to each other."

"I could not follow the conversation, but Amanullah, the previous king, was mentioned by Nadir Khan and the friendly talk turned into a heated argument. Especially when Nabi Khan said that both of them had taken the oath of allegiance to the former king. I remember the last few sentences they spoke to each other. Here is how it went:

" 'Are you willing to take the same oath with me?' the king asked.

" 'Yes, but after certain conditions are met.'

" 'Did you tell Amanullah the same thing before you took your oath?'

" 'No.'

" 'I see. At one time in the past I offered you a bond between our two families, a bond of marriage and you refused. Would you accept it if it were offered to you now by a king?'

" 'It depends.'

" 'Depends on what?'

" 'On the attitude of those who are to be married.'

" 'When you speak to a king, you are supposed to stand in the middle of the room.'

Memories of Afghanistan

"Ghulam Nabi Khan slowly walked to the center of the room and the king finally raised his hand. When the two soldiers began to tie his hands behind his back, he raised his head and addressed the king once more.

" 'Have you ever in your life kept a promise or a word of honor?'

"The king did not answer him, but looked him in the eye and flicked the ash of a cigarette with his long yellow finger, while raising his hand once more. It took only a couple of minutes before Ghulam Nabi Khan was a lifeless mass, every bone in his body broken. Throughout the proceedings, the king sat rigidly with his hands folded on his chest. When it was over, he stood up abruptly and, like a newly-recruited soldier, he stiffly turned around and marched out of the chamber."

After Nadir Khan became king, our school, Habibia, was given a new location. Gone were the rolling hills, the flower beds, the soccer fields, orchards, the lovely stream and the spacious, well-furnished classrooms. Our new school looked like an ill-kept army barrack. On the north, it had a common wall with the office and residence of the prime minister. As kids, we used to shout revolutionary songs under this wall in defiance of the authorities, including the cruel chief of the secret service, whose office was also located beyond the wall. On the south side ran a dirt road east to the airport, a short distance away. Across this road were located the well-kept gardens of the foreign ministry, where we used to play ball in recess time even though it was against the regulations, nailed boldly in white on a black background. To the west was the narrow alleyway which led to the door of the prime minister, where a couple of sentries marched back and forth with their loaded guns slung on their shoulders and a large key dangling from their dirty waistbands. People coming in or going out were searched and their admission cards examined before passing through the door.

The prime minister seldom ventured to walk along the alley but did surprise the lazy bureaucrats in the foreign office with his visits a few times a year. These were events of considerable

Blood Feuds

interest to students who would line up against the railing. The old man, Hashim Khan, permanent Prime Minister of the Kingdom, with his drooping jaws and enormous potbelly, would plod along next to his special secretary. With a pen in one hand and a small pad in the other, the latter would be poised for action, furiously committing onto paper the words of wisdom popping out of His Excellency's mouth. They would be surrounded by six soldiers, two in front, two in back and one on either side. It was the job of a couple of coolies to sweep the alley and keep it wet to protect His Highness from any dust that might cause him discomfort.

On one of these occasions, the water carrier was somewhat late and he was hurrying to finish his job when the party caught up with him. The two front soldiers opened fire. Hashim Khan hit the wet road, his secretary on top of him, protecting him with his own body, while the poor water carrier was on the side the of the ditch riddled through the back. The commotion brought all the school children to the railing and even outside against all orders. I was one of those who had missed the real show. By the time we were close enough to see, the prime minister was being dusted off and conducted back to his residence.

Three months later there was a repeat performance, except that this time two pistol shots were actually fired at Hashim Khan. Neither found its massive target, one missing all human contact and the other causing a superficial wound on the leg of one of the soldiers. The culprit was not caught but more than a dozen intellectuals, among them teachers, writers, students and office workers, were arrested and jailed. They were all accused of being agents and collaborators of the Charkhi family.

The rest of the year passed peacefully. However, early the next year, in April, I believe, we were told that schools would be closed for three days. On the first day, the body of Mohammed Aziz Khan would be flown in an airplane from Berlin. He was the Afghan Ambassador in Germany and the only brother of the king outside the confines of his kingdom. He had been shot and killed

Memories of Afghanistan

by an Afghan student, believed to have been instigated by Ghulam Siddiq Charkhi.

The next day, a line almost two miles long was formed from the royal castle on the road south of Kabul. The bedecked casket was followed by long, black cars containing black-clad passengers of royal blood in various manifestations of grief. Then a regiment of cavalry officers with drawn sabers followed, trying hard to manage their scared horses. High dignitaries were followed by not so high dignitaries in various colored cars and buggies. Then the mass of lower ranks and office holders, followed by unruly schoolchildren hopping and chatting loudly, composed "the mourners." A few friends of mine and I wormed our way in and out among the townspeople, who were lined up on both sides of the road, collecting the latest gossip. Most of them happily, and a few sadly or out of fear, agreed that the Charkhi family was responsible for the deed. In the newspaper, Ghulam Siddiq Charkhi was mentioned as the instigator and inciter of the crime.

After three days of "mourning," an ominous calm descended on the city of Kabul. Everyone was waiting for the axe to fall. It was a warm night, quiet except for the few barking dogs. The decision was arrived at by the remaining four Musahiban brothers: Nadir Khan, the king; Hashim Khan, prime minister; Mahmoud Khan, minister of war; and Shah Wali Khan, the king's special adviser. It was sent to the director of the Secret Service. The terse command was direct and short: "Eliminate all males in the Charkhi family within the borders of Afghanistan in the shortest possible time." In Kabul, the blood bath started that night. The Charkhi house near the Kabul River was surrounded at midnight. Six soldiers from the execution squad entered the house. Women and their daughters were locked up in the large living room, while eight males, ages two to fifty-five, were taken down in the courtyard and tied with one rope. The servants were pushed into their living quarters. The job was accomplished most efficiently in a few minutes with the least amount of disturbance possible. There was some wailing by the female crowd upstairs, their faces pressed against the window

Blood Feuds

panes. The servants, all from the Hazara tribe, stoically watched without understanding, while two soldiers, with pistols aimed against the temple of each victim, pressed the trigger. A young servant boy, Abdul Khaliq, was biting his lower lip and blood was trickling down his chin. His mother was holding his hand tight in her grip. When the soldiers left, the courtyard was full of wailing women holding bloody heads in their arms and cursing the gods in heaven.

The young boy, Abdul Khaliq, fifteen years old, now stood near the corpses gazing at his beloved half-brother, Jamal, only seven years old. Khaliq's mother, a beautiful Hazara girl, had joined the Charkhi family as a servant. She had lived there for the last seventeen years as a concubine to Ghulam Nabi Charkhi. Khaliq and his mother were treated with great respect. He was a happy boy, an excellent sportsman and very popular in Nijat school. Now, in the short space of a few days, he had lost his father and brother. That night he resolved to kill the king himself, who was directly responsible. A little over two years later, Khaliq shot and killed Nadir Khan at a gathering of students.

Meanwhile the blood baths were duplicated in many parts of the country, wherever a Charkhi, as close as a nephew or second cousin, could be found.

In 1932, I was spending a part of my vacation in Guldara, where I met Assadullah and another young man traveling with him, who was introduced to me as Abdul Latif Charkhi. After several happy days of mountain climbing, picnicking and just routine talk, we became good friends. One day I told him about my future hopes and desires, how I wanted go to foreign lands, educate myself and then serve our country. I was carried away with pleasant dreams.

"You are lucky," he said.

"What is your future plan?" I asked.

"My normal life terminated when I was twelve years old. Now I am living only for revenge, to kill, to destroy lives, the lives of those who usurped power and killed all I loved."

Memories of Afghanistan

Looking at the intense dark eyes of the lean youth who uttered those sentiments, I shuddered to think what was still in store for the future of my country.

When Zahir Shah, the only son of Nadir Shah, became king, the orgy of killing extended far beyond the Charkhi family. Abdul Khaliq was mutilated bit by bit in front of the multitudes of the Kabul population. His family, relatives, close friends, some classmates, a few of his teachers and many officials of the Ministry of Education were publicly hanged or shot. Many others just disappeared.

For two years, the grand executioner was Hashim Khan, the prime minister and living elder of the Musahiban clan.

Chapter 14
Nida

It was in the house of my friend Asif that I first met Ismail. The house was a gathering place for the high school students that lived within a mile of our street in Kocha-i-Aliriza Khan. Asif's parents had died rather young, leaving three sons and a very young daughter, a considerable wealth in the form of real estate, cultivated lands and orchards, and a large shop in Kabul which the oldest son had been trained to manage. There were a large number of servants in the house who attended to various duties. Since food of all kinds was available, we were constant companions to Asif and his younger brother, Isa, in the so-called study room. We did study and it was my responsibility to see that Asif not only did his homework but also passed all his school tests. So the various subjects were reviewed daily, especially math, and all were welcome to participate. Usually, one or two of us would recite a newly-composed poem, which invariably concerned the themes of loneliness, separation, or political protest. Sometimes we played penny poker.

During our first meeting, Ismail so impressed me that I asked many questions about him that evening after he left us. He was the most prominent and promising student in Nijat high school. His older brother, formerly the editor of a defunct journal, had been languishing in the Kabul jail for political prisoners. By the end of two weeks, Ismail and I became constant companions. He introduced me to a bookseller who imported Western books translated by Persian authors. I can never forget the three-day weekend when he and I took turns reading *Les Misérables* to one another, finishing the last part leaning on a slab of stone near the top of Kabul's mountains. We gazed into space, sad but exalted, forgetting the little bundle that contained our lunch of bread, cheese and apples. Ismail and I read and discussed many romantic novels, travel books and political volumes. Books on politics were

Memories of Afghanistan

kept away from the open shelves in Mr. Rasul's book shop. They were lent only to very trusted and close friends.

One day I asked Ismail if it were possible for me to go with him to the prison on his next visit to see his brother. He said he had talked to him about me and he wanted very much to meet me, but the guards were instructed to report anyone but close relatives to the authorities.

"However, you are a minor, and if they ask questions, hide your true identity."

It was a gloomy and gray afternoon, with gusts of wind throwing the accumulated dust of the morning right into one's face, when we arrived at the prison gate. The guard inspected the cooked mixture of rice and beans inside the little aluminum pot with his dirty fingers and then searched our pockets for concealed weapons. I felt his fingers dragging sluggishly with moderate pressing over the sides of my buttocks. I blushed but did not object. We were finally ushered into a small room with one window facing the yard and covered with thick, rusty bars. We sat at the table near the center of the room on one of the two small stools facing one another. In a few minutes, the door creaked again and a lump of bent human form was pushed inside. He shuffled to the empty stool and dropped his exhausted body on it. He raised his dreamy yellow eyes to me, at the same time pushing a piece of thin paper toward me with jerky motions of his gnarled fingers, still holding a corner of the paper with his thumb. Here is what was written on it:

ANWAR JAN:
The room is wired. Talk only about the weather and your school.

He pulled the paper toward him, rolled it into a thin cylinder and put it in his mouth. Ismail opened the food package and handed him the little pot. He hungrily started putting lumps of food into his mouth with his bare hands. While he was chewing, I watched his massive beard bobbing up and down. His head was shaved.

Nida

"The only way to get rid of the headlice," he pointed to his head. At this juncture, Ismail introduced me to his brother, Nida, an assumed literary name. Our discussion about school, the courses of study and sports lasted but a few minutes. Nida watched his brother with troubled eyes and sad composure for most of the visit. Then he stood up, put his arm around Ismail's neck and kissed him on both cheeks, whispering in his ear.

When we were outside the prison gate, Ismail told me that his older brother acted quite peculiarly at this particular visit. Nida had told him that he was being systematically tortured and that we should remove his personal papers, now hidden in his sister's house, and destroy them immediately before they obtained a forced confession from him as to their hiding place. We removed the papers in small bundles during the next three weeks to a rocky mountain dominating the Kabul River. We read most of the material before burning it. The papers consisted of memoirs, personal portraits, poems, commentaries on books read in Paris, notes on historical events, mostly the French and Russian revolutions, and an unfinished manuscript of a romantic nature. This last one was the story of a tender love affair. Juxtaposed between the imaginary free Afghanistan where the lovers were supposed to be living and the tyrannical reality in the background, the events assumed a surrealistic dimension imbued with a foreboding of doom.

His memoirs and diaries, annotated and dated, were the most gripping. Here one found sketches of friends and foes, a tender love affair in Paris with a French girl named Nannette, happy memories and sad events. I learned, through reading the diary notes and asking Ismail many questions, that after finishing high school in Kabul Nida had worked on the staff of the only newspaper in Afghanistan, *Anees*. He saw promise for his poor country during the enlightened reign of King Amanullah.

Nida was twenty-three years old when his father took him to France for a trip and left him in the care of his uncle, who was the chargé d'affaires in the Afghan Embassy. For the next four years, he studied literature and political science at the Sorbonne. These were

Memories of Afghanistan

the most eventful and tragic years for his country. In fact, Nadir Shah was the Afghan Ambassador in Paris and lived in the same embassy building as Nida prior to becoming king. Nida wrote him a letter of congratulations and hoped the country once again would walk firmly on the path of progress. The king replied with a short note that he needed the help of people like Nida in his future plans and hoped he would join in this worthy cause after completing his course of study. The copy of his letter and the king's reply were found clipped together among the other diary notations. Nida did come back after graduating two years later. He accepted the position of assistant editor on the same paper, *Anees,* which he had left four years earlier. He also taught literature part-time at the Istiqlal School. Eight months later he was arrested for teaching "subversive doctrines" to students. When I first met him, he had already been in jail for a little over seven months and he was only twenty-eight years old!

Yes, picture him then, lying on his cot, after the ordeal of torture so satanic that the nerve cells refused to transmit pain impulses any more, their main ganglion trunks having been damaged by continuous blows. The central nervous system, still intact, functioned as if pulsating in a silent fog. Memories of bygone days, little bright flashes merging together into a round face, bright eyes of deep blue, short of height, dark brown hair... Nannette. Fragments emerged from the bright past. The waiter with the pencil poised to take the order. "But you cannot leave me alone here in Paris, Nida. You cannot, you cannot, you..." echoed confused, disjointed fragments of thought. "Oh, but why did I? Nannette, why didn't you stop... me?" The dinner of fried chicken and red wine was to celebrate–what–a permanent separation? But maybe for the three years of love-making, walking, bicycling in the Loire Valley from one castle to another...

"You taught me French so patiently and now I can't use it.

"What is the bright mass of whiteness, covering everything?

"A ski slope, that is what. You taught me to ski, too. Remember the tiny room facing the valley. We were so exhausted that we embraced one another and instantaneously went to sleep. But we made love the next morning, bathing in the bright morning

Nida

sun." Then a dull pain and high temperature caused confusion and uncertainty. He was wet with perspiration, but still could feel a warm wetness creeping from his loins down his legs. He tried to capture the thread of the happy past again, but a heavy blackness enveloped him in a net of oblivion.

On a Thursday afternoon, I was to meet Ismail on the side of the mountain to finish our task of reading and burning the diaries. He didn't show up. I found him at his sister's house that night in a state of unbelievable sadness and fear. He told me that the authorities in the prison informed him that morning that Nida had committed suicide two days ago, and he was already buried in the common grave near the far end of the prison wall. He was purported to have hanged himself with his shirt in his own cell.

Ismail was afraid for his own future, and I tried to console him that he was a minor, but in my heart I knew he was justified. It had been the custom of the present Royal Government of Afghanistan to follow one of two paths when they eliminated an individual member of a prominent family–either eliminate all the one-step male members of the same family, or bestow wealth and positions of authority to them and keep them out of the capital and under strict surveillance for a long period of time. Experience had shown that the first option proved to be by far the better and safer of the two. So I was not surprised when Ismail was arrested within two months. But I was really amazed to hear that three months later he was released and sent to the northern province of Mazar.

The bits and pieces of the puzzle began to fall into place in due time. The main outline proved to be incontestable, but the details varied. Ismail was confined in a criminal, not a political, prison. He was raped almost every night by a fresh guard and later by criminals. The only book available to him was the Koran, which he memorized cover to cover. When released, he contacted no one but his sister. He was allowed four days to obtain clothing and food. On the first day of his arrival in Mazar, he drowned himself in a river. His body was found and reported to the local governor who had already been informed about him by the police of the

Memories of Afghanistan

central government. Ismail, like his brother Nida, was buried in an unmarked grave. He had sent a note to his sister merely stating his desire to die, and the last line of that letter, "to wash away the accumulated filth in my young body," still reverberates in my being.

Chapter 15
A Wedding in Kandahar

In the summer of 1932, Kabir Ludeen was one of the three students chosen from Habibia's senior class to study engineering in America. He asked me to join him on a trip to Kandahar as the guest of the governor of this southern province. Our first stop was the famous city of Ghazni. It was a great disappointment to both of us to realize that this dilapidated hillside town of cracked mud houses was once the capital of a great empire, established by Mahmud Ghaznavi, the son of Sabuktagin, a Turkish slave. His empire extended over Khorasan, Transoxiana, and the greater part of northern India. It was under his reign that Firdowsi wrote the great epic Persian poetry *Shahnama*.

We spent the night in a caravansary, where the odor of animal and human manure piled in the yard down below was an unwelcome irritant on a hot night. After washing the dust off our faces, we were conducted by our driver to a restaurant, where we ate shish kebab in the midst of beggars and flies. The sun was still hovering above the rounded hills beyond the vegetable fields to the west. The narrow streets zigzagged through open ditches carrying a thin stream of yellowish liquid alongside leaning walls. The enclosed small square yards gaped into the dusty void above. A sleepy lamb, a cow, or a donkey could be discerned here and there. Semi-naked children ran noisily hither and yon, stopping their games when they noticed us. They begged all around us with outstretched arms, cursing us and resuming their games when we ignored them.

"Look at what your people, the Pathans, have done to this land and the people living in it, a drab domicile, filled with beggars," I told Ludeen.

"Why blame the Pathans? What have the other races done for this country?" he said gruffly.

"Let me tell you a secret and you just pretend you never heard it. In this melting pot of racial diversity, neither I nor an

Memories of Afghanistan

Uzbek, a Hazara, a Turkman, a Tajik, a Persian, a Hindu or any other minority in Afghanistan can get employment in the foreign office, become a military officer or go beyond a certain rank in any government bureaucracy."

"You could be shot for what you just said."

"You want to report me, go ahead."

"For you own safety, I warn you not to discuss these problems in Kandahar. As you know, the governor is an uncompromising Pushtun."

The rest of the way to our lodging we walked in silence.

The land between Ghazni and Kandahar was flat and sandy as we moved south. The temperature in Kandahar must have been at least 125°F, and we ran from the parked bus to the shade of a chaikhana across the street to avoid the burning rays of the sun. The seat of government was an ornate old building under a huge copper dome which had been rusted into patches of warm green. We found the governor in the basement involved in a game of chess. He was a tall man. He had a large nose with a pointed head, bushy eyebrows and hairy hands.

"After a quick lunch, you fellows rest awhile, because tonight and the next three days I am going to show you an area of the country which I think is going to produce more food than we can consume."

The hundred-mile trip west in a Buick station wagon, even on dirt roads, was not uncomfortable. We passed many well-kept gardens and green patches of vegetables. We arrived at a beautiful pomegranate garden with a large stream and a marble house surrounded by green grass and flowering bushes. The next morning after a simple breakfast, we drove westward again for about fifty miles to the Helmand River.

"Bachim, this is the reason for your trip to these parts. See all that water down there. It used to be on the surface of the land and a civilization flourished on its banks. As the water ate its way deeper and deeper, it became more difficult to put it to use. At certain levels, sand took over where man once lived.

A Wedding in Kandahar

Now even their tall buildings and monuments are hidden from view."

"Yes, I would like to build that dam someday that everyone talks about," Kabir Ludeen said.

"You and I are going to tame that river and leave it to posterity as a legacy of the Pushtun contribution."

On the way back, the governor continued his talk about the dam.

"The Helmand is a mighty river. Its tentacles stretch over a wide area, covering almost half of Afghanistan, from the Paghman Mountains east through the Hindu Kush range. The torrents of water collected from the melting snow during the hot weather rush down from the ten- to twenty-thousand-foot-high peaks and fan out from northeast to southwest, from the Kabul area to the sand dunes and swamps of the Seestan Desert."

I clapped my hands and congratulated him on his hope for the future and his knowledge of the geography of our country.

"Well, Anwar Jan, next year will be your turn. What are you going to study in America?"

"Education."

"We can hire teachers. Why don't you also study engineering?"

As if Haji Zaman nudged me, I said, "My temperament leans toward the simple rather than the spectacular. Engineers can also be hired."

The dam was eventually built with American technical and financial help. The accumulated salt of centuries of flooding in the Helmand Valley was not a factor in the calculated scheme of soil reclamation by the experts of two nations. Years later, the thousands of Pathan nomads who settled in the newly-constructed houses could not even raise vegetables in the salty soil. Mr. Ludeen, the chief engineer, stole enough money to build his marble dream house. The governor was given a medal for his services and was then kept in Kabul under house arrest. The king who pauperized the kingdom was already involved in other costly plans.

Memories of Afghanistan

We drove back to the castle in the pomegranate orchard. After supper, the governor invited me to a game of chess on the veranda. It was a moonless night. The stars looked shiny against the pitch dark infinity. Only the murmur of the water in the stream down the slope exerted a discordant note to the quietude.

During the game, an official whispered in the governor's ear. While they talked in the next room, the chief of control, who was watching us play, said, "You are a good player, but I would like you to know that the governor does not like to lose in anything, especially chess."

"Are you implying that you people have been cheating him all along?"

"No, of course not. We treat him as a wise father."

"Some fathers should know how unwise they are in certain respects. As Sadi said a long time ago: to admit one's weakness is a sign of strength," I said.

The game was resumed within a few minutes. The stillness of the night was disturbed by the jarring cry of a human voice in the back of the house.

"Someone is hurt," I said.

The governor looked at his pocket watch and said, "We've all had a hard day and another one is ahead of us. How about some rest?"

In my bedroom I could still hear the howling of an adult man. Early next morning, walking around the building, I noticed some low structures beyond the rose bushes. On closer inspection, I saw a row of ten cages, most of them containing a naked human being tied in heavy chains.

"I wouldn't waste too much time on them if I were you," a booming voice declared. Turning around, I saw a short, muscular man carrying a spade on his shoulder. I was surprised that he spoke in Persian, and more so that he knew that I also spoke in that tongue. As if reading my thoughts, he said, "I am a Persian from Teheran and heard you talking my language."

"Who are they?" I pointed towards the cages.

A Wedding in Kandahar

"Mostly political deviants. Behind those cages, there is a dungeon where, at present, there are half-a-dozen prisoners living practically in their own shit. Once a day a bucket of water and another of soup and bread are sent down the slope. When one of them is brought out for questioning, he is taken to the torture chamber, that domed structure on your right."

"Was the howling last night connected with this?" I asked.

"Yes, the poor fellow could hardly walk, and yet his voice is as robust as the day he came. My friend, the torturer, tells me that the fellow confessed, was given a hearty meal and then put to bed. Today he is going to write his confession in his own handwriting."

"How can you be friendly with a torturer?"

"He is paid to do a job—no more, no less. But there are a couple of sadists here, including the big man himself, who actually enjoy watching human suffering. Hakeem told me that once the governor himself was fondling a mutilated penis in the palm of his hand."

"Who is Hakeem?"

"My friend, the torturer."

"Do you think these people are guilty?"

"Yes and no." Raising his right hand, he said, "Let me explain. They are the men of learning and, therefore, concerned about the backwardness of their country, which is caused mainly by an incompetent elite who are rulers by inheritance alone. The laws are written for their protection. Anyone who challenges these laws is automatically guilty."

"Now, my last question. How come you are only an ordinary gardener?"

"I am an escapee from the torture chamber of Reza Shah in Teheran." He pulled his foot from his left shoe. All the toes were missing. "I have other marks of distinction if you are curious to see."

"No, thank you."

"Once I taught Persian literature and philosophy at Teheran University. The sun is about to rise and soon there will be stirring

Memories of Afghanistan

in the house. The cook told me you are staying here today and most of tomorrow. We might meet again. *Khoda hafiz.** Please be careful with the governor. He is a very cruel man," he cautioned me.

As I turned back toward the main building, the sun rays had already penetrated the bent and knobby branches of the two huge birch trees near the house. The rose scent in the balmy morning air, the green lawn sloping down to the water of the brook and the happy chattering of birds in the pomegranate orchard assumed a stark dichotomy to the indignities meted out to the body and soul of man.

"A beautiful day, isn't it?" Gul Mohammed's voice startled me.

"Yes, it is."

"We have two full days here before returning to Kandahar. I would like to discuss certain problems with Ludeen and you. We will start after breakfast, if you don't mind."

"I don't mind."

Sitting around a table on the lawn, Gul Mohammed asked me if I knew any Pushtu at all.

"Very little, sir," I responded.

"Don't you think that a young man of talent and standing like you should make a serious effort to learn your national language?"

"I never had a chance. No one in Kabul speaks Pushtu and all government transactions are done in Persian."

"We are planning to change all that in the coming years."

"The majority of our population speak Pushtu and it is only fair that the minorities should learn it at least as a second language," Ludeen declared.

"We might have to use compulsion if persuasion fails," the governor said sternly, banging the table with his hand for emphasis. I had two choices before me–one, to lose my temper and damage my future prospects in a nation run by fools, or two, to grind my teeth and bear it. I chose the second alternative, saying as little as possible.

"What do you think of Kandahar?" the governor asked.

"I have not seen much of it as yet."

---

* God protect you.

A Wedding in Kandahar

"My idea is to see this city become the capital of the country. Since the language is exclusively Pushtu, there would be no necessity for a transitional period from Persian."

"I agree with Your Excellency. Persian is a foreign language," Ludeen said.

"You are not contributing much to our discussion, Anwar Jan," the governor admonished me mildly.

"I don't know much about these problems, sir."

"The information I have indicates that you are one of the most aggressive talkers in the whole school system. I promise not to get mad if you disagree with our point of view."

Here my good friend Haji Zaman came to my rescue. I remembered his saying, "Protect yourself by all means."

"I am sure your information is correct, sir. But debates among young people about the pros and cons of simple concepts are far different from discussions pertaining to the realm of national policy."

"I have never seen you being that modest," Ludeen said.

"With you I never am," I answered.

"We seem to be getting nowhere. I thought we all might benefit from a friendly discussion," the governor said.

"And I thought, sir, that by spending a part of our vacation in the great state of Kandahar we would learn a great deal listening to its wise and experienced governor." That seemed to hit the target. Gul Mohammed Khan called the attendant to bring us tea and a bowl of mixed fruits. I asked him to bring the chessboard too, and then managed to let the governor win a spirited game.

"You are an excellent player," he said, and turning to Ludeen, he asked, "Why haven't you learned to play chess? It sharpens the reasoning power."

"I am sure he feels his reasoning power needs no further improvement," I said. Gul Mohammed guffawed and said loudly, "By God, you are a sharp one."

In the afternoon, the intense heat drove most of the people into the cool of the basement for naps. My cautious search for the

Memories of Afghanistan

gardener was a failure. Dangling my bare feet in the cool water of the brook, I was surveying the events of the recent past in my mind, when an unexpected voice across the water jerked me to attention.

"Who won the chess game?" the gardener asked.

"The governor, of course, as usual."

"You will have a good future ahead of you as a politician."

"This seems to be my day. I have been getting compliments from friend and foe."

"Let us walk down a ways to the shade of my cabin, where we can talk at ease."

Wading in the shallow water, I followed him to a low mud-walled adobe, where a tall, lanky dog greeted us with playful barking.

"You have never told me your name," I said.

"My name is Barak Zada and I was born thirty-two years ago in the town of Nishapur."

"Do you have a family?"

"Yes, my beautiful wife and political co-agitator is somewhere in Persia with my two-year-old son. You are young. Get all the education and training you can acquire before embarking on a crusade of righteousness."

"You are the second one giving me this advice."

"What about you? Where do you come from?"

"My name is Mohammad Anwar, born in Kabul eighteen years ago. I feel as though I have lived a lifetime already. I have traveled a long road through disease, hunger, indignity and deprivation. I am a young man and yet I want to rest, knowing that I cannot and must not."

Barak Zada passed me a bunch of white grapes and said contemplatively, "We don't believe in terror, but our rulers do. We lose limbs, go blind and die in our own shit in dark dungeons. Yet they call us murderers and communists. Look at this fellow whose broken body and soul were pushed into a truck and sent to Kabul this morning. He would have confessed to any crime under the punishment he received yesterday. The torturer tells me that the

A Wedding in Kandahar

poor fellow is an educated Pathan. Some papers were alleged to have been found in his room implying a cozy relationship between certain Pathan religious leaders and the representatives of the British Colonial Office in India."

"In a year, if my luck holds out, I shall win a scholarship and study abroad for a few years," I said.

"I've seen enough of the various manifestations of human suffering while a guest in your country. In two or three months, I shall enter Persia and search for my wife and child with my heart full of trepidation. Let us hope each of us will see the end of this nightmare in the Muslim countries of the east."

"Do you think that religion is the main cause?" I asked.

"No, religion, ignorance, greed and hunger are only factors manipulated by our domestic and foreign foes. Historically for thousands of years we have been soldiers in the armies of one tyrant king or another, killing one another to perpetuate a system of tyranny. We must put a stop to it."

He spoke softly, becoming meditative, as if discussing with himself problems that had long stayed dormant in the crevices of his brain.

"How to explain rationally why we do certain things? I could have pursued a quiet life, raised children, maybe cultivated a piece of land. But is procreation the central issue of human existence?" He put his chin on his bent knee. "No, for man life must have a purpose, a purpose not for the hereafter, but here on this isolated round ball of rock, dirt and salty water, hurtling through space, repeating the same motions throughout eternity. Life itself is nothing but a pattern of prearranged molecules, which maintain their integrity only a few decades, if undisturbed. Could the purpose of life be to fight the disturbing elements, be they microbes or other men? I wonder."

"There must be more to life than that?" I said.

He raised his head in surprise, hearing a voice other than his own. "Or you wouldn't be here," I continued, "exposed to the howling of human suffering, isolated from the ones you love."

Memories of Afghanistan

Now, his eyes closed, his modulated sad voice drifted in ripples. "Life's purpose is such a controversial subject! To mullahs and priests, it is to serve the symbol in heaven. To revolutionaries, it is to create Utopia here on earth. To philosophers, it depends which school we are talking about. To some, the aim in life is to seek pleasure, to others it may be contemplation, suffering, maintenance of status quo and on and on. But let me tell you this: until man is free, he cannot attain his potential, and unless he attains that, he will never know what life's purpose is. The aim of our struggle in life at this stage must be to help create a society in which men and women have free choices."

I walked over and put my hand on his shoulder. "I must be going now before they look for me. But I would like to come and talk to you again before we leave for Kandahar tomorrow."

"Please don't. I thank you for giving me a chance to practice my teaching even if it was for a short time."

We hugged each other and without saying another word, I walked away with rapid strides, wiping my eyes when his hut was out of sight. I busied myself during the afternoon and the next morning reading Persian poetry. When we were assembled to leave the next afternoon, all the help lined up to say goodbye. My friend Professor Barak Zada was not among them.

In Kandahar, the governor told us that he was going around the state on horseback on an inspection tour and that his car and driver were at our disposal if we wanted to use them. Ludeen and I decided to take advantage of the offer. Our itinerary included another trip to the Helmand Valley, a drive to Chaman on the Indian side of the border, and short trips around Kandahar itself. During our trip on the dusty trail to the border, Ludeen and I had a violent argument in the back seat of the car.

"Where are all those Pathans that are supposed to constitute more than half the population of Afghanistan? We have driven for hours, and except for a few farmers near the Dori River, no human habitation is visible as far as the eye can see."

"You are a traitor to this nation," Ludeen shouted.

A Wedding in Kandahar

"I am only trying to correct certain historical inaccuracies. If it is difficult for you to discuss these problems, say so. Calling me names does not solve the problem," I said.

"If it were not for these people, the son of a water carrier would be our king today," Ludeen said.

"I would go a step further. If the Pathans had stayed on their side of the border in India, we would still have Amanullah as our king."

"Are you implying that the present monarchy is not as good as Amanullah's?"

"There you go again. This question will, in due course, be decided by the historians. The fact remains that a British-instigated rebellion by the British-armed Pathans has caused irreparable damage to the integrity and well-being of our nation."

"What do you mean, British-armed?"

"Well, they certainly were not Russian-armed."

"They make their own guns."

"That is another fallacy. I have heard of the ingenuity in duplicating a modern gun from rusty iron rods that blow up in their faces on first try. I also saw Belgian guns and submachine guns slung on the shoulders of our conquering heroes on the streets of Kabul. They could only have been provided by the British in India."

The driver said something in Pushtu which I did not understand.

"He says we are getting close to Chaman," Ludeen translated. In a few minutes the car pulled over to a dilapidated chaikhana which also served as a restaurant. The driver said he had to see a friend and would be back in a couple of hours.

After eating our lunch of lamb soup, bread, cheese and onion, we ambled toward the border sign post. A massive log was wedged on a couple of wooden stumps as a barrier on our side and a metal gate a few yards away led to the other side. Both posts were manned by Pathans who were inspecting us with curiosity. I could not help thinking that our beloved King Amanullah had passed through these gates only a few years earlier into permanent

Memories of Afghanistan

exile. These morbid thoughts drove me into the isolation of the car which was parked in the shade of the smelly restaurant.

I pulled a much-used copy of the *Rubaiyat* of Omar Khayyam from my pocket to amuse myself for a while before returning to Kandahar. I used to enjoy the skeptical, taunting and playful philosophy of his poems. But on that hot, dry day, in a desolate outpost where the cracked walls of the adobes and sand merged into one great, gray mass, Khayyam's ironies had a morbid effect on me.

Feeling restless, I pushed the car door open and surveyed the surrounding area. Ludeen was still busy practicing his Pushtu with the guards. Through the parched land on my right, a narrow ditch threaded its way up a mound and beyond, where puffs of blue smoke canopied up the still air like ascending ghosts. Walking toward the ditch, I followed a dusty path, kicking the small stones. Sickly-looking, bent willow trees lined the greenish water in which frogs croaked lazily. Climbing the incline, I noticed camels sprawled on the side of the stream busily chewing their cuds. Back in the field stood tents scattered by nomads, whose children in tattered clothes were playing games. They stopped abruptly as I approached them. A tall and hefty man with a flowing white beard limped toward me with the help of a walking stick. He said something in Pushtu which I didn't understand. Raising my hand, I said, "Farsi."[*] He sent one of the children to fetch Mawlana, a younger man clad in white clothes.

"Who are you?" he asked in Persian.

"I am a student from Kabul, spending a few days of my vacation as a guest of Gul Mohammed in Kandahar."

"The governor?"

"Yes."

Mawlana took my arm and conducted me to a large tent and introduced me to his father, Rashid Khan. Most of the children by now were lined up outside. Rashid, who leaned against a massive pillow on the tent floor, asked me to sit down close to him.

---

[*] Persian

A Wedding in Kandahar

I said, "This is the first time I have been among nomads. Can you tell me something about your life?"

He said, "Life is getting harder and harder these days. The fertile lands in Afghanistan are owned by a small number of landlords. The rest of us have few choices. We either become sharecroppers and live as slaves, or accept a nomadic life, always on the run, pursued by heat, cold, tax collectors, army recruiters and plain hunger. In order to survive, we cheat, steal and sometimes even kill. We are money lenders, abductors, spies and much more. You are a student and you are going to read lots of romantic nonsense about nomads. Don't believe them. Look outside. We raise our own animals, whose milk and meat sustain us and whose wool keeps us warm."

I said, "I have heard that the government is planning to tame the Helmand River and then set aside a good portion of the land for the settlement of the nomads."

Rashid Khan and his son laughed loudly. The young man, Mawlana, raised his hand and said calmly, "Our family once lived in Subzawar, a small town on the Harud River, halfway between Herat and Farah. We had a large parcel of productive land that had been handed down through generations. During the last twenty years, our own Pushtun governors in Herat stole every inch of this land by one pretense or other. Now they are going to give us more land with plenty of water in the Helmand Valley. We all know that the land is salty and nothing grows on it."

I said, "Do the government experts know this?"

"If they don't, they are a bunch of idiots. Of course they do. We have told them and their own experimental farms have convinced them of the futility of raising substantial crops. But the initial ten-year budget seems to be in hundreds of millions of rupees, and they would like to get their share of the windfall."

Back at Kandahar, arrangements were made for us to attend a local wedding feast that night. The outline of the hazy disk of the sun was still discernible above the rim of the dusty horizon. The accumulated heat of the day was oozing out of the baked city into

Memories of Afghanistan

the air above. People who had huddled all day in cool basements, near river banks and in any available shade were stirring once more to participate in the activities of the cool night until curfew time at twelve o'clock, when they would be arrested if found outside their houses. Though the house to which we had been invited was at the outskirts of town, I insisted we walk through the town. In many ways, Kandahar was not much different from Kabul. The same odor of man and animal excrement mingled with that of cooking food–fried, boiled and baked. The noises of the vendors, buggy drivers, children, and beggars were deafening. Again like Kabul, it was a male-dominated society. Even the prostitutes were dolled-up young boys in silk-embroidered clothes. Our movements were considerably slowed down by the shoving and pushing of men and animals, in spite of the efforts of our guide to clear a path for us.

We finally arrived at our destination–a massive door guarded by a couple of energetic men. Two brightly-lit lanterns were hanging from the walls. The sound of music and women singing penetrated the still air. Inside, there was a large, enclosed garden full of well-tended flower beds, patches of grass and huge trees. Lights and decorations hung everywhere. Black smoke bellowed from the top of the kitchen to our right. Musicians were unwrapping their instruments on a large rug spread on a patch of grass in the center. The women were evidently housed in the far end of the garden. The monotonous beat of the dayira and the chorus of shrill voices were still the only sign of active gaiety so far.

We were ushered up the stairway into an imposing chamber. People sat cross-legged on the floor and leaned against the wood-paneled walls. Four large French doors opened into the garden and the bridegroom was sitting next to the farthest one. Evidently, the two seats of honor next to him were reserved for us. He was a well-rounded plump young man in his early twenties. Mahmood, the bridegroom, was the younger son of Shayr Khan, one of the important leaders of the Durrani tribe. When he stood up and shook our hands flabbily, he was taller than he had looked sitting down.

A Wedding in Kandahar

His large, brown, cowlike eyes and big mouth surrounded by thick lips, which he moistened constantly with the tip of his tongue, together with his round chin, gave him a lecherous look so typical of well-fed Durranis. His bride, we learned, was the daughter of Wazir Khan, a well-known leader of the Ghilzai tribe.

An elaborate array of dishes was spread on a lengthy embroidered tablecloth stretched on the floor. Lamb *palow*,* on a large platter in the center, was surrounded by shish kebab, chicken qorma, sparrow meat balls, another dish of rice cooked with saffron and mixed nuts, eggplant with *quroot*† and various delicacies in smaller dishes. This arrangement of food was repeated about every four feet. Then four persons gathered around each collection, using their right hands to shove the food into their mouths.

When stomachs were full, comfortably or painfully, greasy fingers were washed by helpers. In the interim between dinner and tea, sucking noises and burps were commonly heard. Meanwhile the sound of music down on the lawn had drowned out the female chorus. The tabla player was a sight to see. He would be playing placidly, following the soft tones of the harmonium, all the while craning his neck and rolling his eyeballs in an ecstasy of expectation. When the singer ended his cue line with all the power his vocal chords could produce, an interval of suspended calm seemed to prevail. Then the instruments whisperingly climbed up the scale, shattering the quietness in a crescendo of tunes with tabla predominating. The tabla player, with closed eyes and swaying body, contorted himself into unimaginable shapes. Around the musicians on the grass, young children sprawled in every conceivable position. They were mesmerized by the rhythm, the songs and especially the antics of the tabla player.

An hour after tea and cookies, people began to leave in ones and twos, then in droves. I stood up to stretch my limbs before leaving. Mahmood tugged at my jacket and said, "Take a little

---

* A dish of rice with onions and spices–*Ed.*
† A hard, sharp cheese.

Memories of Afghanistan

walk around the garden if you like. In about a half hour we will have a private entertainment for a few of my friends and I would like you to be back in this very room."

The entertainment happened to be boys dancing to the tune of tabla, flute and harmonium, one, two or three instruments playing at various stages of dancing. The windows were shut, lights dimmed and the hesitant wailing of the flute filled the room. A tall, lean youth of about fifteen entered the stage. He wore a red cap embroidered in gold, a silk shirt, cotton pants tight around the hip to emphasize his rounded buttocks. He circled shimmeringly round the room on his bare feet, his hands stretched over his head and his head bent coyly toward his right shoulder. As he warmed up in a gyration of movements, the tabla joined in. The onlookers, mostly young, but a few old buzzards, began to stir, making loud comments of appreciation.

"Ach, my heart."

"You slay me."

"May I be sacrificed for you."

"Have mercy on us."

During the intermission, hubble-bubbles were passed around, bowls of fresh fruits and nuts were replenished and held-back conversation resumed. The groom turned to me and asked, "How do our dancers compare to the ones in Kabul?"

"I am sorry to disappoint you, but this is my first experience."

"Do you like it?"

"It has been a memorable experience."

Mahmood said, "'Wait till you see the star of our show!"

Again the lights dimmed and the sound of the tabla was just audible, as if it came from a far away valley. Then the figure of a youth emerged gradually from a dark corner of the room. All eyes were riveted in his direction. Even breathing seemed to stop. The boy was about the same age as the previous dancer, but more elaborately dressed, and he had little bells tied to his ankles. He shuffled into the center of the room and the bells began to

A Wedding in Kandahar

jingle louder and louder. He stopped for a moment then resumed moving only his hands and the upper part of his body to the soulful tune of the flute. It was one of the most sexually suggestive demonstrations of the body I had ever seen or expected to in the future. I could hardly believe my eyes. A couple of middle-aged men across the room had their hands inside their loose garments and were actually masturbating in public. I also noticed that Kabir Ludeen had an intensely lecherous expression on his face. The dancer then leaned on one knee and stretched out the other leg, turning and twisting his hip, while his dreamy face, mouth half open, was waiting for the momentary orgasm to subside. Then gradually he straightened up in a limp, exhausted way. The flute was joined by the other two instruments and the rhythm changed from languorous to swift, tabla taking the lead. The volume of sound went up and down in cycles, but the tempo of the rhythm did not slacken until the very end. The seductive dancer twirled and twisted around the room, winking and playfully touching the important people. The bridegroom nudged me with his elbow and said, "Doesn't the perspiration on his face look like the morning dew on rose petals?" He neither expected nor received an answer. His shiny, searching eyes did not miss a gesture or expression on the dancer's face or a bending motion of his agile body. The people began to throw fistfuls of paper money to the center of the room, which the dancer disdainfully ignored.

When we left the wedding party, a soldier was assigned to accompany us home. Twice we were stopped along the way by loud orders from two or three other soldiers asking for the "night's name," which was the password. Each time, guns were aimed at us from both sides of the carriage and our guide barked back at them "watermelon," which was evidently the password.

The rest of our ten days were spent in semi-boredom. Gul Mohammed returned from his inspection trip. It must not have been very successful, because he was moody and complained about the smallest details of daily living. The intense heat that started in mid-morning drove all of us, except the servants–the cook and

Memories of Afghanistan

his helpers, the gardeners and the driver–to the cool of the castle basement. The governor's barking reverberated in every corner of the dark room. By candlelight, I tried to read the few books I had brought with me, but the constant noise and interruptions made it impossible for me to concentrate. For the first time I realized how boring and stupid a governor's life was. He either had to be the center of authority and attention, ordering, beating, jailing, or to be constantly entertained. If he said, "How about a game of chess?" it was to be construed as a command. Because I found him dull and unimaginative, I tickled his vanity by saying, "A man of your caliber must have a wider field to apply his ingenuity."

"Ah, I am like a caged tiger whose body cells atrophy at an increasing rate by idleness. Even here in Kandahar, which I understand like the palm of my hand, I receive a list of childish instructions on how to attack certain problems. And I am watched constantly by the spies appointed by the central government. Right in this basement, I am watched for every move I make. But they know that I am the head of Mohmandi, the kingmaker tribe."

I was happy to leave Kandahar, carrying with me poignant memories of failure, stupidity and cruelty, which were the common features of the rule of lawlessness in the land of my birth.

Chapter 16
Unexpected Ghosts

One finds the devil behind every mirror one looks into.
—Haji Zaman

In the fall of 1931, the top five graduating students from Habibia were sent to America for further study. This event made me very happy. I had been introduced to this remarkable land by Thomas Paine. Since then, I read everything I could find about America, its land mass, its strange and restless people and their devotion to freedom. I admired its inventive spirit and loved its Charlie Chaplin. I redoubled my efforts to be a good student, putting more effort into sports than politics. But the signs of political upheavals were crowding us from all sides. Colonialism was beginning to disintegrate in Asia. Fascism was on the march in central Europe, challenging the sluggish old lands that held half the human race in bondage yet called themselves democratic. Our rulers admired the former and paid lip service to the latter. We students had just the opposite feeling. We certainly could not see that a master race would be better than a master who is about to retire.

I entered the last year of high school with trepidation and foreboding. Although still the head of my class, I knew that having been born in the Shia sect, the scholarship might be withdrawn in my case.

On a warm October day, I was sitting on the windowsill of our classroom absorbing the soothing rays of the sun. The whole school had gone next door to the mosque for the daily mid-day prayer. During the last class period, I was requested to go to the principal's office.

"Why didn't you attend the prayer today?" Nabi Khan, the principal, asked me.

"I have not gone to prayer once the whole year."

"Are you aware that you are defying God's command, the government's law and school regulations?"

Memories of Afghanistan

"No, sir."

"You are," shouted Ghulam Nabi Khan, the nicest principal I ever had. "And for this terrible transgression, I have no choice but to punish you for your display of defiance."

For the first time, I noticed a long, heavy stick lying on his desk. He seldom used corporal punishment.

"I am sorry, sir, in the future I will not show myself in public during prayer time."

"You are insolent. Bend over the desk." He picked up the stick.

"Please don't," I begged.

With a quick motion, he landed the end of the stick on my neck. The melee that followed between us, in which two scrawny attendants and the sports teacher joined in rapid succession, resulted in torn shirts all around and a superficial wound on the teacher's neck. Fortunately Nabi Khan, the principal, standing aghast across his massive table, escaped our common indignity. However, he ordered Jameel Khan, the sports teacher, not to wash the blood off his torn uniform. Hurriedly, the principal wrote a letter and sent it with me and Jameel to the minister of education. In the absence of the minister, we were ushered into the office of his deputy, Raheem Khan. When he finished reading the letter, he raised his dark eyes and looked at me through his shaggy eyebrows. With a thin nasal voice, he dismissed Jameel Khan and told him to wash the blood in the stream outside before going home. Then, resting his chin on the palm of his hand, he looked at the garden outside through the low window on his right.

"Do you intend to destroy your life, eh?" Still not looking at me, he continued, "I have been watching your progress through the school system. It would be a shame to cut it short. However, if you want to show how strong you are physically, you should become a professional wrestler." Then, turning his face toward me he said, "Sit down, sit down. What do you have to say for yourself, eh?"

"I am sorry I lost my temper. I hate corporal punishment."

Unexpected Ghosts

"You are comical, you know that, eh? You beat the school attendants, bloody your own teacher, and then calmly tell me that you hate violence. Do you hate it when it applies to you only, eh?"

"I am very sorry," I said.

"Go home now. I'll try to help you, but I want you to report to me regularly about your behavior in future."

A few days later, the minister of education came to our school. He gave me a verbal reprimand in front of the students and teachers and asked me to apologize to Nabi Khan, which I did. He became a helpful friend to me during the rest of the school year.

I was certainly surprised at the turn of events. Only a short time back, I was sure I had lost any chance for a higher education and had even begun to picture myself as a second-rate clerk in dingy and dark corridors, or at best a teacher in one of the rundown elementary schools, barely making enough money to provide for essentials. I could have been blacklisted and completely shut off from any government employment, which for all practical purposes meant no employment anywhere in the country. Instead, help came from unknown and unexpected sources.

A couple of weeks later, in a dark alley of the city, I knocked at the door of Raheem Khan. I was ushered into a room where it looked as if I had interrupted a heated argument. The deputy minister was clad in loose-flowing, white cotton native clothing. He introduced me to Nazeem Khan, the son of a landowner in Maimana, a town very close to the Turkmen Republic of the Soviet Union.

"We were discussing the question of violence before you came in," Raheem said, and, turning to his friend, continued, "Anwar is one of our interesting students. He might even agree with you."

"I would like to know to what I am agreeing."

"To physical violence," Raheem said.

"I am still in the dark," I said.

Nazeem was still studying me in silence. He had a chubby face and large bones–a bear of a man. His eyes were small and

173

Memories of Afghanistan

deeply set; their color could not be told with certainty. He wore a large karakul cap on his massive head and a silk embroidered chapan round his wide shoulders.

"I was telling Moheen* Sahib that any means, including violence, is justifiable against a system of tyranny."

"And my contention is that unless the system itself is uprooted, violence against individuals is counterproductive. I would even go a step further: unless the ground is prepared for a constructive program to go into effect, a free-for-all struggle for power would ensue, even if we are successful," Raheem said.

"That is where I draw the line–the second part of your statement. How could any system allow 'the ground to be prepared' for its own destruction?" Nazeem responded.

I raised my hand (a school habit) and said, "I think Nazeem Khan has a valid point. In this country the mere advocacy of democracy is tantamount to treason. Any gathering of more than three persons is considered a crime."

Nazeem said, "This criminal system of inherited monarchy must be fought at every level. You would be amazed how many millions of dissatisfied peasants march right now under a banner of equal rights for all the people of this land."

"I think you are carried away by your own rhetoric. Most of our people live in the Middle Ages. They are uneducated, unskilled and hungry, and they would march under any banner which provides a crust of bread. They have been hurt and abused to such an extent that a crack of the whip would line them up for the slaughterhouse," said Raheem. He raised his bearded chin contemplatively and added, "Maybe it is too late already. Our buffer status that saved us so far is about to be terminated. The Russian bear is awakening from a long hibernation and is gobbling up any unprotected land within its reach. You are a Turkman. Most of your people are already under Slavic domination."

"What you say is true, but the remainder live under the more cruel, ignorant and sadistic Pathans."

* Deputy

Unexpected Ghosts

"The Pathans, my dear, are not represented by those overfed perverts who have barricaded themselves behind the castle walls, surrounded by a moat filled with stagnant, smelly water. They are the poor, ignorant nomads wandering all over the countryside for a living. They speak an obscure dialect and have not developed a culture to speak of. Culturally, then, we have all been dominated to a great extent by the language and heritage of Persia, as America is by England."

"I apologize for my emotional statements," Nazeem said. "But aren't we going to see our country on the road to a peaceful life and industrial progress in our lifetime?"

"The destiny of a nation cannot be measured by the span of one lifetime. But isn't it lucky to be living in an age of change, eh? With all its unpredictable consequences? There are plenty of resources in our country for our small population. We need native talent, which only education can provide, and this is an extremely slow process," the deputy minister said.

"Moheen Sahib, I am a bit confused," I said. "With all due respect, I beg to disagree with your line of reasoning. The bulk of our intellectual elite are, at this moment, rotting in the prime minister's 'guest houses,' and you are advocating a slow process of producing more educated talent. It sounds to me like a vicious cycle."

"How would you go about it?" Raheem Khan asked.

"I wouldn't overlook education, of course, but our rulers are isolating themselves into a cozy delusion. They instinctively feel that a dissatisfied nation can be held in submission by force, not realizing that they themselves have caused the alienation to begin with. I do not believe in individual violence. It seems to me that a dictatorial monarchy prepares the ground for its own destruction, and it is our legitimate duty to help them do it. But how?"

Raheem Khan turned to his friend and said, "I told you he basically agrees with your point of view."

When we were left alone, the deputy minister told me he was glad I had come. "You should come to see me more often. I'll send my servant to inform you on the way to or from school whenever

Memories of Afghanistan

there are interesting people to talk to. This was proposed to me by our mutual friend, Zaman. The last time I met him, he said, 'Expose Anwar to new ideas'."

At the end of December, another cold winter descended with vengeance on the valley of Kabul. Snow followed by sleet and freezing temperatures caught me unprepared. My shoes were in bad shape but could be mended to last me another few months. My cotton pants tied around with a rope barely covered by a faded jacket were not enough covering to protect me from the next two months of severe weather. My father had developed a hernia that caused him considerable pain, yet he still struggled to open his shop daily in the hope of earning a few pennies. My older brother had a job as a chemist in the mint where he analyzed the silver content of coins. He made a decent salary but did not help the family, though he still occupied a large room in our house, rent-free. I felt trapped and helpless. One night I found Father alone, and began to talk to him about school and the prospect of going to America for further study next year.

"But I have another choice, Baba Jan. I am sure to be offered a decent job if I refuse to accept the scholarship."

He was sitting next to me, covered by a large blanket, with his legs stretched under the sandali. He looked at me intently, his head trembling slightly from another new malady. He put his right hand on my shoulder, his lips quivered and large drops of tears rolled down his emaciated cheeks.

"But you always wanted to study more."

"Yes, but I want to help before it is too late."

"Too late for what? We have been living on this side of hell practically all of our lives. Now you have a chance to pull out of this miserable situation. Take it. Maybe some day you will be able to help others."

I bent my head to touch my face to his hand, which still rested on my shoulder.

"There is a package for you from Shareef, the weaver, over in the corner. He told me to give it to you." Opening the cloth

Unexpected Ghosts

bag, I found a second-hand overcoat folded nicely. The note said, "Please return it next spring; it is rented for four months."

"It is too large for you, but it will keep you warm," Father said.

When I came home the next day I found my brother Wahab shaving in our living room. Relations between us were strained. We hadn't even said "hello" to each other for a long time. Then, without turning to face me, he said, "I hear Shareef sent you a coat."

"None of your business."

"You had better return the coat to him. No charity is accepted in this house."

"What did you say?"

"You heard me the first time." He continued to shave.

"Go to hell," I said.

Before the sentence was out of my mouth, I saw the mirror hurled at my head. I ducked and it hit the window. Without thinking, I picked up the largest broken piece, lunged toward Wahab and jabbed the jagged end almost an inch into his thigh. Leaving the room, I found I had a wide, though not deep, cut on the palm of my right hand. After that day, Wahab and I avoided each other until his wedding day four months later.

That winter, my physical and mental resources were at their lowest ebb. Father's declining health, the lack of primary necessities in our house, and my complete financial collapse drained me so completely that I became victim to a host of maladies. A head cold and chest congestion, accompanied by constant coughing, stayed as my companions through February. Trudging through deep snow in shoes full of holes with no stockings became so arduous that I began to cut classes. Yet I was alarmed that I might not be able to pull through the most crucial year of my life. One day in the school yard, our principal, Nabi Khan, took my arm and directed me to his warm office.

"Sit down over there near the stove. I'll be with you in a few minutes," he said and busied himself with routine school problems. The stove was hot and I was thankful for a much-needed rest.

Memories of Afghanistan

"You certainly cannot get rid of that persistent cold by being out in this kind of weather. I have decided to give you a temporary leave of absence. You will receive your weekly assignment delivered to you by the school attendant. With him you may send back any problems or requests regarding your courses of study. However, we would like you to do something for us in return. I have here in this folder an outline of the programs for the seventh and eighth grades for the coming year. I want you to make any comments, additions, or deletions on a separate sheet of paper. You will be paid a nominal sum for it. Here is your advance payment for one month." He handed me the folder and an envelope. At home, I found that the envelope contained thirty rupees, a considerable sum in those days.

I bought myself a pair of new shoes and two pairs of stockings right away. On the way home, I also bought a large live chicken, which my sister and my stepmother killed, cleaned and cooked to celebrate my sudden good fortune. Years later, I found out that Nabi Khan had given me the money from his own pocket rather than from the school budget.

A few days later, my father gave me a folded piece of paper. A Mahrab Ali wanted to see me about an urgent problem.

"Who is Mahrab Ali?" I asked Father.

"He is the elder statesman for the Hazara* tribe. As you know, the Hazara belong to the Shia sect of Islam, as do we."

"Does he live far away?"

"No. As a matter of fact, he rented a big house just a few blocks from us. He is rich and can afford a better place, but he said he wanted to be close to his co-religionists."

When I met Mahrab Ali, he informed me that he wanted to put two of his nephews under my tutelage. This encounter boosted my income by another twenty-five rupees which I gave to my father. But my reward was far greater than its monetary value. I found in Mahrab not only a charming friend, but also one of the

---

* The Hazaras are descendants of the Mongolians, who had invaded most of Asia and parts of Eastern Europe during the early part of the 13th Century.

Unexpected Ghosts

most erudite persons I had ever met. Of Mongolian origin, he had studied the history of his people, their military exploits, culture, art and customs.

I loved to lean back on a cushion in his living room and listen to his monologue. The topics varied from philosophy, which he called "the love of his life," to politics and history. Sometimes he read from his handwritten books delightful passages on comparative early Eastern and Western philosophies, commenting on the shortcomings of both. Raising his head from the text, he would address me, "You know, Anwar Jan, Aristotle's concepts shackled European thought as rigidly as Confucius did that of China. They both foisted subjective dogmas as eternal truths. The former was overthrown by the empiricism of the Industrial Revolution, and the latter still persists in large measure, though the emerging new China will, I hope, eliminate it there."

"Doesn't any dogmatic religion do more or less the same thing–penalize the process of thought and reasoning?" I asked.

"Yes, of course. And one dogmatic system nourishes another. The Christian Fathers found in the Aristotelian philosophy a gold mine, and the combination produced the Dark Ages in Europe. Similarly, the fusion of the Buddhist cosmology and Confucian ideals of reverence for the traditional past produced a society that for centuries was unable to cope with the problems of the present or those to follow in the future."

I never knew Mahrab to get tired. Sometimes we talked way beyond the 12 o'clock curfew. "Well, it looks as if you are going to spend another night with me here."

"It is becoming a bad habit with me. You will get tired and sleepy in your office," I said.

"I never told you about my important position. I am a member of the House of Elders, an imitation of the House of Lords in England. Since I am only forty-six years old and by far the youngest member, I objected to the word 'elder.' But the rest were not willing to confront the government with a change of name. So, that's where I go whenever the spirit moves. When I get my stomach

Memories of Afghanistan

full of snoring and farting by those pot-bellied ancient specimens, I trot myself home to this dark hole for contemplation."

"Why do you subject yourself to it then? Why not at least go to the pure air of your village in the foothills of the Hindu Kush?" I asked.

"Because there is no one here in Kabul to concern himself with the affairs of my people, the Hazara. In my present position, I can communicate directly with the king himself. Certain small problems do get solved every now and then. Our previous king, Amanullah, did a great deal for us without being prodded. The half-dozen primary schools which he opened in our area stayed closed for two years. Through my constant effort they were finally re-opened."

The appearance of the silky amenta of pussywillows along the ditches north of the city, where I often walked, was a happy sight. The breeze on the upper slopes of the mountains was somewhat chilly, but I longed to get away as early as possible from the dirt and the noise of Kabul to those barren blue volcanic rocks.

One day the school principal asked Kassim and me to come to his office. While there, he handed each of us an envelope. They had already been read and left open by the censor. The return address was "Mason City, Iowa."

"How come you two received these letters?"

"Well, sir, Jamaluddeen, our English teacher, told us a couple of months ago that 1932 was designated as International Brotherhood Year among high school students. He gave us a sheet of paper with names and addresses and asked us if we cared to write to any of them. About four students, including us, wrote. Apparently these are the answers to our letters," I explained.

The letter I received contained a photograph of a pretty girl holding a tennis racket and two sheets of a handwritten letter. The picture was in black-and-white so one could not tell the color of the eyes or hair, but she had a delightful smile on her radiant face.

As I remember, the text of the letter was about her sports, which consisted of swimming and volleyball and tennis. She was planning to go to college next term and study teaching. She

Unexpected Ghosts

had two brothers and was somewhat spoiled as the only sister. In summer she usually went camping with her parents and younger brother. Since I had written her that there was a possibility I might come to the States for further study, she asked me to let her know if it became a reality.

The letters were read and re-read by almost every student in my class, and the picture was studied minutely and commented on by many students. In passing, I would like to mention here that I did go to the United States about seven months later, but I did not contact the pretty girl in Mason City, Iowa. However, strange as it may seem, I did marry another girl who was born in Minneapolis, barely two-hundred miles north of Mason City, and at that particular time she was just entering high school.

Chapter 17
America at Last

In the land of the infidel, at least keep your soul clean.
—Advice from a neighbor

I remember the day when Raheem Khan's servant stopped me on the way to school and informed me that I was expected at the house of His Excellency that same afternoon. It was a clear, calm day. Oranges and bunches of narcissi were already on display in the grocery stores. The winter's accumulation of snow piles had melted away, but there was still much slush and mud from the rainy season to be encountered in the narrow dirt streets. The Kabul River was at its maximum height, its muddy waters occasionally carrying a dead animal. Another few days and the Nowroz holidays would start.

In Raheem's house I met two individuals besides Raheem–my grade school science teacher, Abdul Aziz, and a well-built swarthy man who was introduced as Shah Nawaz, educational director in Badakhshan. Preliminary to any discussion, Raheem turned to Aziz and said, "While Nawaz will be here only a few days, I thought it would be appropriate for him to meet a few of our bright students. That is why Anwar is here." The emphasis was on the last sentence, a hint of danger, and I acted accordingly.

"I hear you are still on top of your class. I am honored to have been one of your early teachers," Aziz said.

"You were one of the best," I responded. Everyone knew that Aziz had a blood relationship to the Royal House. Also, due to an unpardonable digression, he was not a welcome guest there anymore. The background of his downfall, which had occurred only a year previously, was somewhat patchy, but he was suspected of spying.

So, on that particular day at Raheem's house, he had the floor most of the time.

America at Last

"Do you know that tall, good-looking fellow in tattered clothes and matted black hair who roams the streets of Kabul jabbering nonsensically to anyone who cares to listen?" asked Aziz, looking at the three of us with a twist of his eyeballs.

I said, "Yes, I have seen him."

"If you listen carefully, he throws out some gems among the other fragments of disjointed sentences. The one he repeats often is: 'One cannot build on a rotten foundation'." He added, "The poor fellow was accused a couple of years ago of stealing and was jailed. When he was released he had forgotten who he was. They said the headband* did it; this in a country whose prime minister steals in open daylight."

We all looked at each other and kept quiet. Aziz was flustered and tried to remedy the situation by saying, "I am sorry. I talk too much."

"No, that is not the problem," Raheem assured him, adding, "We do not appreciate your crude remarks about our prime minister. I'll let that pass, but if you repeat your impertinent remarks about our leaders, I will personally kick you in the behind. You have abused my hospitality and I remind you that you are not welcome to this house in future." Dejectedly, Aziz took his leave. Shah Nawaz and I roared with laughter after Aziz was out of the front door.

Addressing Raheem, Shah Nawaz said, "May I congratulate Your Excellency for handling the problem with such inspired audacity?" Nawaz had the kind of deep bass voice which demanded respect and attention. He stood up, cracked his knuckles, yawned and said, "With that obstacle out of the way, I hope we can talk more freely now."

"Not that I am absolutely sure he is a spy as is widely accepted. However, he is frivolous and lives far beyond his means," Raheem said.

"So, Nawaz Khan, you come from our northeast state of Badakhshan, which touches the border of the Soviet Union," I said.

---

* A steel torture device which cracks the skull if tightened.

183

Memories of Afghanistan

"Yes, the Amu Darya is the line of division. The Uzbek Republic lies to the north of us, all the way to the Pamir Plateau, which rises to more than 20,000 feet. I live in Faizabad, on the Kokcha River."

"Are you happy there?"

"Not long ago we were. I came here to find out what happened to our hopes and aspirations. The tempo of repression increases with every new governor. We cannot move freely in our own land anymore. Parts of it are declared forbidden territory. Thousands of families have been moved away from the border area without compensation. They lost their homes and their land. They were told that they were being protected from the disease of communism."

"Is it true that they are so bad?" I asked.

"Who?"

"The Russians across the river."

"I would like to explain this point," Raheem cut in. "Any nation that builds a barrier against its neighbor's influence or contact, that nation is trying to hide its own weaknesses. We close our border against the Russian influence and they close theirs against Western Europeans and their ideas."

"You must come to our part of the country, Anwar Jan. It is spectacular. The Himalayan Range entering Afghanistan flattens into a high plain, known as 'roof of the world.' The untamed rivers that originate at its foothills running west and north, entering the deep valleys of pine forests and then meandering through the flat land of our state, are magnificent."

"I hope to see something of the natural beauty of our land someday. So far I have only been exposed to its scarred features and the diseased and maltreated people living on them," I said.

"I hate to interrupt your interesting conversation, but I expect a family guest,"Raheem said.

The last hurdle loomed as a gigantic hill. I felt like a long-distance runner who has to demand more than his system can provide. But somehow the prospect of living with the pain of

America at Last

failure compelled my body to go beyond its reserves for the job ahead. There was only the month of May left before the final examinations would begin–yes, the examinations were as rigid as in Mandarin China during the Ming dynasty. Questions in each subject would be debated by a small group in the Ministry of Education. They would be sealed in envelopes and sent to school principals a few days before the tests began.

On the crucial day, students would march into a large auditorium and sit in assigned seats under the watchful eyes of the inspectors, while the envelopes were opened. There were fourteen to sixteen subjects in each senior grade and every one, except drawing and science, had to be memorized. Since there was practically no teaching the last month of the school year, students would huddle in any corner, shade of a tree, side of a mountain, or on rooftops to memorize sentence by sentence each textbook. Independent thinking and reasoning were frowned upon. Many of the best teachers did not agree with this mechanical system of study, but they were powerless to change it. Their opinions and observations in terms of grading students throughout the course of study amounted to practically nothing.

Each year, I had isolated myself for two to three weeks and painfully tried to memorize as much of the textbooks as possible. This year I decided to go to Guldara. I had received a note the week before from Haji Zaman in response to my letter that he would be happy to see me once more. The sad hint of foreboding in his answer disturbed me.

On a clear day in early May, the bus dropped me at the side of the dirt road that led up the hill to the valley of the roses. Adjusting my rather heavy bundle of books on my back, I struggled my way up to Zaman's house, resting periodically against the stone walls. As the grape vines of the Zaman garden came into view, I heard the barking of the huge black dog, Ghor-Ghory. She ran toward me and stopped abruptly about twenty feet away, still barking. When I called her name, she stopped barking and her tail wagged furiously, though she was still not sure who I was. I put my bundle

Memories of Afghanistan

down and sat on a stone. Clapping my hands, I called her name again.

"Welcome, welcome, Anwar Jan. I have been expecting you since yesterday." The familiar face of Haji Zaman emerged from the shadow of the wall.

"Assalamo alykum, Haji Sahib."

"Wa alykum assalam." We pumped each other's hand while the dog jumped clumsily all over us to make sure she was not left out.

"She has forgotten me since the last time I was here."

"I don't think so. She has lost a good part of her eyesight during the past year."

"Why?"

"Well, she is almost eleven years old, and for a dog of this type, that is quite old. However, her hearing is still sharp. Look at you, growing like a poplar, already taller than I, and your grip is as strong as a vise," he said, grabbing my bundle of books. The dog and I followed him to the house. Rasul, his gardener's son, brought us a dish of talkhan and a pot of tea.

"I know you have a lot of work ahead of you, so the house is yours, and Rasul has been instructed to be at your service all day long," Zaman said.

"Thanks for the help, but I have to warn you that my schedule isn't going to be as full as you think."

"All right, I will be glad to play a game of chess with you every now and then."

"You have to do better than that. You have been a spiritual father to me for many years and I still don't know you as well as I would like to."

"Anwar Jan, life at best is a series of slippery stones in this country. At a certain stage of life, one is bound to slide into the sea of oblivion below. All my adult life I have been dodging obstacles by hiding as much of my life as possible from public view."

All through our discussion, Zaman sounded more reserved and contemplative than usual.

America at Last

"How are your daughters?"

"They are fine and healthy. I have been trying to send the older one to Lebanon for study, but so far the government has adamantly refused my request for a passport and transfer of funds."

My studies progressed smoothly, but Zaman was worried and sad most of the time. One day he told me he had invited a friend for early supper. About five o'clock I was introduced to a boy about my age, who was carrying a baby boy.

"Meet Mr. Saleem and his son, Rauf," said Zaman. "Rauf is eight months old. They own the large farm near your uncle's. Rauf's mother was anxious for you to meet her little boy." Recognizing the dark black eyes of Sharifa on the round and chubby face of the baby, I picked him up and hugged him. After they left us, Zaman said, "I noticed that you recognized the little fellow. For you to meet her son was Sharifa's idea. She always talks about you whenever I see her."

The rest of my two weeks' stay was rather dull. Zaman left casually one afternoon for Kohistan. That night, Rasul handed me the tray of food and an envelope. Inside was a note from Zaman:

Anwar Jan,

I so wanted to make our last meeting a happy one. But happiness is dished out in minute doses in this forsaken land. Forgive me for my hasty departure.

Just before you came to Guldara, a couple of weeks ago, a very dear friend of mine who was a little older than you passed away under torture. About two years ago, his father found some "subversive" literature in his son's room and promptly reported him to the authorities. When he was arrested and jailed, he was legally dispossessed by his father, who occupied an important position in the government bureaucracy. He refused to claim the dead body of his son when it was delivered to his house.

Now you know why I didn't want to inflict you with another week of sadness by my presence. Please forgive me and good luck. I'd also appreciate it if you would burn this note as soon as you finish reading it.

Love,
Zaman

Memories of Afghanistan

The examination did not exert any undue strain on me. I received the highest marks among the three senior classes of the high schools. I was informed that I would be sent to America during the middle of July. My field of study was to be education.

My father was invited to be a guest at a school send-off function. He walked across a large chamber, lifted me up by holding my hands and, in front of hundreds of students and teachers, kissed me on both cheeks, as the tears ran down his beard.

A week before departure we were taken to meet the king. Nadir Shah looked thin and haggard. His voice, emanating from the center of his trimmed beard, was barely audible. His cheeks were sunken, and his long fingers rested on the edge of the gray blanket in which he was wrapped. He reminded me of the ghosts one expected to meet in semi-darkness behind any one of the shrines scattered around the valley of Kabul. Four months later, he was shot and killed by a young student from another school. By then, however, I was thousands of miles away in my little room on 114th Street, near Columbia University in New York.

From Afghanistan I carried with me the memory of my father (whom I never saw again), old and battered by the routine of daily living, hanging on to me to the last minute, and muttering, "My son, make a useful life for yourself."

Part Two

Chapter 18
A Native Returns

In June of 1941 the weather in Bombay was steaming hot as the *President Garfield* approached the harbor. A radiant, tall blond leaned against the railing and squinted at the swarming multitude of frail, dark-brown bodies that were pulling ropes, selling foods of all kinds piled on pushcarts, or running around aimlessly and begging. The noise was deafening. She turned her head slightly my way and said, "The smell here is different than that of Shanghai, where the muddy raw water of the Yangtze River greets you a hundred miles out at sea with a heavy stale odor. Here it seems to be spicy and pungent." Her green-blue eyes were still squinting and the strands of her light yellow hair blazed against the morning sun. One never got tired looking at her face, the prominent cheek bones, the three short vertical white ridges on her partially sunburned forehead and her dimples... always the dimples, even when she did not smile, the bare movement of her lips was enough. Although Phyllis and I had been married for only three years, we had known each other since she was seventeen years old. Now, at the age of twenty-two, she was taking her first trip out of America to far-off lands and an unpredictable future. For me, the trip back home was to fulfill childhood yearnings and hopes.

"Do you have any friends in Bombay?" Lal Babu Ji asked us. We had met a number of Indians on the boat.

"No, sir," I said.

"Then why don't you stay with me for the few days that you are here?"

"Thank you. We accept your generous offer."

"Then we will be looking for you as we leave the ship."

Before we could leave we were lined up for passport inspection. I was shocked to find my wife in the line for the Europeans and myself in the line for the "natives." Interestingly enough, the word "native" was given a derogatory interpretation. As we moved down

Memories of Afghanistan

the plank, Lal Babu Ji was waving to us. He led us to a large black limousine. Without formality, the driver took us to a rich section of the city and stopped in front of a huge, ornate castle. Lal Babu Ji told us on the way that his servants would bring our luggage, but our other belongings would have to be inspected thoroughly in our presence in a couple of days.

The castle was full of dark corridors and large empty chambers. In one of these, our belongings were dumped near two beds and we were told that dinner would be served in two hours. Not finding any chair in the room, we pushed away the mosquito netting and sat on the beds. Gazing around, I saw an empty closet and a statue of Mahatma Gandhi in the corner. While Phyllis lay down to rest, I went out in the bazaar for a stroll. The heat was oppressive. When I had tea in a restaurant, I learned that our host owned half the ships in Bombay and was one of the richest men in India.

For dinner, we entered a small room. Four square straw mats were arranged on the bare floor around a circular board, on which were four small soup dishes and small wooden spoons. We followed the movements of Lal and his friend who sat opposite us. After the soup, the servants placed a dish of boiled rice in the center together with four plates, four dahl bowls and four thin chapaties. All the dishes were very small. While serving the main dish, Lal said, "I hope you enjoyed our Indian food. I have some business to attend to. If you need anything, please tell the servants."

We walked to the restaurant outside and had a good, hot Indian dinner. After that first night, we both knew that the Spartan life of this rich Indian Brahmin was not for us. We put our things into a taxi and asked to be taken to the Afghan consulate, even though we had not alerted the consul of our arrival. Money was running out fast. The consul was surprised to see us, but he did give us a bedroom. While he was busy communicating with the Ministry of Foreign Affairs about the particulars of our trip to Kabul, we spent the next few days in the customs house with the inspectors, both Indian and English. Since we had planned to spend the rest of our lives in Afghanistan, our luggage contained hundreds of books

A Native Returns

and records, a receiver-player set, a baby grand piano, and cartons of pamphlets on gardening, canning and many other necessary and superfluous aspects of living.

"You can't open any of these boxes. They are in transit," I told the Indian officer.

"What do you mean, I can't? Who are you to order me around?"

"Sir, I am not trying to be unpleasant. I am merely stating a clause of international law that goods in transit are to be opened only at the country of destination."

He mellowed considerably, and I suspected it was because he had been addressed as "sir," which was reserved only for the Europeans. He said he would fetch the chief inspector, an Englishman typical of the genus known in Asia as the "colonials." His red hair was covered with a bowler and his pale blue eyes and thin lips were overshadowed by his bushy mustache that curled slightly upward. He carried an ornate, short stick, which he slapped periodically against the palm of his left hand.

"What can I do for you, young man?" he asked. But before I could open my mouth, he said, "Excuse me," and walked directly to my wife, who was inspecting a large slash in one of the boxes.

"May I be of help to you, miss?" he asked, removing his hat and bowing.

"Yes. You may help us greatly if you would kindly let our belongings go through without opening them."

He looked at me and back to her, mildly puzzled. "I can't do that, madam," he said, replacing his hat and resuming the slapping action with his stick.

"Why can't you? They are in transit."

"War-time emergency regulations, you know."

"About how long would it take you to finish the job?"

"Well, if they contain clothes, no problem, but..."

"They are mostly books and records," I said.

"I am afraid it will take a few days. Leave your name, address and phone number at the office. Someone will call you in a few days."

Memories of Afghanistan

In the consulate, we learned that we might be delayed more than just a few days. As we entered the building, Shoayb Khan, the consul, said, "I have been looking for you all morning, Doctor Sahib. Could you come to my office for a few minutes?"

His office was small and cluttered, and the only window faced the noisy street below. Phyllis and I settled ourselves on two overstuffed, uncomfortable chairs.

"Now, may I see your passport?" he asked me. Puzzled, he said, "But your wife is not included here."

"No," I answered. "She has her own passport."

"Oh, an American one? But in our country, we always give only one passport to a man and wife. Madam, do you mind if I transfer your name to his passport?"

"They are both legal documents. Why go through all the trouble of changing them?" I asked.

"No trouble at all. As a matter of fact, our law states that any foreign national loses her nationality automatically when she marries an Afghan."

"How can you make laws applicable to a foreign national?" Phyllis asked. "What happens if a female Afghan marries a foreigner?"

"She loses her citizenship," Shoayb said.

"Well, my wife certainly does not want to give up her American citizenship in this period of turmoil and uncertainty," I said.

"It makes it very difficult for me," Shoayb complained. "I am not authorized to give her an entry visa to Afghanistan."

"This is ridiculous. Why didn't the Afghan government clear up this point with us in New York? I demand that you either give her a visa on her own passport or give her the cost of a trip back to America," I protested.

"You mean that you will go to Kabul without your wife?"

"I will give you my decision after she is out and on her way."

"Doctor Sahib, calm down. I will explain the whole situation to the Foreign Office by telegram. They might make an exception in your case."

A Native Returns

Two days later, the clerk at the consulate gave us two messages–one, our customs inspection was finished, and two, that a Mr. Lateef wanted to see me. I was given his telephone number. Lateef was another Indian, a pearl merchant, whom we had met on board the ship. He invited us to dinner at his house that night.

"Not one of those 'fancy home cooking' affairs again," Phyllis groaned when she was told about the invitation.

"No," I answered. "He is a Muslim and will serve real meat."

During the afternoon, we met with the chief of customs again. He read us a long list of objects that had been confiscated or, as he put it, "not allowed out of India." They included all the books in the German language, those on politics or political economy and those pertaining to Russia or communism.

"I thought Russia was England's ally in this war," I said.

"I'd rather not discuss the subject."

"By the way, on your list was a book called *Soviet Power*," Phyllis pointed out.

"Yes, I believe there is, madam."

"Do you know who wrote that book?"

"No, and I don't care who wrote it."

"It was written by the Dean of Canterbury, Hewlett Johnson," Phyllis said.

"I don't believe it."

"The book must be here somewhere. Go and check the title."

He marched to his office and came back with the book. "You may have this book."

Phyllis persisted. "Why were the recordings of Paul Robeson– 'Six Songs for Democracy'–on your list?"

The poor inspector was furiously wiping the perspiration from his face and neck. "Because they were broken, madam."

"May we have the broken pieces, please?"

"They were thrown away."

"Could it be that perhaps democracy itself is a subversive idea in Asia?" Phyllis questioned.

Memories of Afghanistan

Back in the consulate, we were greeted by Mr. Shoayb with a big smile.

"Madam, your request for a visa in your own passport is granted by Kabul. You may leave any time you desire," he said.

"The sooner, the better," Phyllis said.

"I will send one of the boys to get you the railway tickets for tomorrow then. Your goods will go by a different line. I will take you to a good Indian restaurant tonight."

"Thank you, no, we have already accepted another invitation for tonight," I said.

In the late afternoon, Lateef's son called for us at the consulate. He was a shy, good-looking, lanky chap. He wanted to call a taxi, but we insisted on walking. The factories and offices were closing, pouring their tired multitudes out over the already crowded available space. People were actually moving in waves, the strollers, window shoppers and beggars carried on against their will. Cars and buses crawled on the street. We were finally led to a side street where our movements were less restricted. Lateef's house was in one of the three-storied brick buildings, where he had an apartment on the second floor with a jewelry shop under it. As we entered the building, the odor of spiced cooking, dominated by that of curry, submerged all other scents.

Lateef's wife was a short, swarthy woman. She held a baby on her hip and he sucked on her bare breast, watching us with bright beady eyes. The lady said something in an Indian dialect, and whenever she spoke, the gold ring dangling from her nose wobbled.

"She says that her older daughter is doing the cooking for us," Lateef said. Two pairs of black eyes watched us through the kitchen door.

"Where is the cook?" Phyllis asked.

Lateef called the daughters to come and meet the American lady. There was a moment of fast activity while the cook changed her apron for a beautiful sari. Then she slowly walked in to greet

A Native Returns

us in twangy English, while the younger girl held onto the corner of her dress, covering half her face with it.

"Aside from the interminable heat, how do you like Bombay so far?" the older girl asked Phyllis.

"First I would like to congratulate you on your good grasp of the English language. Our stay here so far has been very hectic and we have not seen much of the city."

"We would be glad to be your guide for a few days and show you some interesting aspects of our city."

"Unfortunately, we are leaving tomorrow."

"How did you make out with Babu Ji?" Lateef asked me.

"We stayed in his castle only one night. We found out that he is very rich."

Lateef smiled and said, "Yes, but there are many richer people in Bombay, especially among the Parsis."

"Who are they?" Phyllis wanted to know.

"They were originally Persians of the Zoroastrian religion who migrated to the coast of India. They are known as fire worshipers, but actually light as opposed to darkness is venerated. Eternal light burns in their temples. Cleanliness of both the body and the soul is the basic tenet of their belief. They therefore expose their dead to the vultures."

"How is this accomplished?" Phyllis asked.

"By exposing the naked bodies on a tall tower."

The hot chicken on spiced rice was good and ample. On leaving, Lateef's wife gave Phyllis a beautiful necklace of cultured pearls.

Next day, our one suitcase and a handbag were put into a taxi. My wife, holding tightly to her cello, and I said goodbye to the consulate people and left for the station. While there, we discovered that we were to travel all the way to Peshawar third class and it was too late to do anything about it.

"Those bastards in the consulate are laughing themselves sick right now," I remarked.

"Don't worry. In a few days all this will be behind us."

"I am afraid, Phyl, that this is only a taste of what is to come."

Memories of Afghanistan

Since there were no reserved seats in third class, I rushed to the compartments to get us seats. One could not visualize the problem of traveling third class in India in the month of June over a thousand miles unless one actually experienced it. The wooden seats (if one were fortunate enough to get one), the burning heat and the noise of the crying babies were only the harbingers of yet-to-come sufferings and indignities. Wind poured red clay dust through the cracked open windows in such quantity that everyone's skin turned copper color. Kids pissed through the open cracks of floor boards, while goats licked one's face, disturbing a much-wanted sleep. There were changes to be made in the middle of the night. The noise of the food venders and the flies that buzzed in and out were a common feature of every stop. My poor wife, resting her head near the pegs of her cello, looked strangely patient.

Finally we arrived in Peshawar on the afternoon of the third day. After a shower and a big meal at Dean's Hotel, we went to bed and slept deeply until a knocking early the next morning awakened me. Answering the knock, I saw a young boy holding a tray of morning tea. Leaving the tray outside the door, I tiptoed back to bed grumbling about the barbaric English custom of pre-breakfast tea. Fortunately, Phyl was asleep and the short, squat figure on the side of the bed was only her cello, guarding her sanity from flying away.

On the second day after our arrival in Peshawar, all our belongings except the piano arrived. The next day we found a truck driver who was willing to take us and a fruit merchant to Kabul. The baskets of Indian fruits were intermingled among the cartons of books and records. On the outskirts of town we were stopped at a road station, our passports were examined and a guard with an English rifle in his hand climbed onto the truck and sat on a box. The merchant introduced himself to me as Kazim ("but they call me Gurg"*). From there on, all conversations were conducted in Persian and I translated them for Phyllis. She told me to tell Gurg that the smell of his fruits was very appetizing. The truck

* Wolf.

A Native Returns

was stopped in the middle of the road and Gurg, with the agility of a leopard, jumped out and entered the back compartment of the truck. He ripped open a few boxes, sending bananas, mangoes and oranges toward the front seat for my surprised wife.

"What's this all about?" she asked me.

"The fruits of your appreciation, my dear."

"My God, if it isn't just like our southern states–ignore the weaker sex, but defend her wishes gallantly and her honor to the death."

"You had better just smile and say '*tashakur*'."

"What is 'tashigur'?"

"It is not tashigur, but ta-sha-kur, and it means 'thank you'."

Gurg and the driver laughed loudly at her first Persian spoken word. The driving resumed and shortly we passed the Khyber Pass' heavy fortifications. I pulled out the camera to take some pictures, but as I aimed through the open window, I felt the cold muzzle of a gun on my neck and, at the same time, heard the word "forbidden" from the soldier behind me. The camera quickly disappeared into its receptacle.

At the border, the soldier left us and we entered the soil of my country seven years and eleven months after I had left it. In a little mud cubicle, our passports were scrutinized by two frontier guards while we waited patiently on the dusty road stretching our muscles. Gurg, a tall, muscular man in his early thirties, leaned against the truck. He had a white turban around his head with the sash dangling on his left shoulder. Another cloth, a red-striped one, was wound around his waist. The sash was used mainly to wipe his nose, but all other cleaning functions were performed by the red-striped cloth, which he unwound for the job at hand. Gurg had large brown eyes topped by thin, black curves of eyebrows that would have suited a female face. His smile was pleasing and his movements fast but graceful.

The passports were returned after both guards gave Phyllis and me suspicious looks. We were on our way into a sea of gray dust, protruding ridges and patches of clay-covered bushes. Only

Memories of Afghanistan

the driver could tell where the contour of the road might be. The rays of the mid-morning sun were getting hot on my arm as we started climbing up a narrow, hazardous path on the bare, rocky protrusion of a much higher mountain to our right.

"Oh, look, look, Hammad, down the hill!" Phyl nudged me. A huge bald vulture was ripping chunks of meat from a dead animal, probably a sheep.

"Big, isn't it?" I responded.

"Are all the vultures as big as that in Afghanistan?"

"I don't think so. I have seen only small ones, and always in groups of five to ten."

The truck lumbered down into another parched valley. I began to think of the recent past, of our lives in the States–of casual walks in Central Park or on Fifth Avenue, of organized living and of a predictable future. Did I have the right to expose the person I loved most to a future full of danger and privation? I had been offered a job by the Ely Lilly Company to do research work on enzymes, and I had asked her opinion. She said the decision was entirely mine.

"You want to do something for your country. Get it out of your system; it will nag, haunt you the rest of your life."

I tried to put the fragments together again. But what about her? She would be forced into a male-dominated society. What was it that impelled me to come back to a land where, for nineteen years, I saw and felt nothing but suffering? I was not alone. Others who had also suffered offered a helping hand, friendship and love. I remembered Haji Zaman after so many years. His letters stopped coming to the States just after I graduated from college in 1936. Why had he stopped answering my letters? My father had also stopped inserting his couple of lines of greeting in the family letter, the last having been dated August, 1939.

"A penny for your thoughts," Phyllis said, and added, "You looked so absorbed. Can you talk about it?"

"I was mulling over our problems."

"Why worry? We will either cope with them or get out from under them."

A Native Returns

"I wish they were that simple," I said, secretly admiring her optimistic outlook and her open defiance of life's obstacles.

"You know, Phyl, in the West one often hears that life is cheap in the East. In a sense this is true. It is either treated as a cheap commodity, as you saw in the tin mines of Malaya, or cheaply extinguished by primitive local despots, as easily as pinching a dancing candle flame. I certainly don't believe that the physiological entity called man is different in different parts of the globe in his aspirations, desires, pains and his longing to reach beyond himself."

"I am sure you are right, but we will try to keep out of trouble."

"But how?" I answered. "The very mode of living is under scrutiny in these parts."

"What do you mean?"

"Well, you remember in America I talked to you about the problems and pitfalls of living in Afghanistan? It just occurred to me that you, as my wife, are expected to wear a chaderi, covering yourself from head to toe."

"You're joking. Do the other European and American wives of Afghans wear that damned contraption?"

"They all do, but you are the first American wife of an Afghan entering the Holy Kingdom, and no one is going to cover your beautiful face."

"But what will happen?"

"It will be interesting to see. You just behave normally, and under no circumstances give up your American passport."

The truck pulled to the side of the road and stopped in front of a decayed chaikhana. Gurg told me that here they prepare better fried eggs and teapot soup than at any other place along the way. Although the sun was hot, it felt good to move around a bit.

"Ay, bastards, haven't you seen a *farangi*[*] woman in your lives? Get us some food!" Gurg yelled at the youngsters. On the side of the shop a thin stream of water rushed down the slope.

---

* Foreign.

Memories of Afghanistan

"Feel the water, madam. It comes from a spring up the mountain," Gurg said directly to my wife in Persian.

"Tashakur," she replied in Persian.

We all had a good laugh. I translated Gurg's statement for her, and she graciously wet her hands and face while smiling at him. He covered his blush by offering her a good length of the red-striped cloth which he unwound from his waist. As we moved toward a patch of grass, we noticed a young boy on a charpayi in the sun, covered with a heavy blanket, shivering violently. His round black eyes followed Phyllis, while his teeth chattered.

"Malaria," I said.

On the grass, Gurg unwound his all-purpose waist cloth and spread it on the ground to serve as a tablecloth. We all squatted cross-legged on the grass when lamb soup appeared on the scene. I was wondering how Phyl would manage her first meal in Afghanistan without a knife and fork when the fried eggs and chapaties were put before us. She used her soup spoon to put the egg between two pieces of bread and made herself a sandwich.

When we were on the road again, we passed the sleepy town of Jalalabad without stopping. In late afternoon, the truck entered the crowded, noisy yard of the customs house in Kabul. My sister, Diljan, and my younger brother, Jwandai, were waiting for us. All our belongings were piled on two carriages and we were on our way home, which happened to be a rented apartment in the center of town. On arrival, we entered a dark enclosure and groped our way up a stairway into an open space. A door led into the living room, which was connected to a bedroom and on the other side, two small structures–the toilet and the kitchen. Jwandai and a young boy who had been hired as a helper kept busy bringing boxes up the stairs while Phyllis inspected the house. I took Diljan aside and asked her to tell me about the rest of the family. She started to cry. Covering her face with both hands, she told me that Father had been dead for a number of years. I put my arm around her shoulders to console her, when Phyl's voice was heard.

A Native Returns

"Hammad, the toilet consists of only a hole in the ground and that is it." When she entered the bedroom, her eyes widened. "What's wrong?" she asked.

"Father has been dead for quite a while," I said.

"You had suspected that," she answered, kissing me and patting Diljan on the arm at the same time. To distract me from the bad news, she said, "You haven't answered my question."

"I thought it was a statement, not a question."

"Stop being a wise guy. How does one manage the process of elimination?"

"One simply squats. It really is a scientific way to accomplish the job. The thighs, each consisting of a single, strong bone (the femur) exert pressure on the lower abdomen, in the same way as two fingers press on a full tube of toothpaste."

"You... you... why, you are reverting to barbarism and backing it up with science, no less! Anyhow, I tidied up the place a bit and kicked the pile of hard mud into the hole."

"You did what? Those hard mud pieces are used to wipe oneself with!"

"Don't tell me that is also scientific. Why not use paper?"

"For two reasons: paper is hard to find here, and it is considered sacred, to be used only for the written word. Now I think we should organize our lives a bit before it gets dark."

"I'll manage the living room, if you'll tell the boys to help me with the heavy stuff," Phyl said.

After a few minutes, Phyl came to the bedroom, dragging a scared youngster of about three with her.

"Look what I found in the kitchen,"

Jwandai said, "That is Faruk, Diljan's younger son."

"Is there another boy hiding somewhere also?"

"No. The other one, Habib, lives with his grandmother."

"What are you two jabbering about? Who is he?" Phyl demanded.

"He is my nephew, Diljan's son. His name is Faruk," I said.

Memories of Afghanistan

She picked Faruk up and kissed and hugged him. In a few minutes, he was following her from room to room, picking up small objects and saying, "That." "That goes over there," and Phyllis would indicate a place.

I sent Jwandai and the hired helper, Noor Gul, to buy supper for six people. Phyllis had decided to turn the living room into another bedroom by night and a dining room the rest of the time. She arranged the boxes of books as seats around a small table for four. Faruk and Noor ate on the floor. Later, Diljan also decided to eat on the floor.

The regular bedroom was assigned to Phyllis and me. At six o'clock sharp as we were busy eating, the public radio outside gave the news:

> Mussolini has just returned to Rome from a meeting with Adolf Hitler at the Brenner Pass.
> Von Papen is in Turkey trying to break the bond of friendship between that country and Great Britain.

The booming noise of the radio for a couple of hours in the morning and from six to ten at night became the most disturbing element in our daily lives. That first night, when everyone had gone to bed, my sister and I spent hours near the pale flame of a candle discussing the tragedies and good fortune of our family. Although he had had a good start, Diljan's husband had been accused of bribery and had been in jail for two years. She and her two sons had been living on the edge of starvation ever since. After Father died, Wahab, my older brother, "legally" transferred the parental house to his own name and then evicted everyone but his immediate family. Dada, my eldest sister, and her family had prospered. Her son, Nowroz Ali, a medical doctor (nose and throat specialist) was becoming rich according to local standards.

When I finally went to bed, the accumulated events of the past and present merged into sharp focus, disturbing my first night of sleep in Kabul after almost eight years.

Chapter 19
Children of Darkness

The booming voice of the mullah on public radio, in Arabic that no one understood, greeted us on the second day of our arrival in Kabul. It was followed by the modulated shriek of a tribal guru in Pushtu that few comprehended either.

"I wish someone would turn the damned volume down. It drives me nuts listening to it day after day," Phyl said.

"You'll have to learn to turn you mind off like the rest of us," I said.

"Trying to turn one's mind consciously away from something is a sure way to pay more attention to it."

"Then do it unconsciously."

"Oh, stop it."

Stuffing all my diplomas (a B.S. and M.A. from Columbia University and a Doctorate of Science from Johns Hopkins) in a cardboard tube, I went to the Ministry of Education. Sayed Abdullah, the first deputy minister, received me warmly. He pulled the diplomas out of the tube, spread them out one at a time on his desk and studied them.

"You certainly brought back an armload of documents with you."

"I hope I didn't go to America just to bring back lots of documents. In certain schools in America, one can buy diplomas."

"Is that so? All documents coming from that country must, therefore, be authenticated."

Abdullah had been two years ahead of me when I was at Habibia High School. He was known to be the dullest student in his class. He looked like a spider, thin long outer limbs carrying a bag of wind in between. He had a small head, thin lips and an Adam's apple on his scrawny, elongated neck. His most distinguished claim to high office was that he was the son of one of the most

Memories of Afghanistan

vicious leaders of espionage in the country. His spies, I learned later, permeated the student body and the intelligentsia.

Four days later, I had an audience with the minister of education himself. Naim Khan was one of the strongest men in Afghanistan at that time. The other two were his uncle, Hashim Khan, the prime minister, and his brother, Daud Khan, the minister of war. Naim was a proportionately-built, tall man. His impressively large eyes and humped massive nose exuded intelligence, rare in his family. He was also assistant to Hashim. We shook hands in his large office.

"Your diplomas show that you pursued two different fields of study, education and chemical science."

"Yes, sir. First I acquired the gift of gab and then I thought I had better learn something of a practical nature."

He smiled and said, "First I would advise you to curb your sharp tongue. Second, I want you to inspect our Teachers' Training School in Kabul. They tell me that no one wants to soil his hands on that mess."

"When do I start? I need to support a family of five."

He picked up the phone and told someone in the Ministry of Education to consider "Dr. Anwar employed as chief educational inspector as of the beginning of the current month." Turning to me he said, "I want you to report to me directly. This is one of my pet projects." As I left the room, a young man who introduced himself as Naim's personal secretary handed me a pass that entitled me to enter or leave the building at any time.

The facts and figures concerning the school were gathered in the Ministry of Education. The Teachers' Training School was a boarding school for four hundred male students. It was headed by Jamaluddeen, an Indian. Most of the teachers were also Indian. The curriculum consisted of sixteen subjects and English was studied as a foreign language.

The facts not given me were more telling as I dug deeper and searched the ashes of a long dead institution, dead educationally and in spirit. I found it to be closer to a criminal house of detention than an educational enterprise. Since the students were selected on the basis of their standing in their respective schools, they loudly resented being fenced in, maltreated and fed unrelated facts in school and meager meals in the boardinghouse. The school's budget was higher than that of any other similar establishment, yet the students were destitute of physical and mental richness. I also discovered that there was a plan afoot to close the whole establishment. Day after day, I visited the congested classes in a rundown building just outside the city limits on the main road to Darul Fonoon (Center of Learning), formerly known as Darul Aman, named after the beloved king, Amanullah. The students were unable to answer even the simplest questions in math, physics or chemistry. Their notebooks, when leafed through, were found to contain a few pages of notes for almost four months of study. In the director's office, I was asked by Mr. Jamaluddeen my opinion about the school. I promised to send him a copy of my report.

"Dr. Sahib, I would like you to become my assistant," the director said and hastily added, "I have a great deal of influence. You will practically double your salary."

"Sir, if I wanted money, I would have stayed in America," I said.

"In the ministry, it was planned to dump this school in your lap to give you and American education a bad name. However, with your help, it can be changed into a model school. Under what conditions would you work here?"

"With all due respect, sir, since you were once a teacher of mine, I would want a free hand, and my first act would be to fire you."

On Saturday morning (schools were in session Saturday morning to Thursday noon), I found no students in the school. One of the guards told me that they had some sort of problem in the boardinghouse. Near the massive door of the padlocked dormitory, two armed policemen were on guard. My inquiries were tersely answered, "We have orders to keep the students in and other unauthorized people out."

In the ministry, they talked of an explosively revolutionary situation in the Teachers' Training School.

Memories of Afghanistan

"Do you know, Dr. Sahib, the rope was already dangling from the walnut tree when the students tried to force their way into the director's office? He barricaded himself behind the door reinforced with chairs and tables, while the guard was ringing the central police station," Sayed Abdullah said.

"Another minute or two, Jamaluddeen's body would have been swinging in the courtyard," the director of control said. "The prime minister is foaming at the mouth in anger. I heard him say, 'These children of darkness do not deserve to become teachers'."

"What will happen now?" I asked.

"There is nothing to do but wait for a policy directive from His Highness, Naim Khan."

Realizing that all authority resided in three individuals, I went to see Naim. In the waiting room were four ministers, the heads of health, finance, interior and mines. They came once a week with their portfolios under their arms to obtain written permission for projects large and small. The announcer who called their names was a huge bundle of fat, a prince (one of King Habibullah's sons) in the previous dynasty. The fat on his thighs hung down to his kneecaps and rubbed together, making his walk extremely ponderous. Faruk Jan called my name, and, before I entered the imposing office, he said, "Dr. Sahib, the first time you were in there you did not follow the proper procedure. You see, when you are leaving His Highness, you should walk backward to the door and not turn your back to him." He gave me a quizzical look when I refused to respond to his silly suggestion.

"Well, do you think it is too late, Dr. Sahib?" Naim asked.

"Late for what, sir?"

"To remedy the situation. Everyone suggests closing the school for good."

"Sir, I don't think we can solve the problem by running away from it. We need teachers. If we close this school, we will have to open another, but the same thing will happen if it is mishandled."

"You think it is all the fault of the administrative authority?"

Children of Darkness

"Partly that, and partly the teachers and..."

"I don't think anyone in the Ministry of Education would agree with your point of view."

"I know."

"Would you take total responsibility for the school if I put it under your complete authority?"

"Yes, but I would want that in writing."

"What?"

"What you just said," I replied and hurriedly scribbled the following on a piece of paper:

> Dr. Anwar is totally responsible for all the activities of the Teachers' Training School in future. He is given full authority by me in all decisions pertaining to this school.

I passed it to him and he inscribed his signature and passed it back to me. With this edict in my pocket, I went to the school's boardinghouse and discharged the two policemen, then entered the huge edifice for the first time. It was a two-storied square structure. Each story on three sides of the square consisted of three dining rooms connected to sleeping rooms in which double bunks were arranged in rows. Students were huddled everywhere in groups. Addressing one small group, I said, "I am your new principal. Will you inform all the students to line up in the yard. I would like to talk with them." In a few minutes they were all down in the yard. I told them I needed their help in running the school.

"The past will be completely forgotten and the future will be in your hands. Together we shall build a new educational enterprise. Our country is poor and cannot and must not fail the children of this land, who are entitled to a decent education..." I went on, appealing to their sense of nationalism and fair play. I could see disbelief and puzzlement on their faces. How could one man change all the abuse and indignity that had been dished out to them daily? I told them to elect about 20 representatives to meet

Memories of Afghanistan

with me that evening in the boardinghouse. One of the guards cautioned me, "They are in a rebellious mood and if something happens to you, we will be held responsible."

"Why should they hurt me?" I asked.

"Nobody knows why they behave badly," the second guard said. "If you can get us guns to protect you, it would be a different story."

"I will not permit violence of any kind in this school. You men may stay away if you want to," I said.

As I was leaving, one of the guards, Ghulam Ali, followed me and offered to stay with me. I thanked him.

When I re-entered the building that evening, Ghulam accompanied me. We entered a large room where a game of poker was in progress. A number of students sat in a circle with small piles of pennies and a rupee or two here and there in front of them. Ghulam seemed surprised at the audacity of the students, who moved not a muscle in my presence. I watched the game for a few minutes, then moved on to another room where some students were smoking. Again I was not shocked and went on to inspect a few bedrooms and the bedding.

I asked some students whether they had elected representatives to talk to me and they said they had. "Please have them come to my office," I said. On the way, Ghulam informed me that the students who had been elected were really the gang leaders. Without asking permission, about 15 students walked into the office and sprawled on every available surface. I told Ghulam to leave us alone.

"Well," I said, "I am probably more pissed off by the way you have been treated than most of you. You have been deeply hurt. I promise that from now on no one will hurt you again."

This statement was received with expressions of disbelief and some raising of eyebrows. I went on.

"As of tomorrow, corporal punishment will be outlawed in this school."

"Under any circumstances?" one student asked.

Children of Darkness

"Under any and all circumstances," I emphasized. "I need your help to make a list of grievances, and I shall tackle each one as fast as possible."

Three hands were raised and I noticed some smiles.

"One at a time," I said.

"Our food is terrible."

"Our clothes come back from the laundry as dirty as ever."

"No one guides us in sports."

"Most of the teachers waste our time and hardly teach."

"The boardinghouse director not only restricts our food, but also our movements to and from the boardinghouse."

I asked, "Is there a separate director for this house?"

"Yes, and he is lucky we can't find him these days."

"We are here to solve the problems of the school, but we cannot do that by threats and violence. Now, let us concentrate on the urgent problems first. I want you to form committees to buy your own food and to keep the boardinghouse clean. I will concentrate on the educational aspects."

On the way home, I was confident that I had the students in a cooperative mood and my mind was filled with plans for the school. As I neared the house, the public radio was loudly proclaiming the defeat of the Red hordes by the mechanized forces of the German army.

"You look like a ghost. What happened?" Phyl said, seeing I was disturbed as I entered the house.

"Hitler attacked Russia yesterday. All that noise on the radio outside is proclaiming the Second Coming."

"I did notice the exuberance in the voice. But Hitler must be out of his mind, taking on the whole world single-handedly."

"Don't underestimate him, dear. Der Führer has many allies even in America."

"How is your school? Any progress?"

"I think I am beginning to reach the students. And how was your day?"

Memories of Afghanistan

"I am making great progress in my Persian. I even learned a phrase or two today. When Faruk causes too much trouble, his mother tells him, 'Boro gum sho,' which means, go disappear."

"You might be learning some Persian, but I'm afraid you are losing ground in English. *Get lost* is a better translation."

The German attack on Russia was followed by a severe attack on my wife's digestive system by Kabul's special microbes. The disease was known as Kabulitis by the small foreign colony and was considered to be the initiation fee one had to pay for the privilege of living there. My poor wife was confined to her bed for three days and was limited to a bland carbohydrate diet.

In Kabul, we had quite a number of foreign-educated young men. From America, three engineers had come back. Kabir Ludeen, being a Pathan, was already the deputy minister in the Department of Public Works. Mir Najmuddeen, a dentist, and Abdul Majid, a microbiologist, were employed in the Ministry of Health. Two doctors of medicine joined us shortly after my return to Kabul. One of them, Abdul Zahir, a Pathan, who later left his field of specialty and entered politics, eventually became a prime minister. About a dozen students came back from France, Germany and England. Some, including Dr. Mir Nisam (probably the best medical doctor Afghanistan ever had) brought foreign wives with them.

In this particular period our lives were rigidly controlled by Hashim Khan, the prime minister. All the foreign wives of Afghans (about twelve) had to cover themselves from head to toe with the cursed chaderi. Since Phyllis was the only one to defy this barbaric regulation, she was not very popular among them, and they predicted dire calamities for our family.

During the first month of our stay, I was extremely busy with my school work. Corporal punishment was abolished. One teacher was fired when he disobeyed this regulation. The directors of the school and the boardinghouse were discharged. Teachers were advised that unless they showed progress, their contracts would not be renewed for the following year. The students were magnificent. When they saw that I kept my promise to them, they began to stir. They formed committees to handle food, health, sports, recreational activities... They met with me daily. They were encouraged to argue for their points of view, and problems were solved by majority rule. I loved those bright and excited rebel leaders whose enthusiasm permeated the fiber of the mass of the sluggish student body and a teaching staff that didn't care.

In the midst of all these activities, I received a note from Hashim Khan's office that the prime minister wanted to see me. When I entered his semi-dark office one afternoon, I had difficulty finding him. The huge chamber was full of expensive Afghan rugs, and a stale odor hung in the air. There were no chairs or tables. In the semi-darkness, I saw a huge bundle on the floor piled up against the wall. Drawing closer, I saw it was the massive body of His Highness. He stared at me in silence. I took off my hat, greeted him, and stood in front of him waiting.

"How long is it since you've been back from America?"

"About a month, sir."

"Talk louder; I can't hear you."

"I said a month, sir," I shouted.

"You have certainly caused a lot of commotion within so short a period of time."

I thought he was referring to the school problems, so I said that they were under control.

"What is under control?"

"The school, sir."

"Who's talking about schools? I am talking about your American wife. I want you to put a veil over her and restrict her movements. All the other foreign wives of Afghans are abiding willingly."

I was boiling inside at the false and insulting statements of this primitive man, and yet I knew he was goading me to lose my temper.

"I don't have the right to do what you are asking of me, sir."

"What do you mean, you have no right? Aren't you her husband?"

Memories of Afghanistan

"Yes, but she is an American."

"Speak up. Don't mumble. Do you refuse to obey the laws of this land?"

"As an American citizen, my wife will not obey any law that restricts her freedom," I shouted.

"Stop yelling at me. I warn you, I am going to hold you responsible for her actions."

"You may do whatever you please with me, but if my wife's behavior sets a bad example for other females, then I suggest you send her back to America."

"Are you saying that you would rather have a free wife away from you in America than a restricted one living with you?"

"I don't seem to have any choice in the matter, sir. Would you like to talk to her yourself?"

"Absolutely not. I don't like your attitude. In the future, I don't want you to walk together anywhere with your wife. She must walk at least fifty paces behind you. Now you may leave."

It was too late to go back to school and too early to go home, so I stopped to see my friend Dr. Mir Najmuddeen at his dental office. No one was in the reception room and the doctor was inside perched on the dental chair reading a magazine.

"Do you have a toothache?" he asked.

"No, I just left the prime ministry and thought you might like to see me."

"I am delighted. You are getting too chummy with Naim. The less you see of him the better. These Musahibans are unpredictable bastards," he said.

"I was with the old jellyfish himself, not Naim."

"Hashim?" he asked.

"No other," said I.

"Hold it," he said, raising his hand. "Before you tell me your tale of woe, you have to listen to mine. A couple of days after the German troops attacked Russia, I was working on the old man, who had a root infection in one of his molars. The minister of health and the minister of court were standing in front of him carrying

Children of Darkness

on a conversation about how long it would take Hitler to finish the job in Russia. The prime minister thought it would take three months and the other two predicted six weeks at most. Finally he turned to me and said, 'I would like you to be the arbitrator in our dispute. Who do you think is closer to the target date?'

" 'I am afraid that neither one of you is close,' I told him.

" 'But either I or they must be closer.'

" 'Not at all, sir. You haven't considered the other alternative. I believe Hitler will lose just as Napoleon did before him.' Well, the conversation stopped and the next day I was fired."

"Are you out of a job now?" I asked.

"Temporarily. I will be transferred to the outpatient department of the clinic for females, where they don't even have a dental chair. Now tell me what crime you have committed to deserve an audience with Hashim Khan."

"My problem is Phyllis, who is supposed to be bundled up like a Christmas gift. Can you imagine putting a veil on the most beautiful face in Kabul and depriving these sexual perverts on the streets of what it means to watch free women walk with as little clothes on as the weather permits?"

"Tell me, what happened?"

"Phyl stays as she is, no veil, but we can't walk together."

"You certainly got off easy."

The Teachers' Training School was changing at a dizzy pace. Even some of the teachers began to do more than was expected of them. The school was not only old, but there was not enough space to handle all the students. A new building had been planned and was about 90 percent finished. It was about a mile away through fields of vegetables and clover, but if one were to reach it by the road, the distance was about two and a half miles. I asked for permission from the Ministry of Education to relocate the school in its new building. They approved my request and allocated eight hundred rupees for moving expenses.

My office staff busied themselves with the details of transporting tons of supplies, consisting of desks, chairs, books,

Memories of Afghanistan

file cabinets, beds and a host of other materials. Because of the wartime emergency, gasoline was not available. The only mechanical transporting system still functioning were carts pulled by bullocks. I was told that the cost of moving would be twelve hundred rupees, allowing 10 percent for breakage, and that it would take five days to complete the job.

I mulled over the problem most of the day and then had a conference with my rebel children. I proposed that they, the school administrators and the teachers move everything. Pros and cons were considered but finally they accepted the rough outline of my plan. I then spread on my desk the plans of the school and boardinghouse and marked all the locations. They were asked to spend the next day acquainting themselves with the details and plan to begin the task the following day. I circulated a notice to all the classes that on Tuesday morning all students and teachers would be expected to be in school two hours earlier than usual. The details of the plan had already leaked, so that no one was surprised at my request.

Practically everyone was in the school yard when I arrived that cool morning in early July. I had talked to the farmer through whose fields we were going to walk. I had given him some money and a promise that we would not cause undue damage to his field. I entered my office and came out with two chairs and a bundle of files under my arm. Addressing the students and teachers who were standing in a huge half circle, I said, "Friends, manual labor is frowned upon in our culture, but today I want you to dirty your hands as an honorable duty. I will be sad if this remained an isolated example. Let us make it the beginning of a change in attitude toward manual labor. I would like to see no interruption in today's study schedule. We have two hours in which to move all our belongings to the new school. There will be guides there to direct you to your proper classrooms." I started toward the clover field with my chairs and files. The job took an hour longer than I had planned, but by ten o'clock classes were functioning normally in the new school. From that day on, I earned the coveted title of *divana*–madman–in the Ministry of Education.

In the afternoon of the moving day, I congratulated the student leaders and gave them the eight hundred rupees that had been allotted for moving as partial payment for a two-day feast at Chilsotoon (a public garden just outside the city proper) the following weekend. Twenty-five hundred rupees more were collected before the weekend, which was one of the most memorable occasions in my life. Those children, who barely six weeks earlier in a rebellious mood had almost hanged a man, played music on their crude instruments and sang their local folk songs. They played games and, above all, they laughed as children should.

Chapter 20
Nationalism

With the approaching end of the second quarter of the twentieth century, an entirely new mood of expectancy was permeating the fiber of power politics in the Middle East. It was feared or hoped for, depending on one's economic status, but it was never fully understood. We were told by some that a "yellow peril" would replace benign imperialism, and by others that the little Japanese were proving, if proof were needed, that the difference between a civilized and an uncivilized man was that the former possessed a gun with which he coerced the latter into becoming a beast of burden. However, only a few understood that there were easier ways to exploit the resources of the continent than by brute force: Let the kings, little dictators and sheiks do the dirty work for which they would be rewarded with arms and money.

In the Muslim countries of the Middle East, the ruling dynasties were all prepared to welcome Hitler's victorious army. The leaders of Arab nationalism, lush with oil royalties, were fearful of the impact of a Jewish democracy in Palestine on their feudal privileges. Reza Shah in Iran was exiled for his intrigue with German agents.

In the *Khodadad*[*] Kingdom of Afghanistan, nationalism manifested itself in an expectedly bizarre way. Hashim Khan and his two young nephews were pressing hard to make Pushtu the language of the whole nation. They realized that with the decline of British power in India, the supremacy of a small minority of Pathans among the other minorities, which constituted the bulk of the population, was becoming untenable. However, it is one thing to purify a nation's language, as the Turks were attempting; it is quite a different story to replace it with a primitive dialect devoid of all the prerequisites for a language. Pushtu had no literature of

---

[*] God-given.

Nationalism

any significance, no published books on grammar, fiction, history or science.

In Afghanistan, problems were solved by edicts. Let there be a dam and eventually there was one. If it didn't work, it was someone else's fault. So the edict was issued that people learn and speak Pushtu. Then and only then, committees were formed in the Ministry of Education and the Department of Communications (newspapers and radio) to give the edict an image of form, if not the reality of substance. The following decisions were issued by these committees and approved by the authority in power:

All government employees must study one hour of Pushtu every morning from 8 to 9 before the start of the regular day's work. No one thought to see that there were not enough teachers who could read and write the dialect to serve all government departments in Kabul, let alone the other provinces where Persian was spoken. Since a day's salary was deducted for a day's non-attendance, practically no one missed these popular stag tea parties. The Communications Department valiantly attempted to put out a few crude pamphlets in Pushtu as a starter. Since my school was closed in October, I was immune from Pushtu or its penalty for the time being.

It was also resolved that there should exist a Pushtu encyclopedia, in which all fields of knowledge were summarized. All twenty-four volumes of the *Encyclopaedia Britannica* were to be translated. The cost was authorized by the prime minister, Hashim Khan, and was duly publicized in the newspapers as another gift to his proud people who were thirsty for knowledge (hungry for food would have been more to the point). There was probably not one competent translator in Afghanistan who knew enough English and also the equivalent words in Pushtu. At least 90 percent of the words, concepts and ideas in science, the arts, and literature had to be invented in the Pushtu dialect before any translation could be attempted. So this phase of the work was shelved for the future, and translation began in Persian. This should have been considered a mean trick and the perpetrators

Memories of Afghanistan

should have been hanged or at least exiled (which they would have greatly appreciated). Here was the Persian language, destined to be downgraded, raising its ugly arm to receive yet another shot of the serum of knowledge.

There were a couple of subsidiary benefits to the foes of ignorance and tyranny that escaped even the scrutiny of the more sophisticated servants of the monarchy. A number of very competent intellectuals were unemployed and in great need of money. My good friend Dr. Mir Najmuddeen could not practice his profession because Hashim Khan did not like him. He became such a competent translator that he almost went blind. One day I carried a huge bundle of his translations to Naim Khan to prove what a devoted and hard-working person Dr. Najmuddeen was. He was reinstated to his old job.

A shrewd operator in the Communications Department cooked up a deal with the superintendent of the political prison (where some of the great minds languished in idleness), who allowed the inmates to translate parts of the encyclopedia into Persian on a three-way equal basis (among the superintendent, the prisoner and the middle man). The government paid fifteen rupees a page. Some of the inmates not only earned a large amount of money, but were able for the first time to buy some of their necessities from the outside world with the help of the superintendent.

After a couple of years and the expenditure of a large sum of money, a meeting was called to assess the translation of the knowledge of the ages that had so far been made available in Persian. Ghulam Hussein Khan (once a classmate of mine) chaired the meeting and tempers flared hot and heavy.

"It is the most ridiculous accumulation of facts and figures I have ever seen," one member said. "There are hundreds of pages devoted to the British monarchy and hundreds of others to obscure personalities that I don't give a damn about. Our total history is covered by less than a page and even that is distorted beyond recognition."

"But you voted for it in this very room," said another member.

Nationalism

"I voted for decency, not for shit."

"Gentlemen, please let us correct our past mistakes and hope that this time we are on the right track."

The meeting continued all afternoon and into the night before a compromise resolution surfaced. It stated that from then on, only selected portions of the encyclopedia would be translated. It left out the crucial point of who would do the selection. Later Ghulam Hussein Khan decided that selection would be done by topics. Certain articles would be eliminated entirely; others would be condensed or left unchanged. No one bothered to get permission from the owners of the *Encyclopaedia Britannica*. Years later, the masses of disjointed articles in various handwritings and different color inks filled three walls of shelving in a large room. By then everyone was sick and tired of the project and happy when the government finally terminated further financial support.

By far the most damaging policy decision was to introduce Pushtu into the school system, not as a primitive language to be studied and improved, but as *the language*. Starting with the first grade, every year the entire curriculum of the progressively succeeding grade would be taught in Pushtu. This policy was in full force when I returned home from America. My further investigation convinced me that the ignorant rulers of Afghanistan could not have damaged the education of the children of the country more if they had merely closed a grade each year in a country in which probably more than 95 percent of the population could not read or write. It was a great shock to me, only five months after my return, when I realized that my educational activities would be a futile exercise.

Phyllis and I discussed our future on a cold night in our new apartment on the second week of December, 1941. Our radio was softly playing the Schubert Quartet No. 13. Radio Kabul devoted half an hour to Western music every evening for the benefit of the small but influential group of foreign residents. Although the sequence of movements was not followed in proper order, we tried not to miss them anyway.

Memories of Afghanistan

"You knew the unpredictability of our situation here before we arrived," Phyl said.

"Yes, but I didn't realize what an awful mess we got ourselves into. I knew there was corruption, ignorance, privation and cruelty. But I didn't know that these terrible calamities were actually planned and followed through as national policy," I said.

"I don't believe that at all. I don't think your ruling class is that smart."

"But, my dear, their masters just across the border certainly do not want a revival of the anti-imperialism of the Amanullah era in the uncertain climate of the Near East. Students have been the bitter foes of the status quo and the entrenched power structure." At that very moment, our music on the radio was cut off abruptly and an excited announcer declared:

> Radio Kabul has just learned that Japan's air armada dealt a devastating blow to the American naval forces in Hawaii.

"Oh, my God," I said.

"What happened?" Phyllis asked.

"Japan has attacked the American forces in Hawaii!"

"What? Stupid, stupid... stupid."

"Who is stupid?"

"The Japanese warlords, who else? Roosevelt has been itching to get involved. Japan solved his problem for him."

"The news commentator said that the American navy is almost destroyed."

"Who cares? We shall build enough to destroy the poor bastards' island fortress and then some."

"We should be there to help the war effort."

"Yes."

The next day I went to the Ministry of Education. Everyone was in a festive mood.

"Your country has been almost finished in the first blow," Abdullah told me with a wide grin.

Nationalism

"I thought Afghanistan was my country," I said.

"Sorry, I meant your wife's country."

"If I remember correctly, some of our very astute leaders predicted that Russia would be conquered by the German army within six months. Now the six months are almost over and the Red Army, with the help of Father Winter, is driving the Germans out of some of the captured cities and towns."

"Are you in favor of communists?"

"I thought we were discussing warfare rather than political beliefs."

"I am not ashamed to say that I believe in monarchy," he said. Dr. Annus, a Turkish-trained mathematician, joined us, but Abdullah was watching me intently for comments. I finally obliged him.

"You, sir, would be happy to believe in any political system under which you happened to be born. But I pick and choose under any form of government, accepting only those features which pass the moral test and rejecting all the rest."

"Ah, Doctor Sahib, what standard do you employ to test your morality with?" asked Dr. Annus. He continued, "An act could be moral in one country or in one historical period and yet completely immoral in another time or place." Dr. Annus was a remarkable young man. Although he had a close family link with the ruling dynasty, he gave me the impression that he resented the connection. He had a philosophic bent and discussed ideas not as weapons with which to harm, but to generate more ideas.

"Well, Annus Jan, you're talking of morality in religious terms. I am concerned with it only in its human application. Forms of government change; religions are modified or discarded, but the human desire to avoid pain and seek safety, food and pleasure remains fairly constant. The concept of morality will also stay unchanged when it is applied to these tangible needs."

"What are you people talking about?" asked Abdullah. Annus and I looked at each other, realizing that our silence rather than our answer would be less damaging to his stiff composure. But he persisted.

Memories of Afghanistan

"Don't you have a sense of pride in your nation?" Abdullah glowered at me. Annus graciously answered his question.

"What do you mean, sir? Are we supposed to be proud of our backward ways, our illiteracy, our diseased and oppressed people, or our lack of freedom? Can you mention a few things that we have to be proud of?"

"We should be proud of our leaders, our religion and our land," Abdullah said, and looking at me asked, "Don't you think we should be proud of these, Dr. Anwar?"

"Well, sir, nationalism is a two-edged sword. It cuts both ways. It can compel people to kill, burn babies, hate and invade other nations. Germany is a good example. Or it can be manipulated for the good of a nation, for people to help each other, for peaceful construction, and respect for the rights of other people living in other lands," I said.

"And which nation represents your second category?"

"None that I can think of, I am afraid."

Chapter 21
Of Sex, Sorrow and Other Things

The Teachers' Training School closed at the end of October. Due to the lack of transportation facilities and the shortage of wood, winter vacation became the general rule for all the schools.

My salary of 600 rupees ($30) a month was barely enough to cover the cost of food and clothing for our family. The government provided us with a rent-free apartment—the entire top floor of a modern building just across from the Nijat High School. This was one of the few buildings in Kabul that had a flush toilet.

I remember the day when I came home and found Phyllis quite agitated.

"What happened? Did my compatriots give you a hard time in the bazaar?"

"No, by now I am used to their leering expressions when I shop. It is much more sinister than that. I was invited to Brishna's house for tea, where a few other foreign wives of Afghans were present. Mrs. Brishna asked me if Naim Khan had been a good student. I told her that I had never met him. She said that I was teaching him English at his house. I told her that she was mistaken, that I didn't even know where he lived. She calmly told me that I should not deny it because I had been seen often entering and leaving his house. 'Now we know why your husband, who belongs to a very low class, receives the highest salary among all the foreign-trained students plus a free house to live in,' she said."

"This is pure stupidity and jealousy, my dear. Don't pay any attention to it."

"How can you say that? My circle of friends is very limited as it is. What hurts me most is that the other women didn't say a damned thing. If they only knew how I hate the guts of the bastards in the royal household who treat the poor people of this land like dirt, these dames would not accuse me of having sexual relations with them."

Memories of Afghanistan

"You're taking this very hard, Phyl. Gossip is the name of the game. I feel sorry for these young girls from Paris, Berlin and London who have entered the primitive life of Kabul, where there is no entertainment of any kind. On top of this, they are forced to cover themselves with a veil whenever they step outside their houses," I said.

"Why the hell don't they come outside without the veil? What would happen to them?"

"Their husbands would lose their financial security."

"You are firm in not allowing a veil to be put on me."

"Ah, but I am from a poor family and have nothing to lose."

King Amanullah had sent some very young students to Turkey, of all places, for study. When they returned to Afghanistan, they were in their middle twenties. They had very little useful education and were completely ignorant of the land of their birth. A couple were employed in the Teachers' Training School for the primary grades, located in the beautiful valley of Paghman. This school was under the supervision of Turks. The curriculum, the method of teaching, and the qualifications of the teachers, I learned later, were primitive and devoid of sense or of excitement.

One of the Afghan teachers in this school had been under investigation for almost a year for sexual perversion. He had been accused of having sexual relations with some of his young students. He was neither caught in the act, nor did any student openly admit a sexual affair with him. But the notorious chief of the Secret Service, Ghulam Faruk Khan, was determined to punish the teacher, Abdul Ghafar, to serve as an example to the free people of the land, where women, the normal partners, were permanently banished into the dark confines of their four-walled adobes.

I was one of those selected to pass judgment on the case. The others were from the higher echelons of the Ministry of Education. We were given a copy of a thick report to familiarize ourselves with the "facts" of the case in advance. On the day of the hearing, I was about a half an hour late, thinking that almost nothing would

Of Sex, Sorrow and Other Things

be performed on time. But the excitement of the subject under discussion evidently had impelled everyone to be at the meeting as early as possible. I entered the roomful of jovial people, who had already dispensed the wrath of God on the sinful.

"You are somewhat late, Dr. Sahib," His Highness, the Minister of Education, said.

"Yes, I have picked up some bad habits in America. Could someone give me the gist of what has transpired."

Everyone looked gravely at Naim Khan who, with a nod, energized the secretary to read the punishment clauses.

> It is resolved that Abdul Ghafar, the perpetrator of the crime of sexual aberration, as documented in the attached report:
> 1. Be discharged of all his duties as a teacher for life.
> 2. Be required to pay the expenses of all his educational training abroad.
> 3. Be sentenced to serve a minimum of two years in jail.

All eyes turned to me, the mad doctor, and it was obvious they hoped I would drown one of these days in the dirty pool of my own sarcasm. I seldom disappointed them.

"This is ridiculous," I said. "The report is full of innuendos, misinterpreted remarks, unproven accusations and is plain silly. The teacher was found sitting with a student under a walnut tree! Any day they may find me with a student in my office or any other place. He is accused of walking with a student all the way from Paghman to Kabul! He told the student on the way that he had perspired, and on and on... Now, if the Chief of the Secret Service, who is sitting among us, can't find more useful work for his agents, they should all resign and save the government some needed money."

"Your sweeping indictment of my father's department is unjustified. I would also like to remind you that he is a proven servant of the monarchy," said Abdullah in his twangy, pitched voice.

Memories of Afghanistan

"I was not questioning your father's loyalty, sir, but only pointing out that in a country like ours, where sex deviation is an accepted pattern of life, much effort and money has been wasted on what is obviously a doubtful case. This is plain hypocrisy. I myself was attacked as a sexual object three times between the ages of eight and sixteen by some of our deprived males."

"Dr. Anwar is absolutely right. Homosexuality is most prevalent in any society where females are kept away from males, such as among the navy and army personnel and prison inmates in all countries. In the Muslim countries of the Middle East, it involves the total population. By the way, homosexuality here is as intense among the females as among the males," said Hashim Shaiq, an exile from central Asia and a professor of psychology. The people in the meeting calmed down a bit and some began to reminisce about their own pasts. Even His Excellency, the Minister of Education, added his own touch of humor.

"I remember our teacher of religion in Istiqlal School who used to touch our faces and even our butts playfully in the classroom," he said.

"I was offered money if I went to the house of the Arabic language teacher," another member said.

Still another added, "I was forcefully dragged and raped in a dark alley near my house."

I noticed that Ghulam Faruk Khan, his son, and a few Pushtu authorities were squirming uncomfortably in their seats. I raised my hand and said, "Those of you who were not the victim of sexual aberration in your childhood or youth, please raise your hand."

"I strongly object to being put in this undignified situation by our foreign-educated young men," the chief of the secret service said, and then he walked out of the room. The minister of education also excused himself and left. I followed him on my bicycle to his office in the prime ministry.

"I don't like your sarcastic attitude," he said as I entered his office.

Of Sex, Sorrow and Other Things

"A human life was at stake, sir. I merely tried to show that a disease cannot be cured by an offering of human sacrifice. We will have a large percentage of our male population that indulges in homosexuality as long as we lock up the females."

"You could have accomplished a great deal more if you had approached the problem calmly and with patience. I think I know why you followed me here so quickly. You want the teacher to be pardoned."

"Yes, sir. I will give him a job in my school and take the responsibility for his future conduct."

"Provided you take charge of the school in Paghman also."

"What about the Turks who are now running it?" I asked.

"When their contract time expires, you may rehire them or send them home to Turkey."

So I acquired another 250 students and all their problems, which kept me busy those cold nights of the succeeding three months of the winter of 1942.

At this particular time there already were a few American teachers in Kabul, forerunners of a contingent of an American Embassy rumored to open soon. The number of foreigners in Kabul was increasing rapidly in those early days of the Second World War. Foreign legations were distributing their daily propaganda sheets to a select group of influential Afghans. The pattern of social gathering among the different nationalities took shape in a peculiar fashion. The English, French and Germans had socialized before the war. After the war started, the Germans were rejected, but when France was invaded by the German army, the Germans were accepted and the English rejected. The Russians and the Japanese were not accepted at any time, the former for political reasons and the latter for racial. The Americans accepted or rejected individuals purely on a personal basis.

The most remarkable group of foreigners were the Jewish refugees from Germany. Whether they had been sausage factory owners in Stuttgart, dentists in Bremen, teachers in Berlin or engineers in Hamburg, one found them to be men of culture and

Memories of Afghanistan

dignity. They were what I had always associated with being an educated German, who was interested in music, in literature, good food and interesting company. The Jew's suffering was beyond belief, and yet he carried a residue of love for the land that caused it.

Phyllis and I selected our friends from the hodgepodge of domestic and foreign people. The choice was limited both in number and in quality. Since outside entertainment was nonexistent and home gatherings were confined to dinner parties, a game of bridge or listening to recorded music, we were thrown into one another's arms to dissipate some of the suffocating boredom. I remember a tea party at our house for a small number of American teachers.

"Hey Hammad, the minister of education sent me your diplomas for evaluation," said Robert Paine, a high school English teacher, grinning at me.

"Is that a joke?" I asked.

"No joke at all, honest. I've got all three of your diplomas on my desk."

"What are you going to do with them?"

"Nothing at all, just look at them for a few days. They do look pretty with their red ribbons and all, you know. One of these days I'll send them back with a note giving you a high grade–if you are good to me."

"I think you should tell them the truth–that with only a bachelor's degree you are not qualified to judge the value of my diplomas."

"Are you out of your mind? It's not my problem if your high officials are stupid."

Another teacher, Mr. Hoffman, joined us. He had a hefty frame and the fold of pale flesh below his rounded chin was pushed upward by his heavily starched shirt collar. While listening to us, he rhythmically wound and rewound his Phi Beta Kappa key, which was attached to a thin gold chain, around his forefinger.

"Robert is absolutely right. He will lose face if he does what you suggest. Your people pay a great deal of attention to saving face," said Hoffman.

Of Sex, Sorrow and Other Things

"If *we* are to be blamed for the bad habit of face-saving, why are you afraid that Robert might lose face?"

"You don't seem to understand. We acquire some of your traits in order not to embarrass you."

"A man of principle, that Hoffman!" called Mr. Fry from the other side of the room.

The initial excitement of the first few months of my return to Afghanistan wore off rapidly and a mood of hopelessness took its place. I felt trapped and isolated. I also blamed myself for exposing my young wife to privation and hardship without any compensating values of any kind. The school opened and I plunged myself into work to forget the reality of living. Phyllis was hired in the girls' school to teach hygiene and sports. She had learned enough Persian to make herself understood.

One day, Phyllis met me at the door when I came home and told me that a young nephew of mine had been on his way to see us when a horse kicked him. He was taken to the hospital near the school. I rode my bicycle back to where I had just left, about two miles away. At the hospital, I was informed that the Turkish doctor suspected internal bleeding and at that moment was operating on the little fellow. I joined his family, who were allowed inside the operating room. I saw the white face of my nephew Kazim, with his guts all piled up next to him on the operating table. Unable to watch the butchery performed in the name of saving a life, I walked out of the room, and as I paced the corridor of the hospital I visualized the body of my rugged and beautiful land carved and decimated by self-appointed butchers who did not know any better. I waited long enough to kiss Kazim's hot brow when he was laid in bed. Two days later we buried him in sandy soil near the mountain, the first of so many others that followed during the next two years of our stay in Afghanistan.

Chapter 22
Phyl's Foibles

In our new home, Phyllis was consulted on everything from home furnishings to clothes, food, hair styles and health. Here we loved her, laughed at her Persian accent and tried to make her as happy as possible in a strange land. Our relatives and friends (except for one, Kaka Nabi) were cautious and watchful to see what would happen to us. To buck a tyrannical system in a primitive society was considered risky at best. And, for the most part, they stayed away and waited for the inevitable outcome. Meanwhile, Phyllis attracted a host of children through her open kindness.

In most houses, children were treated as second-class citizens. They seldom received love and kindness. They were fed last and abused physically for small deviations from the norm. Of course, there were some families in which children were loved and treated with respect. Among our closest relatives we encountered both varieties. My brother Wahab had two children, Zubaida and Mahmood. Zubaida's mother was divorced and, at this particular time, Zubaida was living with her stepmother. Zubaida was a wild girl of the streets at age seven, dirty, hungry, abused and abusive. Mahmood was happier living with his poor grandmother, who also took care of Habib, the older brother of Faruk, who was living with us.

One day Diljan declared that Habib was going to spend a few days with us. Phyllis stripped him and threw away his clothes, cut his hair short and asked me to prepare a hot bath. I filled the corrugated iron tub with water, put the home-made steel resistor in it and waited the customary two hours for the water to get warm. The resistor, which looked like a large welding gun, was originally constructed for us to modify the high-voltage electricity so that we could operate our American radio and turntable. Since the resistor became red hot, we began to dip it in a pail of water. Consequently we had a supply of hot water available to us for all uses.

Phyl's Foibles

Well, the poor, scared Habib was cleaned, deloused and outfitted with new clothes. During the following days and weeks and months and years, Habib became a permanent resident of our domicile. His thin frame and sunken cheeks filled up in time, but it took a long while for him to realize that food did not have to be stolen and could be had for the asking.

One day, Phyllis tried to get from Diljan the dates of her children's birthdays.

"When was Habib born?" Phyllis asked.

"Let me see. I think... four years... no, wait. Five, yes, five," said my sister.

"Are you sure?"

"Well, it was the year my husband was promoted."

"Do you remember the month?" Phyl asked in desperation.

"Why not? It was not snowing, so it couldn't have been winter. I remember now. It was spring."

"But what month in the spring?"

"What month? It was an early spring month. Yes, I remember the petunias were not yet in bloom."

Phyl gave me a furtive look, wrote two dates on a piece of paper and passed it to me. I turned to Diljan and told her that Habib was almost five years old and had been born on August 10, 1936, and Faruk was two years old and had been born on March 8, 1939. Diljan looked at me gravely and said, "Phyllis is a very smart girl."

So we planned an elaborate party for Habib, our first birthday party. During the succeeding two weeks, various gifts (mostly clothes) were bought, wrapped in colored paper and hidden in a box in the corner of our bathroom. Phyl had mentioned Habib's party to some of our foreign friends and they contributed generously in cash, which we tied separately in little cloth bundles. The night of the party, after supper, the living room was darkened and Jwandai walked in holding a large, round cake aflame with five dancing candles. We all sang, first in English and then in Persian, the birthday song. Habib was so anxious to open his presents that the

Memories of Afghanistan

cake was set aside for later. He kept ripping open parcels and piling them to one side–clothes, candies, cash, and games. In the middle of the festivities, Faruk jumped up bawling and ran to his mother yelling, "I want MY birthday now." As usual, Phyllis came to the rescue. She said, "Stop crying and listen to me. Habib will share some of his presents with you, if you promise to do the same on your birthday." Faruk was listening carefully. "Will you?" Phyllis asked. He nodded his head vigorously.

Phyl's next candidate was my brother Wahab's rejected son, Mahmood. One afternoon in the early summer of 1942, as I climbed the stairs to our apartment, I noticed a little boy, naked to the waist, running down the steps. I grabbed him.

"Mahmood, where are you going?" I asked.

"Let me go, let me go," he kept repeating.

"Hammad, is that you?" I heard Phyllis call.

"Yes."

"Have you seen Mahmood anywhere?"

"He is in my arms, and he stinks of kerosene."

"Bring him up here. I was delousing him and he disappeared when I went for a comb."

Poor Mahmood had no option then but to submit to the brute force of two adults, one holding him tightly against a small stool and the other trimming his curly black hair as close to his skull as possible.

"Look at the damned lice crawling in his lap."

"Hold on to him while I get rid of the mess," I said.

"On your way back, check to see if the water is hot."

"The water is just the right temperature," I called from the bathroom. As I pulled the black elongated resistor out of the tub, Phyllis came in, dragging the unwilling child by the hand. Mahmood saw the resistor in my hand hanging like a fat snake, and howled. Meanwhile Phyllis was trying to pull off his Afghan pants. Somehow the cord got entangled and, in the ensuing struggle, wrapped around his penis. I threw the resistor to the floor and ran for scissors. The poor child was sure we were going to

Phyl's Foibles

mutilate him bit by bit. I grabbed and pinned him down on the floor while Phyllis cut the cord.

"OK. He is safe, dump him in the tub," Phyllis said. Then, sniffing the air, she asked, "What's burning?"

"I don't smell anything," I said.

"You never do, but I smell a cat or a dog burning."

"Oh, stop that."

"I do and I see smoke right behind you."

I jumped around and saw the resistor burning the edge of our *namad*.* While I was unplugging the resistor, I noticed Mahmood try once more to leap for freedom, but Phyl caught him by one leg, his unprotected rump missing the sharp edge of the tub by inches. "Oh, no you don't. You go or stay only after you are clean," she said. The cleaning procedure, including toenail trimming, was accomplished without further mishap. But Mahmood turned out to be one of our failures. He ran away as soon as the opportunity came.

We next tackled Wahab's daughter, Zubaida. She was a dirty tomboy of the dark alleys. Her divorced mother could not afford to keep her and the stepmother could not tame or domesticate her. One day, my older sister Dada, her husband and her son Dr. Nowroz walked into our apartment and dumped the dirtiest, smelliest lump of human flesh one ever expected to see in our living room.

"Doctor Jan, this girl needs your wife's attention more than anyone in the city of Kabul. Besides, she is of your blood and flesh," Agha Mirza[†] said. After my father died, the husband of my oldest sister and already the father of a well-known medical doctor, became the head man of our growing tribe. In spite of his fancy title, he could neither read nor write, and he felt a little uncomfortable in this exalted position. Like my father, he had been a shopkeeper all his married life and had accumulated innumerable children, but no wealth. Whenever he spoke, he took a deep breath and when he finished the sentence, he emitted a sigh of relief.

---

* Soft rug.
† Learned father.

Memories of Afghanistan

I thanked Agha Mirza and asked Zubaida if she wanted to live with us. All the while she was watching Phyllis from behind her thick, matted black hair, which covered most of her face. She paid no attention to me. Phyllis beckoned with her finger and Zubaida moved toward her. I insisted on written permission from her father before embarking on another cleaning operation. That afternoon, Doctor Nowroz brought it from Wahab, but by then Phyllis was already in the midst of cleaning and delousing the little girl.

It took both Phyllis and Diljan all of three days to complete the job, but the result was worth it a thousand-fold. Zubaida was one of the rare beauties one encounters only a few times in one's life span. Phyllis promptly enrolled her in the school where she was teaching.

In the summer of 1942, my wife came down with obstructive jaundice. She lost weight rapidly and her whole body tone began to turn yellow. No competent doctors were available in Kabul, but fortunately about this time a remarkable German-trained Afghan physician, Dr. Nisam, appeared on the scene to treat her and gradually restored her to health. During this troubled time, Zubaida was Phyl's constant companion. She prepared her diet of starchy food, boiled and cooled her drinking water and helped with small items of shopping.

Wahab must have seen his beautiful daughter out on the streets, because relatives began to drop hints every now and then that he wanted her back in his own house. For a beauty like that, he must have reasoned, one could demand a fortune for dowry.

On a hot day in mid-June of 1942 when I came home I heard loud noises in our apartment. I ran upstairs and heard Wahab yelling for his daughter. As I entered the bedroom door, an earthen water jug hit the wall, missing Wahab by inches. I could not believe my gentle wife was capable of such violence. I told Wahab to leave my house and instructed my younger brother, Jwandai, to throw him out if he resisted. Phyllis, who had lost forty pounds and looked like a yellow ghost, lay exhausted and trembling under her white sheet.

Phyl's Foibles

"Where is Zubaida?" I asked.

"She is hiding under my bed."

"Come on out. Your father is gone." Zubaida crawled out from under the bed holding her bloody nose in her hand. She had been slapped across the face by her father. Before we left Afghanistan for good at the end of 1943, because of the pressure of relatives, she was returned to her father. Later we heard that she had been married in her early teens to an official more than twice her age for a substantial amount of money. She had a brood of children before she was twenty-two years old and lived unhappily thereafter.

The marriage of one of Dada's many daughters, Fukhraj, took place around this time. She asked Phyllis to make her a wedding dress. "I want to look as beautiful as you in those lovely dresses you wear," she complimented Phyllis, who agreed to take on the job. Soon our living room became a sewing circle. Material was scattered everywhere. Phyl was busy measuring, cutting and stitching, while females of all ages gathered around, gaping and commenting on the ingenuity of the farangi. At one point when Phyl began to cut the cloth, the bride-to-be jumped up and yelled, "*O dukhter, chi mekoni?*"*

"Let go of my arm. Don't you see that I am cutting away the excess cloth?"

"Tell her, Doctor Jan, that I have spent a lot of money for this material," my niece told me.

"But it won't fit you properly and then you won't look as pretty as Phyllis on your wedding day," I explained.

"What can I do with the small pieces except to throw them away?"

"Give them to your sisters for dressing dolls," Diljan suggested.

"*Tu divana shudi?*† Using this material for dolls!" she said, jerking the cloth off Phyl's lap.

---

* Girl, what are you doing?
† Have you gone crazy?

Memories of Afghanistan

"You know, Hammad, except for you and Diljan, the rest of you family don't amount to much," Phyl said in English.

"Thanks for the round-about compliment. What do you want me to do?"

"Get this crazy girl out of the house before I lose my temper."

I remember a day when I came home around 5:30 in the evening and found Abdul Raheem Khan and his male secretary outside my house. He was a rather quiet man. His title was Director of Two High Schools, and his offices occupied the ground floor of our building. I parked my bicycle against the wall of the building and shook hands with him.

"You are usually home by now. Are you waiting for someone?" I said.

"Not particularly," he answered.

I looked at him, puzzled. But he playfully told me that half an hour earlier he and his secretary had had to jump out of the window to get out of his office.

"What was the problem?" I asked.

"Tomatoes."

"Tomatoes?"

"Yes. Your wife has barricaded the house with tomatoes. Go look inside."

I walked up the steps and peeked into the hallway. Sure enough, tomatoes were piled up the steps and against the walls and closed office doors.

"I don't understand it."

"Neither do we. We just waited to see how you would manage to get to your apartment."

"Your wife had no problem," the secretary said.

"Is she upstairs?"

"Yes, when she paid the donkey driver after he unloaded his tomato bags, she said, 'God damn,' took off her shoes and stockings and walked through the pile of tomatoes."

"I had better do the same. I am very sorry and apologize for any inconvenience my wife may have caused you."

Phyl's Foibles

Upstairs was unusually quiet. Diljan was holding her two sons by the hands and they were waiting to see my reaction. In the living room, Phyl greeted me with a big grin.

"What is this all about?"

"I just told the guy to give me fifty cents worth of tomatoes and he unloaded the tomatoes, grabbed the money and disappeared before I could say boo."

"Fifty cents! Darling, that is almost ten rupees!"

"He was cute. Big brown eyes. Did I ever tell you that I married you for your big brown eyes?"

"You are impossible!"

"I know," she said, kissing my left eye.

"Awaz," I yelled. He was our new servant. He appeared through the kitchen door. I told him to bring baskets, bowls and any other container he could find. "We'll all pitch in to carry and pile the tomatoes in the backyard until we find some use for them."

Chapter 23
My Brother Jwandai

When my mother died, Jwandai, at the age of six months, became my complete responsibility. No one forced him on me. It just happened. So, for almost two years, wherever I went, he was on my shoulders, his feet dangling around my neck. His weight increase, being gradual, went unnoticed. However, my bones must have been soft and fragile in those two years when I was six, seven and eight, because they gradually bent under the constant pressure. I am still, half a century later, stooped somewhat forward.

After he reached the age of two, Jwandai had to hustle through life alone, like the rest of us. He was a chubby little boy, not as precocious as I, but just as dirty. In school, he did not show any exceptional talent in any subject, but whenever he found a piece of paper, he would always draw the shapes of objects around him, so he entered the art school.

He was a happy child when paper, colorful crayons, water or oil paints were put within his reach. He went wild splashing contrasting colors side by side, pulling, pushing, merging and submerging one color into another. He had entered the second year of art school when we parted for eight years. In America, I used to follow his progress through the mail. In fact, he was the link between the family and me. Father would write to me only a line or two with his shaky hand in the margin of Jwandai's letter. And through the years he developed a remarkable singing voice and became a featured singer on Radio Kabul. As his style of writing became more complex, but less lucid, his paintings took a turn towards the gloomy and forlorn. A year before graduation, he was kicked out of the school for insubordination and lack of interest. His income from singing supported him through a year of intense experimental work in the type of painting in which he was interested. He had some little success commercially and the

My Brother Jwandai

art school employed him as a teacher, the same school in which he had been a student barely eighteen months earlier.

When I returned to Afghanistan, I found Jwandai a spent individual, physically and mentally. His singing voice was still pleasant but seemed to have stopped developing. His sad folk songs left us feeling alone, desolate and crying. At the age of twenty-one, he had almost reached the end of the line in painting. The dead weight of society had crushed the hopes of so many who aspired to provide an element of richness even where the essentials of life were lacking. Jwandai was no exception.

Phyllis and I encouraged him in his painting. Phyl told him it would be very pleasing if the big empty wall of our living room were covered by one of his paintings. He agreed to accept the project. There was a desolate hut on the slope of the rocky mountain, visible in winter from our living room window. The hut had been built by someone and then abandoned. There was a steep footpath to it from the road that ran next to the Kabul River, which in winter-time looked not only hazardous but inaccessible as well. The hut sloped slightly to one side and its ceiling had been gutted by the weight of the winter snow. Jagged black-blue rocks dominated it on two sides, throwing elongated dark shadows during sunrise and sunset. This Jwandai chose to paint for us.

Jwandai's living had no definite pattern because he had no goal. The relentless struggle for existence had transformed him, like most youths of the Middle Eastern countries, into a grabbing, cheating, lying and sex-starved dreamer. Those few who, exposed to educational facilities and humane contacts, developed an urgent desire to correct the inequities of the past in one fell swoop were the tragic misfits who died young. Jwandai was not one of these. He was a romantic dreamer who built his castles on the shifting sand of his imagination. Poetry of escape, music of loneliness, painting of desolation and one-dimensional romantic novels were his spiritual nourishments. He tried to bring a semblance of order into his daily tasks of teaching, painting, and entertainment, but it was haphazard and only partly successful. He played all our

Memories of Afghanistan

Western music records and chose a couple to which he listened day after day. They were Brahms' Double Concerto and Bloch's *Schelomo*.

One day we came home and found the painting of the hut-on-the-mountain hanging on the wall of our living room.

"Poor guy, the poor, poor boy," Phyllis commented.

"What are you mumbling about?" I asked.

"As if there is not a ray of sunshine in his life."

I said, "Look at those early morning sun rays hitting the sharp slabs of stone. Did you know that he used to get up at four o'clock in the morning and walk there just to catch the very first rays?"

"Yes," she answered. "But the sun was used only to emphasize the shadows. Look at them–like black lightning slashing through the cabin. The jagged rocks, standing like so many black-clad monsters. The sun is just a prop in the background."

"Boy, you sound ominous as hell," I said.

"It is, it is," she insisted.

Phyllis' sense of foreboding became a shocking reality in the following days and weeks. Jwandai developed certain mannerisms and idiosyncracies that became a part of his nature for the rest of his life, withdrawn, shy and unconcerned with his clothes and needs.

Eventually, he managed to own that shack on the mountain. He added a couple of bedrooms to it and every year repaired the damage caused by the previous winter's snow.

Years later, he married a pretty girl and raised a family in a rented house in town. His beautiful wife, being artistically inclined, danced her way into a divorce. Jwandai managed to find suitable husbands for his two daughters, then went back to his hut and became a hermit. I was told that his artistic creation was unusually remarkable at this particular time. But it was abruptly extinguished, leaving him brooding like a pinched black candlewick smoking in the dark.

Jwandai came down to town only to pick up his most essential requirements or to take bunches of wild flowers to his daughters.

My Brother Jwandai

"The hut was in bad shape," he wrote to me. "One bedroom had slid away quite a distance into a gulch. I had to bring it back stone by stone to its original place. This time, with the help of the money that you sent me from America, I bought some cement and poured it on the foundation rock. Hopefully, my hut stays put this time so that I can resume my painting a little earlier next spring."

Chapter 24
There Is Order in Chaos

Phyllis started her teaching with a great deal of worry. What if the children didn't like her or, even worse, didn't understand her Persian? What if she didn't get along with the other teachers? What if...?

Her school, the only school for girls in the country, was not too far to walk. But to save her time, I suggested a bicycle as a means of transportation, to which she doubtfully agreed. Since no woman's cycle was imported to Afghanistan, we had difficulty locating one. Finally a friend of mine found a female bicycle frame to which he added the other necessary parts until it functioned as a neutral machine.

During the first few weeks, Phyl was a menace on the dirt roads of Kabul. She was particularly troublesome to donkeys and mullahs. The poor policeman who stood at the bridge intersection kept a close watch on her. Whenever he saw her approaching, he blew his whistle and yelled, "Watch out! Here she comes!"

"Why pick on mullahs and poor donkeys?" I asked.

"Because they are both sluggish in their response. The donkey is only stupid, but the mullah is obstinate as well."

In school, Phyllis learned that she was the only college graduate among all the foreign teachers, including the principal. Her salary, on the other hand, was only three hundred rupees ($15) a month, about one-tenth the wage the other foreign teachers were getting. Those who married Afghans were given the low-scale Afghan salaries.

But Phyllis began to enjoy her teaching. One day she told me that she was teaching her class the dangers of being exposed to microbes and other harmful microorganisms.

"The students just don't believe me when I tell them that the exposed water in the river and the side ditches are full of these organisms. Could you set up a microscope and slides for me to do a demonstration?"

There Is Order in Chaos

After the experiment, I asked her, "How did it go?"

"Oh, great! It scared the daylights out of them to see the blob of an amoeba propelling itself with a series of contractions, or the paramecium darting all over the place in a drop of water."

It was interesting for me to observe how complicated one's life could become in a marginal society, where the meager resources were distributed (grabbed) according to one's rank. Barely enough was left for the producers' supply of energy to maintain the next seasonal cycle.

"Sir, last year you gave me a free hand in the affairs of the Teachers' Training School. I assumed that it also involved the expenditure of the budgeted money," I said one day in Naim's office.

"No, that would be quite unusual. It would disrupt the workable procedure prepared for us at considerable cost," Naim Khan said.

"Who prepared it?"

"An Italian expert whose name I have forgotten."

"He certainly introduced more paper work and a more complicated and time-consuming system," I said. "Personally I don't like to handle money, but I am trying to run a boarding school. Problems with delays and bottlenecks take up too much of my time."

"I'll tell the director of control to expedite your requests without any delay whatsoever."

I thanked him and left. Five days later, the director of control in the Ministry of Education came to my home for a friendly chat.

"Doctor Sahib, I have been admiring your knowledge and, if I may add, your courage from a distance, so-to-speak. I thought to myself it is about time to meet the good doctor face-to-face. Your admirable scheme, which His Highness Naim Khan instructed me to follow, is beyond doubt ingenious." His phraseology of flattery was getting on my nerves. I tried to terminate his stay, but tea was already on the way. I began to change the subject but with very little success.

245

Memories of Afghanistan

"I have a young brother in your school. He thinks you are a unique person, yes sir, this commodity is rare in our poor land. What is your salary, if you would kindly forgive my impertinence?"

"You already have that information," I said.

"Indeed I do, yes, indeed. I only wanted to hear it from your own lips. A very small sum, isn't it? A man of your stature should have a big house attached to a beautiful garden, servants and..."

"Wait a minute. What are you driving at?" I asked.

"Nothing evil. I would like to be an instrument in your hand to provide these luxuries that you deserve more than anyone else in this country. I have a man in my office, one of your co-religionists from Chindawol. I would like you to appoint him as your controller in the school as a link between you and me. He will handle your finances the way you want... and..."

"But that would be stealing the money appropriated for the education and welfare of my school children," I objected.

"I wouldn't put it that bluntly, sir."

"How WOULD you put it?"

"With due respect to your integrity, sir, let me add that this practice of skimming the milk, so to speak, runs through our society from top to bottom. Do you suppose that a minister of the realm lives on his meager salary of one thousand rupees? He spends more than that on his garden shrubberies every year."

"What if I were to report you to the higher authorities?"

"You wouldn't do that. It is not in your character to be counted as one of their spies, and besides, you hate the ones on top, our high priests of crookedness. Now I am convinced more than ever that my brother is in good hands. Thank you, sir, for the tea and the conversation."

After he left, I sat near the window facing the road on which a few dilapidated buggies were pulled by scrawny horses. Down below near the ditch, my nephew Faruk was busy with a mud pile, his undergarments scattered around him. Across the road, children six to eighteen were running and shrieking on the paths and the grassy meadows of the Nijat School. Farther back, the Kabul River

There Is Order in Chaos

made a slight bend. The spring foliage cut the view of the dark gray mud houses of Chindawol, where the bulk of the Shia sect of Muslims lived. Then the mountain, like a gigantic wall, shot straight up. Its jagged, blue-black ridges jutted sideways, reflecting the rays of the late afternoon sun. Traces of the crumbling ancient walls, zigzagging up the mountain like giant pythons, could still be seen. They had been built by some king to protect his royal prerogatives, but eventually his dynasty had crumbled like the walls themselves.

My mind wandered around and about the follies and the foibles of man in general and my own people in particular. A carnage of killing and destruction had, at that particular time, engulfed the whole of Europe and the Far East. And in this barren stretch of the Middle Eastern land mass an outward calm prevailed that belied the tension of bare existence.

Outwardly my school was a great success. In order to bring the study load within manageable levels, it was divided into two categories–science and social studies. The subject matter was cut from sixteen to twelve in each department. Some subjects, such as English, methods of teaching and practical agriculture, all students participated in. I personally taught chemistry to the science students and a course in the philosophy of teaching to the social science group. Religious studies were abolished. There was enough money to expand sports and recreational facilities and to establish a well-stocked library.

Poor teachers were weeded out and replaced by new ones. Turkish teachers were unwilling either to work under the new, demanding situation or to leave the country voluntarily. I found them to be poorly prepared in their subjects. By holding them responsible to show progress in their classes, which they could not, they were forced to terminate their contracts.

Among the newly-hired teachers there were some remarkable individuals. Our agriculture expert and the psychology teacher, both newly-hired from India, were excellent. There were some domestic teachers who did outstanding work.

Memories of Afghanistan

One teacher I would like to remember in a special way. Bob Allen, who had previously taught English at Robert College in Istanbul, was at this time serving in the newly-opened American Embassy in Kabul. He was dissatisfied with his work and accepted my offer of a job as an English teacher. He not only did an outstanding teaching job but became one of our constant companions. Bob was a romantic idealist and dreamed of spending a good part of his life in the foothills of the Himalayas sitting on rocks, playing the cello and contemplating life in general.

A clause in the contract obliged the school to provide him with lodging. We rented a house for him which had a garden and six bedrooms, each painted a different color. Bob ignored the bedrooms and occupied the servant quarters which hung over the garden and offered a magnificent view of the mountains. He asked if I could also find him a housekeeper and a gardener. My uncle's image flashed in my mind for one of the jobs.

My uncle Abbas was about sixty-five years old. He no longer roamed around the countryside seeking warmer cities in winter and cooler ones in summer. Since my return to Afghanistan, he visited us once a month, one or two days after each payday. Once I found him in our kitchen having a lively conversation with Diljan. I patted him on the shoulder and slipped an envelope containing a few rupees in his lap.

"Kaka Jan, I found a job for you," I said.

"What kind of a job?" he asked gruffly.

"A very good and easy one. I don't like to see you live in the dirt and filth in the old city."

"The way I live is no concern of yours," he said stubbornly, without looking at me.

"He is only trying to help you because you are our uncle," my sister said.

"Be quiet. Since when are women allowed to interfere in the affairs of men?"

"Anyway, Mr. Allen, the American teacher, needs a housekeeper. You will have a good, clean place in which to live.

There Is Order in Chaos

The pay is generous and the work, well, there is hardly any work at all, just to watch the house and keep the strangers away."

"You suggest that your own uncle work for a farangi? I am surprised at you."

"Robert does not mind working under me in the school."

"I am not working for no Robert," he said, turning his head one side and spitting against the kitchen wall. He left the house abruptly without saying goodbye. He was at our house a month later for the handout. After we left the country, he carried on his meager existence into his mid-seventies without seeing a doctor or a dentist. One day my sister was informed that her uncle was dead. She found him curled up in the corner of a dark room in a caravansary. His only wish had been to be buried next to my father.

The social activities of the Teachers' Training School were channeled through the many clubs that were formed. Two of these clubs, in which I participated, produced far-reaching consequences which culminated in my escape from the country of my birth. One was the Debating Club and the other Justice.

The Debating Club met once a week. The procedure was to select one speaker (among competing students) a week in advance. The criteria for selection were originality and content. I had given the students a wide range of topics to be discussed provided name calling and personal attacks were not employed. As I remember, some of the topics were:

Critique of the Afghan Constitution
Causes of Backwardness in the Middle East
The Three Evils: Faith, Hope and Charity
What Is and What Is Not Constitutional Monarchy?
Why Not Teach History Rather Than Fairy Tales in School?
Race and Religious Discrimination in Afghanistan
Why Are Some Born Privileged?

Usually about thirty to forty-five minutes were devoted to the speaker and then questioning and general discussion took as much

Memories of Afghanistan

as two hours. I remember the day when the students almost forced me to the platform. I talked on the great historical changes since World War I. From that day on, routinely I spoke for about half an hour each week on such topics as the rise of fascism in Europe, the Russian and the Chinese revolutions, the decline of colonial empires and the twilight of absolute monarchy.

The Justice Club was my idea of introducing the judge and jury system to the school, familiarizing the student body with such concepts as prosecutor and defense, witnesses and proof of innocence or guilt. Since there was no legal system in the country, the students were pleasantly surprised at the rights of an accused person in other countries.

I remember a theft case. A student had lost money gambling and was accused of stealing money from someone in the boardinghouse. The accused consistently denied the charge. The case was tried one afternoon a week, each Thursday, for a full month. A witness was introduced by the "prosecutor" who had seen the accused searching in a box of clothing in a bedroom that was not his own. On that same day, he was alleged to have purchased two packs of cigarettes and again lost some money in a card game.

In the middle of the fourth session, the accused finally confessed his crime and offered to make full restitution and accept his punishment. Since corporal punishment was strictly forbidden in the school, the judge was in a quandary. He came to my office to discuss the matter.

"Well, sir, I talked the matter over with other students. We all feel that we actually don't have the authority to kick him out of school or even confine him in a separate room, which is really a form of corporal punishment," he said.

"I am afraid I can't be of any help to you," I said. "You are the judge. I cannot possibly interfere in this affair. The court has to come up with a fair decision."

There Is Order in Chaos

"I realize it is my responsibility and have come up with the only decision I can think of, but I am afraid it might be too severe," he said.

"May I ask what it is?"

"I am going to pass sentence that the accused find his own way to pay for his crime."

"I hope you aren't thinking of isolating him from all social contact."

"Of course not. That would be a cruel punishment. We are going to treat him as normally as in the past."

At first, the accused thought he had gotten away easily and that it was all a joke. But guilt started to gnaw at his conscience. In a week, he was in my office, asking for punishment.

"It is unfair. I would like to pay for my crime rather than live under a perpetual state of guilt. The nicer my friends are to me, the lousier I feel."

"What can I do about it?"

"You are the school director. Put a stop to it."

"How can I stop other students' attitudes toward you? Have they done anything to hurt you physically?"

"That's just it. I wish they would do that. Instead they are extra nice to me or at least that's how I feel. Please help me," he pleaded and started to cry. I promised to help him.

To resolve the problem, I held a series of meetings with the judge and other student leaders. I was anxious to avoid a suicide case in the school. The problem was finally solved at a mass meeting in the boardinghouse one evening. I spoke of poverty and how it compels people to cheat and accept bribes. I told the students how I had participated in stealing when I was a young boy. A few other confessions from student leaders followed. Then the young fellow in question joined us, the small circle of confessed thieves, and hundreds of students applauded loudly.

In the course of normal discussion one evening in the Justice Club, a student was accused of spying for the government. Next day a delegation of the club's membership came to my office.

Memories of Afghanistan

"Sir, we are facing a technical difficulty. We would like to discuss it with you before pursuing the matter further," Abdul Rauf, a student leader, declared.

"I am listening," I said.

"Can we expose and prosecute a spy?"

"Whaaat? Spying for whom?"

"For the Ministry of Education."

"Are you sure?"

"Quite certain, sir. We are still digging in for further details."

"I consider this a very serious matter. I would like you to give me all the information you have collected so far. Let me mull it over, talk to the student in question and then I'll tell you how to proceed. If this is true, I am sure it is not an isolated case. There must be others involved."

That phrase "many others involved" energized the club members into an intense search for spies in our school. The case snowballed into an unmanageable situation. The club members claimed:

- That they had found nine other student spies.
- That Abdul Rauf, the inspired student leader, was in fact a spy.
- That they were reporting directly to Ghulam Faruk in the Ministry of Education.

I confronted Abdul Rauf with the facts and figures in the case. It did not require any pressure before he confessed.

"But, Doctor Sahib, we were told that we would be performing a great service for our country."

"To put your buddies behind bars, to destroy their lives because they criticize a governmental mistake? Don't people in the government ever make mistakes?"

"I now see that I equated the welfare of our country with that of the government."

"How much were you paid?"

There Is Order in Chaos

"Forty-five rupees a month, sir,"

"How many students are involved?"

"At present, seventeen students, sir."

"At present?"

"When you took the job there were only four."

"Do you think we should prosecute each and every one of you?"

"The Ministry of Education knows that we were discovered and Ghulam Faruk himself told us not to worry about it."

"I see. How do you feel?"

"I feel ashamed of myself and I am willing to become a witness for the prosecutor."

"I believe you."

During the next two weeks, I held a private meeting with each one of the other sixteen accused student spies. Three said they would resign from their duty as spies if given a chance. Five admitted they did it for money because their families were poor. Six insisted that by serving the monarch they were, in fact, serving their country. One adamantly denied being a spy and one threatened me with dire consequences if I persisted in pursuing the matter any further. The last one was an interesting case, a remarkable fellow.

"Doctor Sahib, you do not seem to understand either your country or human nature. Your saccharine moral concepts make me sick. I am not serving these morons who are sucking this nation dry of substance, rather than keeping it healthy to provide power–power to use for good or evil."

"Like Hitler, I suppose?"

"Exactly. I come from a rather poor family like yourself and I shall use every conceivable trick, spying, cheating, lying and harming others who stand in my way, to get to the top. And if I die trying, the exercise will be worth it. I have one advantage that you lack. I am a Pushtun. So don't get in the way. Just do what you are hired for, teach us how to read and write."

Memories of Afghanistan

"Thanks for the advice. You may go now," I dismissed him.

I had a heated meeting with the members of the Justice Club, one that dragged on all afternoon. I told them that I had decided to discharge all the students in question, except Abdul Rauf, who would resign from his spying job. Most of the students accepted my decision except two who insisted that there should be a mass trial.

These two, Ghulam Jan and Ali Akber, were excellent students. They were rather awkward in sports, but there the similarity stopped. Ghulam was tall, talkative and outgoing. He came from a well-to-do Tajik family from the northern province of Mazar. He spent money lavishly and was very popular among the students. His outward flippancy and loud belly laughs were surface manifestations of an inner core of steel determination.

Ali Akber was shy and unassuming. His poor family of sharecroppers lived on the outskirts of Herat, where he went to school. He belonged to the minority sect of Shia Muslim. He seldom spoke in meetings. He was short of stature and had dark, sad eyes that turned attentively toward each speaker. He read many books and wrote poetry in his spare time, and at the age of twenty, was respected in the school as a leader.

Arguing with these two about the concept of justice and the art of compromise reminded me of my old religion teacher, Amir Khan, when I was even younger than they. I saw the same unshakable determination in their attitude to accept calmly whatever was inevitable.

"You keep saying that the truth must be pursued at any cost," I said, "but don't you see that the cards are stacked against you? If there were a remote chance of an equal fight, I would gladly join you. I am not a coward."

"Sorry, sir, I did not imply cowardice when I used the word 'cautious'," Ghulam Jan said.

"I was just thinking of a teacher of mine, Amir Khan, who would have gladly taken your side."

"What happened to him?" Ali Akber asked.

There Is Order in Chaos

"He was stoned to death."

"What was his crime?"

"Uncertainty. He taught religion, but would not accept any dogma on its face value. I had another teacher, a friend rather than a teacher, who cautioned me to protect myself at all cost because there are so few of us."

"What happened to him?"

"Haji Zaman was tortured, killed and forgotten. So what choice is available in this land whose unsung heroes are not even remembered?"

Both students graduated with honors a year later. Ghulam Jan became the director of the school system in Mazar. I never heard of him again. Ali Akber stayed in Kabul as a teacher. Many years later, a delegation of Afghan teachers studying the educational facilities in Iran met with me in Teheran. One of these teachers told me that Professor Ali Akber's only son had died a few months earlier at a student demonstration in Kabul against the oppressive system of monarchy.

While I was preparing the discharge papers for the sixteen student spies, I received a request from the American Legation asking for permission to send an observer to the next trial held in the Teachers' Training School. This request was politely rejected. A letter was sent to the Ministry of Education calling their attention to the fact that the school, of which I was a director, could not inculcate the ideals of a teacher in the mind of a youth who let himself be exploited as a spy. Therefore, all sixteen students listed on a separate sheet may not attend this institution.

I was mildly surprised that the ministry accepted my decision without protest.

Since spying for the government carried a stigma of the worst kind, I was deluged with requests by the families of these boys to reconsider my decision. These were sent to the Ministry of Education without comment.

One morning a fully uniformed colonel entered my office without formality.

Memories of Afghanistan

"Are you the boss here?" he asked, pointing his finger at me.

"No one is permitted in this office armed. Leave your revolver outside and then you may come in."

"I was sent here by General Omer Khan."

"I don't care who sent you here. Leave your revolver outside if you want to talk to me," I said.

He untied his revolver and passed it to one of the two school guards standing near the door.

"Now tell me what you want," I said.

"The general wants his son, Kasim, to be reinstated right away as a student in this school."

"Tell the general we do not accept spies as students here."

"How dare you talk about the general that way?" he asked, patting his empty revolver case.

"Obviously you were going to intimidate me with a weapon. Get out of this office. Your weapon will be returned to you through proper channels."

"I can't leave without my revolver."

"Then I'll have to throw you out."

"Please send the weapon to my home."

"All right. Out now." He scribbled his address on a piece paper and left it on my desk. I never heard of General Omer Khan again, but I did hear from a much more ominous source a while later.

Chapter 25
A Dream Collapsed

In the summer of 1943, a subdued mood of despair prevailed among the aristocracy of Kabul. The intense internal rivalry between the king, Zahir Shah, and his uncle, Hashim Khan, the prime minister, was a favorite topic of discussion in the tea shops. Here was the king, almost thirty years old and still confined to the royal palace performing only ceremonial functions. He was searching for a way to break out of his isolation. The only individuals permitted to have contact with him were his doctor and a painting companion. Dr. Zahir (no relation to the king) was a shrewd operator from Laghman, a province famous for its rogues. He was a graduate of Columbia University Medical School. As the king's personal physician, he saw to it that his distinguished patient constantly received a dose of politics along with his colored pills. These ideas incubated for some time in the dull cranium of His Highness before he was able to grasp the reins of power he was told were rightfully his. Dr. Zahir patiently waited until he, too, received his reward of the premiership of the country. But that happened long after I had escaped.

The king's painting companion was Khair Mohammed, a teacher in our school.

"Doctor Jan, the poor king is a pathetic, nervous wreck," he confided in me.

"Tell him the only thing that holds the house of cards together is the symbol of royalty that he carries," I suggested.

"But isn't it awful, Doctor Jan, that such a weak bastard carries this exalted symbol? I think Doctor Zahir must be feeding him more than medicine, because lately he has been mumbling disjointed phrases such as 'I'll show them the gate one day. Authority must flow from only one source–the king. Alexander, at my age, had half of Asia at his feet'."

"Do you think he will do it?" I asked.

Memories of Afghanistan

"I think so, Janim.* If his cousins, Daud and Naim, who are the supreme powers now, are toppled, and if you are chummy with one of them, you might be harmed."

"But I am just an innocent bystander," I protested.

"You are neither innocent nor a bystander. Look at the transformation of this school. No, sir, you are a menace and a threat to both camps. I wonder that you are still alive."

"Thanks for the compliment. And try to pick the winner."

The other event which was disturbing to the rich and powerful was that at this particular time Germany was in trouble. Cologne was a smoldering city and the Krupp Works in Essen had been blasted by a thousand planes.

I remember a conversation at the dining room table in the prime ministry. It was noon-time when I finished my discussion with Naim. Those present were Hashim Khan (the prime minister), Ali Mohammed Khan (minister of foreign affairs), Mirza Mohammed Khan (minister of finance), Ahmad Shah Khan (minister of court) and Latif Jan, a businessman and director of the construction and woodworking industries. The food was ample, varied and delicious.

"Anything new about the war?" Hashim asked, turning to his foreign minister.

"Well, sir, it looks bad everywhere. Japan got a punch in the face in the Battle of Midway. Rommel's Africa Corps was defeated at El Alamein."

"How could the Atlantic powers be so blind as to guarantee the success of Bolshevism over half of Europe and most of Asia?" Hashim asked, glowering at no one in particular.

I did not participate in the discussion, but inwardly felt a sense of joy at their pain of future foreboding. But all this bad news did not seem to dampen anyone's appetite. Hashim Khan hardly chewed his food. His chubby hand literally pushed the meat, vegetables, bread and all sorts of delicacies into his mouth to disappear downwards into his protruding barrel. Finally the dishes

---

* My dear.

A Dream Collapsed

were cleared and *firni** and cardamom tea were served. A relaxed mood prevailed. When everyone was picking at his teeth, burping, or noisily sipping tea, I noticed the minister of court stand up. All eyes turned toward him. He bent his head to one side and began to recite a humble eulogy to "our wise and resourceful father [not God]. He provides us with food while famine and starvation are so common around the world. He gives us peace while half the human race are killing one another. Where but in this land can one see justice? Where but..." When he finally sat down, I said, "Wazeer† Sahib, have you read today's paper?"

"No, Doctor Sahib, did I miss something?"

"I think so. If you had read it, you might have altered your speech. Last night alone, two people died of starvation in the city of Kabul. One was a child, a boy six years old."

The ominous calm that followed was finally broken by the prime minister, who lumbered up off his padded seat, threw his napkin on the table and wobbled out of the dining room as fast as he could manage. The rest of us filed out of the room in silence, one at a time. Near the gate, the director, Latif Jan, caught up with me.

"Can I give you a lift? My buggy is just outside," he said. I accepted his offer.

"Doctor Sahib, may I speak bluntly with you? We know each other only from a distance."

"Be as blunt as you want to be."

"You are like a person who takes pleasure from inflicting pain on himself. There is no Persian word for it, but there must be one in English."

"Masochists," I provided.

"Yes. Anyway, it gives me pleasure to tell you that you have a great many influential admirers. They like your style of work, your unusual and unorthodox methods and above all, your honesty. But

---

* A cream pudding.
† Minister.

Memories of Afghanistan

I must warn you that nothing will save you if you keep on hacking at the foundation of the monarchy."

"Are you referring to my comment on the speech of the minister of court?"

"Not at all. He is a fool and an unofficial court jester, even if he is the king's father-in-law. Your comment was pungent. It would have been ignored if it were not symptomatic of your total attitude toward those in power. You and I both come from very poor families. It took me almost twenty years to get where I am. In spite of the fact that you are from a religious minority sect, the Shia, you practically jumped from the gutter to the promised land in one swoop."

"Let me also be blunt," I answered. "Your promised land has no appeal for me, sir. My only aim in this country is to be of some help to the forgotten people who nursed you and me to manhood. The ones on top bore me to death."

"We are approaching your house. You would do me a great honor if you would let me drive you to my house so that we can finish this interesting conversation."

I agreed. Latif Jan's house was on the outskirts of Kabul, practically at the end of the wide dirt road to Darul Fonoon. This straight and pleasant road had been lined with beautiful tall poplars, with thick foliage and luscious flower gardens behind them when we first arrived from America. They were kept green by sprinkling water from the ditches on either side of the road. The people of Kabul often fled to this oasis on late afternoons to get away for a few hours from the noise and the odor of the old city. Those who could afford it would go by buggy to the end of the road and promenade around on the garden paths surrounding the imposing six-story buildings. Phyllis and I would also often mingle with the crowd of walkers on weekends. One day we found the trees had been chopped down and the bushes pulled up, exposing the well-kept houses behind them to public view.

Two theories were given for the destruction. One was that the prime minister was afraid of snipers hiding behind the bushes and

A Dream Collapsed

trees, since he had been shot at a number of times. The other theory was that since the road, gardens and buildings were originally built by Amanullah, the deposed beloved king, they had to be destroyed. This latter sounded more reasonable to me, because people did flock there in droves to dream and talk of their lost hopes and future despair.

"Here we are. You seemed to be deep in thought," Latif Jan said.

"Yes. Which theory do you believe in?" I asked, vocally continuing my thoughts.

"I am afraid I don't understand your point."

"This gloomy wasteland that once was lush and pleasant."

"Oh, that. I'd rather not talk about it," said the director. "My driveway is long and the house is still secluded and surrounded by nice plants. You'll see."

"You see, my dear director, you can enjoy life in your plush home even though it is surrounded by wasteland. I'd rather be a part of the wasteland."

The house was indeed magnificent, with its large red marble columns, hardwood floors, huge windows facing a well-kept garden and a large porch covered with a colorful canvas tent.

"Now, getting back to our topic of discussion," resumed Latif Jan, "this is not a bad country to live in when one learns to close one's eyes to repression and inequity..."

"And degradation and murder and torture, and... and... one has to close one's eyes permanently in order not to see the daily indignities heaped upon the helpless population," I interrupted emotionally.

"Doctor Sahib, if I were you, I would leave this land as soon as possible. With your ideals and emotional make-up, I am surprised that you are still alive."

The next few days passed as in a dream. One afternoon, I received a telephone call that Hashim Khan wanted to see me within two hours. Fear gripped and compressed my body, causing sweat to pour out of every pore. At that moment, I decided that I could no longer live in the land where I was born. I remembered a

Memories of Afghanistan

fragment of a conversation I had had with my father almost twelve years previously.

"Dad," I asked, "wasn't it a misfortune when your father left his tribe of Benua Khuza'a, near Mecca in Arabia, walking three thousand miles eastward, to settle finally in this Godforsaken land? Couldn't he have gone westward and found a better place?"

Father looked me in the eye and said, "Bachim, if he had done that, you wouldn't be here to ask this question. You are a restless boy. Who knows which direction you will travel?" It just happened that the land I finally adopted (America) was about the same distance away whether I traveled east or west.

Answering Hashim's phone call, I entered his chamber only to find him in a nasty mood. I removed my hat and stood in front of him. He was propped up on a square box with colored pillows. While he was marshaling his thoughts, his eyes were on me and his left hand was brushing his well-manicured goatee.

"Now what do you have to say for yourself?" he exploded.

"In what respect, sir?"

"What's that?"

"I said, in what respect?" I yelled. His wide open eyes looked at me with surprise.

"You have the nerve to ask that question. You have committed more possible crimes in two years than most persons manage in a lifetime. You teach communistic ideas to your students. You insult devoted servants of the realm. You question those in authority. Neither you nor your wife seem to obey the laws and the regulations of the country. And you have the nerve to ask for particulars."

"Let me answer them one at a time, sir."

"Don't raise your voice."

"I am sorry."

"What's that?"

"I said, I am sorry. Let us take the accusations one at a time."

"I don't care how you take them. There are enough to choke you."

A Dream Collapsed

"I have never taught communism to my students nor to anyone else. I have talked of democracy and freedom to them."

"They are all the same to me. Now you admit it yourself, that instead of inculcating the ideals of monarchy, you are advocating foreign ideologies?"

"But sir, I am staying strictly within the boundary of our own Constitution. It entitles every Afghan to be a free man."

"Yes, free to give his life for his nation and his king."

"And also free from unlawful arrest, from being spied upon and..."

"Stop," he interrupted. "I know all about your democratic court procedures in the school. It is subversive and must be stopped immediately. And who says we cannot have spies? Show me a country that doesn't have spies."

"In our constitutional monarchy..." I persisted.

"In what? Speak louder."

"In a constitutional monarchy, one is protec..."

"This is a constitutional *absolute* monarchy. Don't you ever forget that!"

"But..."

"There is no *but* in it. And if you don't stop contradicting me, I will call a soldier and order your head chopped off right where you are standing. Now get out of my sight. You may never set eyes on me again."

His last threat was a prophecy. I never saw him again because barely three months later, I was out of his slave land.

After that interview, I told Phyllis what had transpired in those last few decisive days of my life.

"I also have something to tell you," Phyl said.

"If it's bad news, tell it to me later."

"Depending on how you take it, it could be either good or bad news."

"OK, my mysterious darling, tell me."

"I am pregnant."

"What?"

Memories of Afghanistan

"Yes, the doctor says it is definite." "Then," I said, "I might just as well tell you the rest of the story."

"Is there more to tell?"

"Yes. After I received the prime minister's message that he wanted to see me, I broke into a profuse perspiration out of pure animal fear. I have never before experienced this feeling and I hope never to again. I resolved then and there to leave Afghanistan for good. I hope this pregnancy won't put a crimp on it."

"I told the doctor to keep it secret."

"Good, because, do you know that if the baby is born here, they can legally keep him? We have just a few short months to get the hell out of here."

Chapter 26
A Message from Rahman

Rahman was the head of the only psychiatric center in the city of Kabul when I returned from America in 1941. This was a sad year for mankind. Fascism was triumphantly radiating in Central and South Europe and had been burning the very ground in North China. Meanwhile, Afghanistan was dozing in a state of torpor, trying to forget the pains of living.

In the squalid bazaars, a few third-rate spies representing various nationalities could be easily spotted, because they were dying to be recognized as such even if they had to imitate the heroes of the latest third-rate spy thrillers. The newly-arrived staff of the American Embassy collected their fresh load of gossip through their Afghan cook and sent it in diplomatic pouches to Washington as recent crucial developments in that part of the world. The male members of the Afghan royal family enjoyed their shindigs behind the brick walls of the British Legation, rubbing shoulders with His Majesty's civil servants. They washed down the lamb kebabs with gin and lime after a spirited game of tennis.

"I think you chaps should make a deal with Hitler so that he can turn his full attention toward the menace in Russia," our rather hefty prime minister, Hashim Khan, said to His Excellency, the British Ambassador, who deftly sidestepped the issue with a broad smile, saying, "Your Majesty is a shrewd observer of contemporary events."

In the inner city where dark and narrow alleyways were hugged by cracked muddy walls, lived, nay crawled, thousands of little urchins with raw eyelids and runny noses, half-naked and barefoot, always barefoot, gambling, stealing, cursing and trying to put something, anything, in their protruded bellies. Rahman and I once lived among these outcasts. How we managed to be counted among the very few who succeeded in living long enough

Memories of Afghanistan

to get educated and finally understand the causes of our misery has been covered elsewhere.

It was but a little walk from the school where I was the principal up the slope of a dusty road to the tree-lined path leading to Dr. Rahman's sanitarium. The 150-odd patients covered practically the whole range of mental disturbances. Walking into his office one late afternoon, I found Rahman with his feet propped up on the corner of his desk and his head resting on the palms of his massive hands. He greeted me with his usual "What has one to do, Doc?"

Turning his head slightly toward the large window overlooking the garden below, he stretched his left hand and mumbled more or less to himself, "The lucky bastard. Do you see that man gesturing with his hands and carrying on a monologue?" Without waiting for me to respond, he proceeded: "He was a teacher only three months ago. He has a wife, a young son, and a large debt. From what I have been told, he also possessed a conscience and was a good teacher. Doc, take the road he did and I will take good care of you here. You have been back from America for almost two years and I assume that by now the hopelessness of the situation must be quite evident. You see, you can go back to the life you left behind. You are married to a beautiful American girl. As for me, I am riddled with a disease far more serious than those of my patients in this nut house–the disease of hate. The morons who rule over this land will not come to terms either with us or with themselves. The tragedy of our country is compounded by the inferiority of its ruling class."

"But if they are as stupid as you claim, couldn't we use them and channel their energy towards productive plans?" I chimed in.

"No. You and I and the likes of us are a threat to their existence. Besides, there are plenty of intelligent people who are willing, for one reason or another, to serve them devotedly. Look at some of your own friends who were educated in foreign countries. By the way, I want you to come a little earlier tomorrow. I have a surprise for you."

A Message from Rahman

Entering the office the next day I noticed another man, a chubby patient with protruding brown eyes and bare feet, sitting next to Rahman. He was introduced to me as the Son of Babrak. I found him somewhat reserved but quite intelligent.

Rahman said, "Pay no attention to his clothes or his bare feet. Last year in a fit of anger he killed the son of a tribal chief. But Babrak himself, being a general in the army, interceded to save his only son from being hanged. So they declared him insane for the time being and sent him here. You see, he himself is a major general."

"What is the mystery of the bare feet?" I wanted to know.

"My father," said the general, "was a tough man and he proved it by living and leaving a legacy among the tribes of the frontier. To prove his physical stamina he vowed when he was a young man not to cover his bare skin against the rocky terrain. I carried on the tradition at first to please my father, but later on to expiate for the sin of my countrymen who serve British imperialism."

I was not convinced, and I steered the discussion away from political to social and educational matters. But unfortunately Rahman could not be stopped. "One tribal chief after another was trained by the British in India and foisted on our poor country as their ruler-agent. Even in the Afghan wars the spearhead of the British army was always one or another of the frontier tribes. They were defeated twice by soldiers gathered in the west or north of the country."

The Son of Babrak excused himself abruptly. I squirmed uneasily in my chair, but Rahman was evidently not at all disturbed. I cautioned him once again concerning the uselessness and danger of loose talk, but he abruptly cut me off. "You pursue your education and I shall follow my instinct and attack the problem my way. You are at the end of your rope but you hate to admit it. With Pushtu as the official language, you can't even talk to your own students let alone educate them."

I saw Rahman twice more before I left Afghanistan, once six weeks after his arrest and again a month later.

Memories of Afghanistan

After many days of inquiring, I located the prison where he was kept. It was not very far from my school. The prison was an unimposing structure, an ordinary mud-walled enclosure with four small watch towers where passers-by could see a couple of soldiers dozing off in the bright hot sun of Kabul. Through my contact with the chief of police, I was able to see Dr. Rahman in an isolated cage in the "first tier" in a damp cabin illuminated by a small electric lamp dangling from the ceiling by a thin cord. He had lost a lot of weight; his massive frame had shrunk, leaving large bones hanging awkwardly. The large beautiful eyes looked larger than ever. A tangled long beard covered his ears, mouth and neck. I foolishly asked him how he was.

"What has one to do. Doc?"

"You look pale," I said.

"The sunshine is for the hard criminals who live on the ground floor. All the politicos live in the first and second 'tiers,' the two underground facilities." His voice was discordant and rough, and in spite of a large blanket wrapped around him, he seemed to shiver periodically.

I asked the guard who was watching us if smoking was allowed. He nodded his head. I lit two cigarettes simultaneously and passed one along with the half-full pack to Rahman through the metal bars. He raised his hand to show the guard the pack. The guard ambled close to the cage, took the pack away, fingered it, and put it in his pocket.

He turned to me and said, "Anything you want to give to the prisoner, you must leave in the office, upstairs. That is the rule." He walked back to his seat.

"Don't bother. I will never see it," whispered Rahman.

Four weeks later, I saw the ghost of the man I knew, sitting on the same stool in the center of this cage. He did not respond to me at all. He was rigid, and he looked through my right shoulder at the semi-dark wall behind me. I spent my allotted time staring at him hoping to elicit a response of some kind after I failed to make him talk. When I got up to say goodbye, I noticed two droplets of

A Message from Rahman

tears rolling down his cheeks, getting entangled in fluffy white hairs on both sides of his mouth. For the first time, I realized that during the short interval since I'd seen him last, a good part of his hair had turned white.

Two years later, in America, when Dr. Rahman's image had become a dim painful memory, I received a letter from India. Opening the envelope, I found two pieces of paper–one yellow, written with ink covering about two-thirds of one page with no greeting or signature; the other was a piece of paper with blue parallel lines, torn from a notebook, written on both sides with no date or signature, but starting with the word, "Doc." I am going to jot them down verbatim:

> I was a guard at the prison you used to visit. I knew Dr. Abdul Rahman Khan very well. He was kind to my sick brother and helpful to his poor family. He gave me the piece of paper I have mailed you and another with your name but no address. It took a long time to find your address in America. The dear doctor had instructed me to send the letter to you if I could. I gave some money to a truck driver to mail the letter from India. Please do not try to find me. Our friend, and many other brave young men, are dead or dying every day. I am only thankful to Almighty God that our friend's mother did not see him alive before she was told to collect and carry his remains in a sack at night.

> Doc. My eyes are beginning to fail me recently. Ah, the bastards have perfected the art of inflicting pain. But let me tell you something about the environment in which we survive, the 60-odd political prisoners. We are segregated from all the other types of prisoners who inhabit the ground floor. There are two layers of underground structures where the light of the sun never shines. There is a central hall on the upper floor surrounded by a corridor about six feet wide. A staircase directly connects this to the ground floor which serves both as entrance and exit. On the opposite side, a door opens into the central hall connecting it to the inmates' quarters and also blocking the corridor from either side. The inside wall of the corridor is dotted with one-way glass covered from the inside with a heavy steel screen. The reason I am explaining this in great detail is that

Memories of Afghanistan

here in this hall, all the atrocities a human mind can conceive are practiced on the political prisoners, while the sadistic officials, informers, members of the secret police and occasionally a minister or a member of royalty stand behind the glass partitions and watch the show without being seen by the prisoners.

The total number of our co-conspirators stays remarkably constant. A while back (time has no relevance here) a typhus patient was brought in and his body lice exposed to us in various ingenious ways. Twenty-six cases of typhus developed among us causing nine deaths. Replacements were prompt. Among the newcomers for the first time we encountered six high-school students, ages 17 to 19. They were assaulted and raped on the ground floor and then brought here after going through the process of "acclimation." One of the six lived only a few days, cause of death unknown.

Oh yes, I must not forget to tell you about the plushly decorated confession room, where the head of the Secret Service or one of his two famous assistants would hold a bi-weekly session with one or two of the politicos, as they call us. I was ushered before the chief himself shortly after your first visit. The sunlight was painful to my eyes when I entered the room.

"Ah, Doctor Sahib," singsonged a tall man in military uniform, a good imitation of a German Gestapo. He goose-stepped to the window and pulled the shade down. "Now that's better, isn't it?"

I did not answer. He took my arm and directed me to a soft chair. The short-legged table in front of us was covered with dishes of fruits and nuts. At his insistence, I gingerly played with an apple.

He was polite and helpful in conducting me through a delicious meal, and for two hours, he avoided talking about the matter that was urgently pressing in our minds. Finally, he dismissed the soldier who was serving us and, with the cup of tea poised in midair, he said, "See that sign on my desk? It is as simple as that."

I strained my eyes to read the bold letters:

CONFESSION
REPENTANCE
FREEDOM

I confessed, "I have been an outspoken critic of our government, sir, and you already have that information. I shall do my best to be constructive in the future."

A Message from Rahman

"That is an excellent start," he continued. "Now, if you just give us the names..."

"I have no names!" I snapped.

"Be reasonable."

"I have no names."

"Please."

"No names."

He abruptly walked to the door and called the guard to take me back to my cell.

"We shall have another chat when you are more reasonable," he snapped.

Shortly after this incident, I was one of the three prisoners conducted to the Central Hall. I am going to spare you the gory details, but when we were carried away from that hall, each of us left behind an inch-and-a-half of our tongues, which were neatly arranged on a piece of paper on the edge of the walnut table. Now you know why I could not answer your questions during your last visit. I am so tired. What has one to do, Doc?

Chapter 27
Escape

"Your shadow is already down there leaning against his bike," Phyl said.

"In this snappy cold weather? I feel sorry for the poor fellow."

"He is wearing a heavy *posteen*.* With the collar turned up, he looks like a wounded bear," said Phyllis, still looking out of the window of our living room. I joined her. The Nijat School, like all the other schools, was closed for the winter. The gray day and the desolate road out there reflected the mood of the time.

For the last two weeks, our house had been under constant surveillance. The prime minister was anxious to put me behind bars as soon as possible, I was told.

Four years back, while working on my research project at Johns Hopkins University in Baltimore, I had been the victim of an explosion which finally blinded me in one eye. For the last few weeks, the damaged eye had begun to ache and water constantly. I was warned by two eye specialists that I must receive treatment as soon as possible in India or Europe. No facilities were available in Kabul. Sympathetic reaction could set in, causing complete blindness. This tragic incident provided me with an excuse to leave the country for "a short time." Naim Khan gave me written permission for medical treatment in India.

Not to cause any undue suspicion, I had to leave Phyllis behind as a "hostage." I was sure she could leave the country even though the Afghans considered her one of their citizens. She carried an up-to-date passport and the American legation would surely help her. However, knowing the mental pattern of the rulers of my land, I made sure that my wife did not become the victim of national or international irregularities. Afghan law considered her an Afghan citizen by marriage. It would be dissolved legally by mail. Divorce by remote control, from India!

---
* Lambskin coat.

Escape

"Aren't you ashamed of yourself adopting their savage ways?" Phyllis asked.

"Not adopting, my dear, but employing. All means are justified for the attainment of a just end."

The last three months of 1943 was the saddest period of our lives. My physical and mental anxieties and Phyl's pregnancy and the thought of an uncertain future were oppressing us to the limit of our endurance. Yet we had to put on a false appearance of cheerfulness which was puzzling to the rest of our family, who were unaware of our inner tensions and thoughts.

One day Phyllis entered the living room and picked up Faruk, who by then was almost five years old, and kissed him exuberantly. "I'll miss you very much," she said in English.

"You know what, Phyllis Jan?" he asked in Persian.

"What? Tell me."

"When I grow up big like my uncle, I will marry you."

"And I will wait for you as long as you want me to."

"*O bepadar*,* you told me the same thing. How many wives do you want?" asked his mother.

"Two," said Faruk, raising up two fingers.

Leaving our children at home and at school at the mercy of elemental forces beyond their grasp was one of the bitterest thoughts we carried with us to America. Children the world over, wherever love, care and food are denied them, are more than a mere loss. Their fragile bodies and minds are bent and distorted beyond repair. We resolved to save as many as possible. Eventually all of my sister Diljan's five sons and four grandchildren were rescued. Only America could provide the means to make this possible. Faruk found out, when he grew up "even bigger than his uncle" that he was unable to marry Phyllis Jan. But he did marry a lovely girl most remarkably similar to the woman he had known in Kabul more than thirty years earlier.

The third week of December, 1943 was morbidly depressing. Dark clouds, chilly winds, a lack of fuel and the rising cost of food

---

* Fatherless one.

Memories of Afghanistan

were telling on the scantily dressed, half-starved population. The only bright spot for us in this gloomy tableau was the war news. The end of fascism was in sight.

The American legation was decorated for the Christmas holidays. We were invited to a party there, but I could not tell them that I would be unable to attend. My passport with a four-month visa to India had been received. A friend in the Ministry of Post arranged for me to travel by mail truck to India within three days.

In the next two days, I visited two locations which confused the poor spy who followed me. The first was the tomb of Babur (Zahiruddin Mohammed), a descendant of Timor Lane. He had entered Kabul at the beginning of the 16th Century. Although he eventually conquered most of northern India, defeating the Pathan emperor of Delhi, he always came back to the cool climate of the foothills of the Hindu Kush, where he wrote poetic anecdotes on the beauties of animals and plants. The Mogul dynasty that he founded produced some of the greatest emperors India had ever known. But Babur died in his favorite land of the mountains, where he was buried in a garden only a couple of miles from our house.

There I leaned against the tomb's marble column for almost an hour watching the piths and knobs of the huge birch and mulberry trees. These trees looked to me as if they had been standing there when Babur was still alive, more than four hundred years ago.

The little soldier who had followed me was huddled in his lamb coat next to a low bush facing away from me. I walked up to him and tapped his shoulder. He jerked his body in a sudden motion facing me.

"It's time to go. I am sorry I disturbed your dream."

"Doctor Sahib, I am sorry to do this to you," he said, extending his hand palm up and grinning. "I have no choice," he said.

"Could you end today's report by adding: 'The pygmies are trampling the land that giants used to tread upon'?"

"What does it mean?" he said.

Escape

"They will know," I said, walking away from him.

The next day he followed me to Bala Hissar, where my family graves were scattered in the silty soil on a ridge dominating a swamp where the royalty used to go duck hunting when I was a young boy. We walked at a slow pace dodging pedestrians until we were out of town. He followed me, pushing his bicycle about fifty feet away. Near the graveyard, he caught up with me.

"Doctor Sahib, you are not a cooperative person. You have made me fail in my duty as a spy."

"How can I do something wrong when you have been obviously behind me every step of the way these past two weeks?"

"I have been following you for six weeks now, not two. After a month of useless search, I surfaced to find out something about you from your own lips."

"I am sorry I have been such a disappointment to you," I said, busying myself with repairing my father's grave. Those of my mother and her children scattered around her had been flattened and mostly washed away into the gully down the slope, where human bones of every size and shape were bleached white by the intense light of the sun. My companion, whose name I didn't care to know, busied himself with oiling the joints in his bicycle.

Early next morning I walked out of our house and boarded the mail truck, carrying a valise packed with undergarments and socks, four hundred Indian rupees and a toothbrush. I drew a sigh of relief when we crossed the border. Next morning, I sent Phyllis a telegram telling her of my safe arrival.

As planned, she immediately asked the American legation for permission for her to leave Afghanistan.

A few days later, I located a mullah in a mosque who spoke English of a sort. I told him that I was a Muslim and wanted to divorce my wife. He looked at me suspiciously from head to toe, leather jacket and all.

"You a Musulman?" he asked, pointing at me with his finger.

"Here is my passport. Look for yourself." He put on his glasses and held the passport away at arms length. "Mohammad

275

Memories of Afghanistan

Anwar," he mumbled to himself. "Pathan?" he asked, raising his head. I nodded.

"Where is wife?"

"In Kabul; she is a farangi from America."

"Difficult matter. A very difficult matter."

I realized that we had arrived at the crucial bargaining point. I pulled a ten-rupee note from my pocket.

"Would that cover your customary charges?" I asked. He took the note from me, looked at it and said, "No, my charge is fifteen rupees, and five for another witness." He folded the bills carefully before stuffing them into a small purse. When he fetched his assistant as a second witness, I showed him the "document" which I had already prepared in the hotel. A sheet of paper containing the sentence: "I, Mohammad Anwar, divorce you, Phyllis Anwar," repeated three times. The mullah not only signed the "document" but took out his seal from a side pocket, rubbed ink on it, and pressed it next to his signature.

I sent the divorce "document" to Phyllis and boarded a train to Lahore where we were supposed to meet at a friend's house. More to calm my nerves than to kill time, I read Galsworthy's *Forsyte Saga*, and most of Gibbon's *Decline and Fall of the Roman Empire*.

I was quite agitated when New Year's Day passed with still no news of my wife. She finally arrived on the eleventh day of January, 1944, in a buggy. We hugged each other in the courtyard of a small Indian house for a long time, while the driver waited patiently for his fare.

"What happened? Why did it take so long?"

"The Afghans wouldn't give me a visa and the American ambassador was unwilling to help."

"But why? Wasn't it his duty and obligation to help you?"

"Yes, but he said that since it is a newly-established legation, he didn't want to get entangled with the internal problems of the country."

"So you were the sacrificial lamb for his peace of mind. Then what happened?"

Escape

"Your divorce 'document' certainly did the trick. After everyone told me it was hopeless till you came back, I personally went to the Foreign Office with that sheet of paper. They consulted with one another for a whole day. The next day I had my permission to leave the country. The American ambassador told me that the divorce was illegal and that I must apply for a legal one in America as soon as possible. I just smiled at him."

"Well, I am glad we are together again," I said.

"Hammad, can we see the Taj Mahal at Agra before going home?"

There we were, one pregnant and the other without a valid visa to America, thrown into the turmoil of wars and revolutions, practically destitute and facing an uncertain future, still unwilling to miss seeing a work of art.

It was magnificent.

Afterward

By Keith Anwar

Capitulation, imprisonment or flight from his native country–these were the options facing Mohammad Haider Anwar at the end of 1943. He might well have risked imprisonment had he not been responsible for the welfare of his wife and their first child, as yet unborn. But accommodation to the regime, the eventual path of most of the idealistic students who returned to Afghanistan in the '30s and '40s, was out of the question. An inability to bend his principles, a compulsion to speak out when silence was prudent and a disdain for conformity all were etched into my father's character at an early age and stayed with him to the end of his life.

My father's world-view took shape around the age of 15, after the fall of the reform-minded king, Amanullah, and the twice-fold pillaging of Kabul, first by the ultra-reactionary forces of Bacha-i-Saqao and then by the city's "liberators" under Nadir Khan. The author tells how he happened upon a treasure of looted "infidel" books, including *Jean-Christophe,* the monumental novel of French radical Romain Rolland. To Rolland, "the great men are the men of absolute truth," he read in Gilbert Cannan's preface. "Jean-Christophe must have the truth and tell the truth, at all costs... It is his law." This code of integrity was a lifeline for a youth beset on all sides by corruption and treachery.

Soon afterwards he devoured the works of Tom Paine, the pamphleteer of the American Revolution. Paine's acidly anti-clerical *The Age of Reason* must have had a profound effect on one who had seen his own religion teacher buried under a shower of stones. The Enlightenment ideas that Paine popularized in this and other works engendered hope in the boy for an Afghanistan freed from religious fundamentalism and tribal backwardness. It was in this period that my father became a staunch atheist and an opponent of monarchical rule.

Afterward

Around this same time Mohammad found himself required to choose a surname, since, like most Afghans, he had been born without one. Instead of taking a name from his ethnic or family roots, as tradition would have suggested, he selected *anwar* (brighter, more luminous), a word implying the light of knowledge and truth. It was an apt surname for someone who felt himself surrounded by obscurantism and ignorance. Indeed, throughout his life my father was to value education far above material wealth, repeating time and again that knowledge was the one possession no one could take away.

In 1933 Mohammad Anwar was sent to the United States to study education in preparation for a career in Afghanistan's Ministry of Education. While attending Columbia University in New York he began to visit friends at a boarding house on Riverside Drive, where political and philosophical discussions would rage over the dining room table. It was here, in 1936, that he met 17-year-old Phyllis Davidson, the landlady's daughter, who was a student at Hunter College. Friendship gave way to courtship as Anwar completed his master's degree in education. The relationship continued after he moved to Baltimore to pursue his real interest–science–at Johns Hopkins, where he hoped to become a physician. In 1939 Phyllis and Hammad, as his friends called him, were married. By the time Anwar's scholarship money ran out two years later he had managed to earn a doctorate of science.

The "land of opportunity" must have had a powerful allure for a young man bred in the filthy alleys of Kabul, especially one who was being offered a promising and well-rewarded career in private industry by the time he received his doctorate. But Depression Era America taught Anwar a few lessons about the limitations of capitalist democracy as well, from the Scottsboro Boys and lynch mob justice in the South to the industrial war against the unions in the North. Angered when the so-called democratic countries refused to back the Republic in the Spanish Civil War, he tried to join the Abraham Lincoln Brigade so he could go to Spain and

Memories of Afghanistan

fight, but he was barred by his status as a foreign student. At their respective campuses the young couple came into contact with the Communist Party. While Phyllis became an activist in the Young Communist League at Hunter, Hammad remained on the party's periphery, sympathetic but skeptical.

Like many students from Asia at that time, Hammad was impressed by the social and industrial advances the Russian Revolution had brought to Central Asia, which only one generation earlier had been on a par with Afghanistan. And he shared many of the CP's values; some, like an uncompromising stand for women's rights, were progressive, while others–the Stalinist dogma that homosexuality was a pathology, for example–were not. But he decided that dialectical materialism was a sham and rejected the Marxism the CP claimed to uphold. Though he would find himself like all opponents of the Afghan monarchy branded a Communist, Hammad's politics would best be described as left nationalist.

But Afghanistan had never been, and still wasn't, a nation. It was a calico conglomeration of ethnic peoples topped by a feudal monarchy clinging to power through the conjoined policies of severe isolationism and decentralization. Hashim Khan, who as prime minister ruled in the name of his nephew Zahir Shah, sedulously curried the toleration of the khans and mullahs, particularly among the dominant Pushtuns, by excluding foreign influences, reining in modernization and acceding to tribal prerogatives at the local level. The *ulema** enforced Koranic law throughout the country. During this period, young men who returned to Afghanistan from their studies abroad armed with notions of forging a unified republic to lead Afghanistan into the modern world ran up against a mud wall of resistance.

My parents entered Afghanistan just as world events were undermining Hashim's already unstable regime. The German invasion of the Soviet Union in June, 1941 had brought simultaneous pressure on Afghanistan–from the Soviets to the north and from British-occupied India to the south–to sever relations that had

* Islamic clergy.

Afterward

developed in previous years with the Axis powers. Kabul itself was a cockpit of intrigue, swarming with foreign and government spies. Hashim responded to these diplomatic difficulties by cracking down on his own population. Under such conditions, the modernizing aspirations of independent-minded civil servants courted pitiless repression.

Central to the tribalism and Islamic fundamentalism perpetuated by Hashim's policies was the role of women–as chattel. A woman was not just a valuable slave forced to perform the drudgery of household work as well as tend fields and raise livestock, she was a commodity to be traded–to pay off a blood debt, to raise a clan's social standing or to cement a tribal alliance. The irreplaceable guarantee of a woman's worth was her "virtue," enforced through rigid seclusion (*purdah*) and veiling. In Kabul at that time, all female Afghans, including the Western wives of Afghan men, appeared in public only under the tent-like chaderi. "The day I arrived in Kabul," my mother recounted in 1980, "there was a demonstration in front of the palace by the mullahs. They had gathered to protest the fact that the rich ladies were making their veils out of silk and that was sort of revealing when the wind blew. And anyhow women's ankles showed and the men standing on the corner could tell whether they were young or old or rich or poor."

In the midst of this atmosphere of fundamentalist reaction, Phyllis' decision–with Hammad's encouragement–not to wear the chaderi was indeed courageous. By year's end two other foreign women married to Afghans had shed their veils, but they apparently relented under pressure in short order. Phyllis was undaunted. "People here hold their breath at our daring," she wrote home in early 1943. "Firstly–no veil. I hope you realize how deliciously revolutionary that is here. First time in History. Second–I go to the movies!!! Thirdly–I go swimming!!!! And now–a bicycle. At each step they've said, 'You can't get away with it.' Then after several months they adjust, so I guess they will again, this time." But in Hashim's eyes such behavior was an intolerable attack on one of the pillars of his rule–the enslavement of women.

Memories of Afghanistan

In late 1943 Hammad was summoned before the prime minister and ordered to veil his wife. Like Jean-Christophe before his own Grand Duke, Anwar stood his ground; it was a simple matter of being true to himself. But where his fictional hero faced ostracism, the consequences looming over Anwar were potentially fatal. He came away from the encounter shaken and doubtful about the prospect of internal reform in so refractory a society. A letter he wrote to the Davidsons in New York around this time was infused with a sense of futility:

> "Our second year stay in Kabul, which so remarkably coincides with the second year anniversary of the treacherous fascist onslaught on the U.S.S.R., passed very calmly. While the liberty-loving people [have] sacrificed everything to preserve their way of life, we, Phyl and I, were thrown by the hand of fate into this remote corner of oblivion and darkness. We wanted so badly to play our little part in this great world drama. Day after day we hear of misery and oppression that are destituting the human race and day after day our hearts are torn by the morbid thoughts of our uselessness...."

As 1943 drew to a close, my father found his every step being dogged by government spies; arrest was imminent. He devised a means of escape via British India under the guise of medical necessity, but getting his wife out proved more difficult. The Islamic divorce Hammad and Phyllis turned to as a means of freeing her to travel on her American passport had the unintended outcome of casting her into social limbo. The government still considered her an Afghan citizen. Under Islamic custom a divorced woman must return to her own family, but Phyllis lacked that option. And the newly-opened American consulate did not want to make any waves in her behalf. So she was adrift and unprotected in a land of ubiquitous and institutionalized misogyny. It took a strong will and a lot of nerve to get through those desperate weeks and finally pry a visa out of the authorities.

Afterward

My parents' flight from Afghanistan was the beginning of a new life for Dad. It wasn't easy. Their first son, who was named after Robert Allen[*] and called Butch, was born with severe cerebral palsy soon after they reached America. Denounced as a Communist by the Afghan embassy in Washington, my father was the subject of FBI investigations for several years. Even after he managed to become a naturalized U.S. citizen, there were reminders of his precarious status, like anti-communist slogans scrawled on our windows or the charred remains of a three-foot cross we found on the front lawn one morning. Nevertheless he built a successful career as the top biochemist of a huge international soft drink corporation. In the 1960s he patented an inexpensive soy-based drink he hoped would aid the fight against malnutrition in the Third World, only to see it shelved by his employers as an unprofitable flight of fancy. Such frustrations led to his early retirement in 1973, when he began to write his memoirs.

He had completed this work and was seeking a publisher when the so-called "Saur Revolution" in April 1978 overthrew the last of the Musahiban rulers, Daud Khan. "Dad is entranced with the Afghan 'revolution'," my mother wrote to me. "To him having ethnic representation and a woman in the cabinet makes it a true-blue Marxist revolution. So he wants to go there and offer his services." Heading the new regime was the People's Democratic Party of Afghanistan, comprised of left-leaning intellectuals, some of whom had served in the Daud administration, and Soviet-trained military officers. Though these elements were clearly attracted to the Soviet Union, under which their Central Asian neighbors to the north had enjoyed a standard of living and cultural level far above those pertaining to Afghanistan, they were not in any way "Communist." Nor were they Soviet puppets. Their ideas of modernization were heavily weighted with the backwardness of Afghan society: throughout its existence the PDPA was riven

---

[*] See Chapter 24. Allen later became a professor at Columbia University's Teachers' College, authoring *English Grammars and English Grammar* and other books on linguistics.

Memories of Afghanistan

by bloody factional warfare that had as much to do with ethnic animosities as political principles.

Yet, for the first time in its history the country was ruled by a regime proclaiming women's equality and taking measures to bring it about. From the standpoint of the tribal leaders and mullahs, it was bad enough that the regime freed women from the chaderi, recognized their right to divorce and set a limit on the bride price. But the law mandating universal education–including little girls!–was intolerable. Tribal khans immediately saw the threat the PDPA reforms posed to their power and, spurred on by village mullahs, struck back with ferocity, burning down hundreds of schools and assassinating teachers, in some cases by flaying them alive. Thus began the world's first civil war to be fought in the main over the question of women's rights.

Among its other reforms, the government decreed equal rights for all ethnic groups in Afghanistan and ordered a redistribution of land. While the latter decree benefitted the vast majority of dust-poor peasants, the regime had no means to implement it in the far-flung villages and isolated valleys of Afghanistan. Nor were the poorest peasants themselves–often in debt peonage, totally dependent on the khans for seeds and irrigation, and in thrall to the mullahs–in any position to claim their due through collective action. This was a country, in fact, that had never experienced a single agrarian revolt of any size by oppressed peasants. In many places where the government did attempt to enforce the land reform measure, the results were calamitous, both for the representatives of the regime sent into the countryside and for the peasants who followed their lead. The PDPA's reforms, minimal as they were, overreached the social forces available in the country to implement and enforce them.

Yet the localized tribal revolts mounting against the PDPA would never have developed into a nationwide Islamic *jihad* without nourishment from the West. Today, after the criminal and horrific World Trade Center attack, the persecution of Muslims has become as American as apple pie. But before 9/11 all American

Afterward

administrations–Republican and Democratic alike–had encouraged Muslim reaction as a weapon against "godless Communism." John Foster Dulles' Cold War manual *War or Peace* (1950) articulated that policy: "The religions of the East are deeply rooted and have many precious values. Their spiritual beliefs cannot be reconciled with Communist atheism and materialism. That creates a common bond between us, and our task is to find it and develop it." In Afghanistan they developed that bond to the tune of over $1 billion a year, doled out–in the biggest CIA operation in history–to a rogue's gallery of Pakistan-based *mujahedeen*, or holy warriors. Among the principal recipients of this largesse was one Osama bin Laden.

As the CIA-armed opposition grew, internecine fighting broke out between the party's Khalq (Masses) and Parcham (Banner) factions, which left many party members exiled, jailed or dead. Around this time my father met Hafizullah Amin, second in command in Kabul behind Nur Mohammed Taraki (and, like Dad, a former principal of the Teachers' Training School in Kabul), at a reception in New York City and asked him for help entering Afghanistan. But his visa request remained dormant–which was probably fortunate, as Amin was too busy eliminating PDPA rivals and conspiring against Taraki to have tolerated a troublesome iconoclast from the U.S. By 1979 the PDPA regime's military was disintegrating, with army commanders defecting to the opposition in the western city of Herat and in Kunar province on the Pakistani border. In September Amin assassinated Taraki and seized power.

The government was on the brink of collapse when the Soviet Union decided to intervene to prevent the formation of a virulently fundamentalist Islamic regime, backed by the West, on its southern flank. In the last week of 1979 the Soviet Union moved the Red Army into Kabul, executed Amin and installed a new PDPA government led by Babrak Karmal. This intervention not only averted a mujahedeen takeover; it created the possibility that Afghanistan would be incorporated into the centralized and planned economic system of the Soviet state, much like the Central

Memories of Afghanistan

Asian republics to the north. I remember showing my father a copy of the Trotskyist newspaper *Workers Vanguard* and asking him what he thought about the headline: "Hail Red Army!" Smiling sheepishly, he said, "Pretty good." He knew that only the Soviet presence had prevented a mujahedeen bloodbath. However, like many Afghan nationalists he still harbored the vision of a self-sufficient, modernizing Afghanistan. Events had already stamped this perspective as utopian.

The following March, at a public forum commemorating International Women's Day at Harvard University, Phyllis Anwar gave a speech in which she recalled the desperation of her female relatives in Kabul: "[O]ne of them once said to me that she didn't care who invaded the country. *Anything* would be worth it to get rid of a life like this. Now I spoke to her about this recently and she's changed her mind because the Russians have come in and she says there's violence. She sees tanks and shooting and says it is violence, and she does not realize that every single day of her life has been violence. Violence of the most degrading kind. The thing that happens to women is the complete destruction of the person..." (*Women & Revolution*, Spring 1980)

The Red Army's intervention paved the way for an astonishing change in the status of Afghan women. Under the PDPA, women encountered vast opportunities to escape the stifling seclusion they had known for countless generations, emerging as students, workers, professionals and activists. By 1988 there were nearly a quarter of a million women employed, making up 40 percent of the doctors and 60 percent of the instructors at Kabul university. In 1984 Indian journalist Patricia Sethi (*India Today*, 31 July 1984) visited the village of Bagrami outside Kabul, where "a chadri-clad woman at the water tap rushed off when I tried to talk to her":

> "But five 15-year-old girls, carrying rifles and claiming to be members of 'the civilian brigade to defend the revolution,' talked to me at length. They spoke fervently and passionately about their revolution and what it meant for young women of Afghanistan: it

Afterward

meant 'an education, freedom from the veil, freedom from feudalists who want to keep us down,' said Khalida. 'We do not want to become the fourth wife of a 60-year-old man, existing solely for his whim and pleasure'."

Such women, armed as members of the Revolution Defense Group militias, played a key role in the 1983 defense of Urgun against a sustained mujahedeen assault.

The Soviets and their PDPA allies were implementing social programs that appealed to wide sectors of the population, as my father saw for himself when he visited the country in 1982. He found Kabul at peace, the population going about its business without fear. He visited some officials from the old regime, friends from his school days, who vituperated against the PDPA, of course. Dr. Anwar attended an assembly of students held in his honor at Habibia High School, where, he later wrote, "It was a rewarding experience for me to take the role of the devil's advocate in opposition to the new Afghan social system, while a picture of Karl Marx looked sternly at me from the top shelf of a bookcase. A few students sided with me, but the great majority vociferously defended their new system." He summed up his visit by observing, "My impression was that, for the first time in Afghan history, dedicated, intelligent and hard-working leaders are serving the people and not themselves" (*New World Review*, March-April, 1983). Though he may have overstated the altruism of the PDPA leadership, this was nevertheless the closest Afghanistan has ever come to forging a modern nation out of its disparate peoples.

Although the Soviet intervention in Afghanistan had been ordered by Moscow's rulers out of narrow self-interest, it went against the grain of Soviet foreign policy, which since Stalin's days had been based on peaceful coexistence with the capitalist West. Most Western pundits, perhaps believing their own propaganda about "Soviet expansionism," were shocked in 1986 when Mikhail Gorbachev announced that the Red Army would be withdrawn from Afghanistan in short order, come what may.

Memories of Afghanistan

In 1989 the last Red Army troops crossed the Amu Darya back into Soviet Central Asia, defeated not by the mujahedeen but by their own rulers' policies. This retreat was only the first in a dramatic chain of events that led to the fall of the Soviet Union's Eastern European allies and the collapse of the Soviet Union itself within three years. Ironically, the last PDPA chief, Najibullah, outlasted Gorbachev in power.

Wall Street is bullish on Russia these days and hopes for a big oil bonanza in the former Soviet republics of Central Asia. But for working people in these countries the return of capitalism has been a calamity measured in unemployment, homelessness, collapsing life-expectancy rates, and intercommunal violence. Multiply these factors a hundred-fold to get a picture of how Afghanistan fared under the Islamic "freedom fighters." My father, who was stricken with Alzheimer's disease by 1989, did not witness the fall of Kabul to the mujahedeen in 1992. He didn't see the city pulverized by indiscriminate bombing, the massacre of ethnic minorities and the driving of women out of work sites and off the streets. For the next four years the contending armies of mujahedeen turned Kabul into a living hell and drove away most of its population. The country became a fractured wreck in a constant state of inter-ethnic and religious warfare. M. H. Anwar's death in 1993[*] roughly coincided with Afghanistan's demise as a viable entity.

Into this inferno rode the Taliban—on Pakistani-supplied tanks and with Washington's blessing. The Clinton administration initially placed its hopes on the Taliban's ability to pacify Afghanistan. As one U.S. diplomat put it, "The Taliban will probably develop like the Saudis did. There will be Aramco, pipelines, an emir, no parliament and lots of Sharia law. We can live with that" (quoted in Ahmed Rashid, *Taliban: Militant Islam, Oil and Fundamentalism in Central Asia* [2000]). The State Department's belated discovery that the Taliban treated women worse than draft animals seems to have been precipitated, in part at least, by the realization that there would be no Aramco and no pipelines. The Taliban regime

---

[*] Phyllis Anwar died in 2002 after her own battle with Alzheimer's disease.

Afterward

was pleased to accept arms and aid from its American-allied benefactors in Pakistan, but it was not willing to soften its hatred of the non-Muslim West. Under Taliban rule Afghanistan became a school of Islamic holy war where former mujahedeen passed along the training and arms they had received from the CIA during the anti-Soviet jihad. This was the culture medium of Al Qaeda–a Frankenstein's monster produced, in the final analysis, by Washington's drive to roll back the Russian Revolution.

The Bush administration responded to the attacks of September 11, 2001 by raining down 1.2 million tons of bombs on Afghanistan and turning the ruins over to some of the same mujahedeen who had ravaged the country in 1992. In Afghanistan today, under a regime shielded by U.S. troops, women are still commodities to be traded into marriage and labor, still subject to stoning for "crimes" like adultery, still excluded from public life and shrouded in the veil. Throughout the country rape by armed gangs of "freedom fighters," as President Reagan called the mujahedeen, has become commonplace, and girls as young as eight years old are being forced into marriage. On the streets of Kabul, squads dispatched by the Ministry of Religious Affairs persecute women for "un-Islamic behavior." If, as the 19th Century utopian socialist Charles Fourier once said, "The degree of emancipation of woman is the natural measure of general emancipation," then Kabul and other Afghan cities have retrogressed 12 centuries in as many years.

The events in Afghanistan by themselves–leaving aside how the rest of the Third World has fared since World War II–mandate a negative verdict on the words my father wrote from Kabul in 1943: "America is becoming more popular every day in these parts of the world, and everyone is hoping that the high ideals that are cherished and put [forth] forcefully in speech and print will be put in practice as soon as the war is over." Such were the expectations of some at the dawn of the era of *Pax Americana*. Today many are aware that the highest ideal, the "prime mover" if you will, of U.S. foreign policy, is profit–both in its immediate realization and in the long-term stability of the system that produces it. Whence comes the irony of five American presidents, Democrats and Republicans alike and all self-styled defenders of the "Judeo-Christian tradition," fomenting Islamic reaction. It's a sick joke, but nobody's laughing in Afghanistan.

April 2004

About the Author

M. H. Anwar (1914-1993) grew up in the slums of Kabul and overcame fierce ethnic and religious discrimination to win the rare opportunity to attend college in the United States. His unique perspective on Afghan society was enriched by his own experiences, first as a street urchin, petty thief and drug courier, later as an idealistic teenager watching his country slide from the promise of modernization into the pit of religious fundamentalism, and finally as an official in the Ministry of Education and administrator of its teacher training institute. In 1943, facing imprisonment by Afghanistan's monarchical government for his espousal of democratic reform and commitment to minority and women's rights–expressed in the refusal to force his American-born wife to wear the head-to-toe veil–Dr. Anwar fled into exile.

Printed in the United States
23878LVS00001B/49-180